A BIT OF ME

DENISE VAN OUTEN

WITH TERRY RONALD

EBURY
SPOTLIGHT

1 3 5 7 9 10 8 6 4 2

Ebury Spotlight, an imprint of Ebury Publishing
20 Vauxhall Bridge Road
London SW1V 2SA

Ebury Spotlight is part of the Penguin Random House group of companies
whose addresses can be found at global.penguinrandomhouse.com

Penguin
Random House
UK

First published by Ebury Spotlight in 2022

www.penguin.co.uk

A CIP catalogue record for this book is available from the British Library

ISBN 9781529109979

Printed and bound in Great Britain by Clays Ltd, Elcograf S.p.A.

The authorised representative in the EEA is Penguin Random House
Ireland, Morrison Chambers, 32 Nassau Street, Dublin D02 YH68

Penguin Random House is committed to a sustainable future
for our business, our readers and our planet. This book is made
from Forest Stewardship Council® certified paper.

Dedicated to my Nanny Mary, always in my thoughts, and my dear friend Nicki Waterman, whose presence I still feel whenever I walk on Hampstead Heath, where we used to train.

CONTENTS

CHAPTER ONE

'This one has been here before'

'This one has been here before.' That's what the midwife told Mum as she handed her a new baby girl, seconds after I was born in a Basildon hospital. 'Just look how awake and alert she is.'

I wonder if she might have been right? By all accounts, I achieved all the usual baby milestones earlier than expected. I was sitting unaided at five and a half months, crawling at six months, walking at nine months and talking in sentences at eighteen months. Perhaps I'd done it all before. Or perhaps it was because I had an older brother and sister to keep up with and didn't want to get left behind. Well, I have always been quite competitive.

I was a happy, contented toddler, but always on the go. As soon as there was music playing, I'd start jigging around and had a thing for spinning continuously on the spot without getting dizzy. This, I'm told, was quite fascinating to watch, and might have been an early hint at my passion for dancing, which started when I was very young.

I remember my mum and dad always working incredibly hard. In fact, their commitment to work and providing for the family is probably where I get some of my drive and work ethic from. They first met in an East End pub in the summer of 1964. Mum, Kathy, was 17 and working as a copy typist for a Dutch pharmaceutical company in the city. My dad, Ted, was three years older than Mum. A 20-year-old lad who was working at the London Dock, Wapping. They were from the same area of London, both born and bred in Stepney, which these days is known as Tower Hamlets. They married four years later, in 1968, and rented the top part of the house from a private landlord, with another family living downstairs. I recall Mum telling me how anxious they both were because the family below them weren't the cleanest of people. This was particularly concerning when Mum became pregnant, carrying my older sister, Jacqueline. One of the biggest problems was that there was only one toilet in the entire house, which they all had to share, and Mum and Dad's neighbours often left it in a terrible state. On top of that, the flat was running alive with mice.

When Jacqueline was six months old, my parents decided enough was enough as far as their dreadful living conditions were concerned. It was time to save up for a deposit for a home of their own. This meant that Mum had to go back to work, while Dad took on an evening cleaning job as well as his regular job at the docks. It took them a year and a half until they'd enough to put down a deposit on a house in Corringham in Essex. They chose the area so Dad could transfer his job to the nearby Tilbury Docks. Mum, meanwhile, kept up two cleaning jobs.

By the time I came on the scene, they lived in an ordinary semi-detached house in Howell Road, Corringham. Back then, it seemed like the whole of Essex was made up of ex-East Enders who'd taken the leap and moved a bit further out of London in search of a better life and more space. My dad was a docker, and he certainly saw moving his job from the docks in the East End to Tilbury Docks in Essex as a brand-new beginning. Also, like many East Enders, much of my close family lived on the same street as us. My auntie Teresa lived opposite with my cousins, Sarah and Daniel, and Nanny Mary and Granddad Bill lived six doors down. They were my maternal grandparents. Nanny Mary pops up a fair bit in my story; she was an important part of my life and a significant influence on many of the things I did in my early career. I spent so much time at her house when I was a kid. Whenever my mum couldn't immediately locate me, or my sister, Jackie, and brother, Terry, she always knew where to look. We could always be found at my nan's place – it felt so comfortable and safe there. Among her many other talents, Nan was well known by friends and family for making the best carrot cake. Whenever we turned up at her house, she'd stick a cake in front of us, which was another excellent reason to spend time there.

I also went to church with my nan most Sundays. My family are Roman Catholic, my primary school St Joseph's was a Roman Catholic school, and I took my first Communion around the age of eight or nine. However, the restrictions of sitting still in a church were often problematic for a child who found it hard to concentrate or stay in the same spot for more than a few minutes at a time.

• • •

My sister, Jackie, went to dance classes, taking ballet, tap and modern dance. By the time I was three, I had told Mum I wanted to go too and ended up joining the baby ballet class. Not long after joining the class, I gave Mum and Dad a scare when I went missing with my friend Claire, aged four. Claire lived a couple of doors along from us in a small terrace block, and we'd often play together. On this particular day, I asked Mum if I could go play at Claire's house, and she watched me as I tottered down to Claire's with my doll's pram and went inside. Parents always seemed so much more relaxed with their kids back in the seventies and eighties, don't you think? All the way through my childhood, I had a lot more freedom than I'd give my own daughter, and my friends tell me the same about their childhood in comparison to the way they are with their own kids. It's just the way it was back then; it feels like a different world now. Perhaps it's something to do with all the scary bad-news stories we're constantly alerted to on social media as well as the news.

A couple of hours after I'd gone to Claire's house, Mum walked up the road to collect me, only to have Claire's mum explain that we'd both left to go back to my house half an hour earlier. Of course, our mothers were panic-stricken, frantically running around the streets calling our names, getting more worried by the second. As time went on, more and more people joined in the search, neighbours, friends and passers-by, but still, we were nowhere to be found. Eventually, Mum called the police, who asked for a description of us, including what we were wearing and when and where we were last seen. By this time, everyone was separately worried. We've all seen those news stories when kids go missing, and we've all been sad and horrified when we hear about the ones that turn out badly. As a parent, I can only imagine what Mum and Dad must have gone through that day. Eventually, a police car came around the corner of the street. The policeman driving told our mothers that we'd been found on the other side of Southend Road, which was a fairly busy road.

'I told them Mummy and Daddy are worried about you,' he said. 'I said to get in the car, and I'll take you home, but the little one wouldn't hear of it.'

That was me, of course.

'No! I'm not allowed to get in strange men's cars,' I'd said, point-blank refusing to go with him.

A little while later, Mum says she remembers seeing a policewoman walking towards her with both of us girls, determined-faced and pushing our dolly prams. It turned out that I was the orchestrator of the entire missing-children saga, encouraging Claire to tag along with me to show her where my dance school was. All in all, the two of us had walked over two miles, crossing a busy main road there and back.

As proud as I'd been to show off the location of my class to Claire, my time at baby ballet was relatively short-lived. A few months after I started, I told Mum I was bored and didn't want to go any more. It wasn't that I didn't like dancing; on the contrary, I loved it. It was just that baby ballet wasn't challenging enough for me any more. I wanted more. Just a few months later, I was ready to dance again, as long as I could move up to the next class. The problem was that class was for five years plus, but I was insistent that I could hack it, despite my young age. In the end,

Mum gave in, deciding that she would pretend I was already five, just to get me into the class. Then, worried we might be rumbled, Mum and Jackie went through the syllabus with me quite thoroughly so I'd be able to keep up with the other kids in the class. I knew I wasn't supposed to make it evident that I was already well-versed in a lot of the set work and, at first, was quite convincing in my charade. Everyone just thought I was a fast learner, able to pick things up quickly and easily. The problem came when the school principal observed the class and asked our teacher which pupils she thought were ready to advance to the exam class. Our teacher called out a couple of names and then called my name.

'Denise hasn't been in the class very long but has been doing remarkably well,' she said. 'I think she could take the exam.'

Unfortunately, you had to be six before you could take the exam, so Mum decided she had best come clean and tell them that, at that point, I'd only just turned five. It all worked out for the best, as I did end up in the exam class, taking the exam as soon as I was truly old enough.

• • •

As you can probably tell, I was a proper little achiever, always wanting to do my best in whatever I tried. I really have no idea why this was the case; there was this little fire in me that made me want to push myself forward. Once we could swim the width of the small pool (doggy-paddle style) in my swimming class, we received a badge to sew on to our swimsuit. Usually, any child who completed the swim would get a badge, but on the day I was due to attempt the swim, our instructor announced that the badge system was under review because they only had one badge in stock. He decided that the fairest way to solve this problem was to get the participants to race, and only the winner would get the badge. The stakes had been raised. Mum says she remembers me glancing over at her with a look of absolute determination: I'd doggy-paddle like my life depended on it and win the race, bagging the coveted badge. I did my best and ended up winning it, but once the race was over and the badge awarded, I spotted another little girl crying because she hadn't got one. I felt terrible and offered to give up my badge so that she could have it. The girl's mum, however, wouldn't hear of it.

'Denise, you won the race, so you must keep the badge,' she said.

Mum smiled, agreeing that I could have the badge, but I think she felt quite proud of me for wanting to share my success.

I was just six when showbiz beckoned. A local newspaper was advertising for children to audition for a new musical for kids, *Miss Fits' Misfits*, written by a local guy called Mike Nash. Recognising my eagerness to try new things, Mum asked me if I wanted to try for it. Of course, I said I was up for it. I'd already had a small part in our local panto, *The Old Woman Who Lived in a Shoe* at the Towngate Theatre, Basildon, the previous Christmas, but this would be my very first singing audition. Everyone who auditioned had to sing the same song: 'Any Dream Will Do' from *Joseph and the Amazing Technicolor Dreamcoat*. I learned the song and practised every minute I could before the audition. My hard work paid off; I was cast as one of Miss Fits' misfits, playing the part of a fairy with a broken wing. The role required me to keep one arm bent with my hand on my shoulder throughout the performances. I even got to sing my first solo, hilariously titled 'Flying Round in Circles'. The moral of the story was that everyone is an extraordinary individual, no matter what their circumstances.

That was it, I was off. I'd performed my first solo in front of an audience and from then on there was no looking back.

CHAPTER TWO

Kids who were into singing and dancing weren't exactly the norm

I gave my mum and dad the second big scare of my childhood when I was eight years old. While I was practising hard for a ballet award, I got terrible pains on my right side. I didn't tell Mum and Dad about the pains; perhaps I was worried it would affect my chances of going for the ballet award. During a ballet lesson leading up to the exam, we were all doing barre work while our teacher walked along the line of pupils, instructing us, one at a time, to pull up while placing her hands on our tummies. When the teacher got to me, I screamed out in pain. I had no idea what was happening but immediately burst into tears. Mum came and took me home, assuming that I'd pulled a muscle or something. An hour or so later, it was clear that was not the case, as the pain grew worse and I turned a deathly shade of white. Desperately worried, Mum and Dad rushed me to the hospital, where doctors diagnosed peritonitis caused by a burst appendix. As it turned out, it was lucky they'd acted so quickly. The consultant told Mum and Dad I'd been fortunate because I might not have made it in another couple of hours. He also told them I had a very high pain threshold, having played down the pain I must have experienced for so long.

By this time, my mum had also registered me at a child's modelling agency called Tiny Tots. Along with all the other tots, my picture was in a modelling book, so if a casting director wanted a cheeky eight-year-old blonde girl, I might get picked out from my photo and then go for a fitting. If they liked the look of you, the next thing they'd check was if the clothes fit. There could be another five or six kids who looked just like me at the fitting, so it was dog eat dog. I learned fast, and had plenty of tricks up my sleeve when it came to fittings. I usually had some devious way of making sure everything fitted me. If there was a skirt that was a bit too long, I'd run to the loo and roll the waistband over until it was just the right length. If I had to look young, I'd ask my mum to put my hair in plaits to make me look cute, and if I had to look a bit older, I'd ask her to do me a top-knot to add an air of sophistication. On a couple of occasions, I got caught out, but, even then, I still got the jobs, just for being so resourceful and cheeky.

One of the reasons I was so confident and outgoing was because my older sister, Jackie, was the opposite. She struggled in social situations and was quite shy. I always felt very protective of Jackie because she was so timid, even though she was the older sibling. If we were in a room full of people and somebody directed a question at Jackie, she'd get embarrassed, so I always felt like I had to jump in and save her. I'd end up answering for her because I could see how uncomfortable she was.

I certainly wasn't shy. I loved being in front of the camera, whether it was in a photographic studio or on a film set of some kind, filming an advert. It wasn't just that I didn't feel self-conscious; I also really enjoyed being in the company of adults. I suppose I was a bit of an old head on young shoulders, so I loved chatting to and getting to know the team or the make-up and wardrobe people. On many of the shoots I did, my nan, Mary, was my chaperone.

Perhaps my enthusiasm for adult company at such a young age was why I never felt like I was missing out on a normal childhood. Often, I couldn't play in the street or the park with other kids in my neighbourhood because I had a casting to go to or a photo shoot or a commercial to do. It didn't bother me because I loved working and enjoyed being around all those fascinating older people who inhabited the world that I longed to. It did, however, make me stick out a bit as far as the other kids went. I've heard people say that they met their best friends when they were five years old and have kept these same friends throughout their lives. I don't remember having close friends from primary school; certainly not any that stayed with me. Looking back, I wonder if that was because I was so focused on what I was doing outside of school, coupled with the fact that I just loved hanging out at my nan and granddad's house and being with my family. Whatever the reason, I think some of the other children around me thought I was a bit of a weirdo.

With all the TV talent shows around now and the significant impact of the internet, there seems to be an abundance of young people dying to get into the entertainment industry. Everyone wants to be on the telly. You can't look at your iPhone without an

Instagram story or a TikTok popping up, with someone doing their thing, hoping to entertain and perhaps, with luck, go viral. Maybe they were always out there; they're just more visible now they have all these different platforms – I don't know. When I was growing up, it was a little more unusual to want to entertain, which meant that kids who were into singing and dancing weren't exactly the norm – well, certainly not in Basildon anyway. I suppose that was why I got the mickey taken out of me on a fairly regular basis. I remember walking out of my front door and hearing a kid saying, 'Oh, here she comes, the model', followed by much giggling from their mates. It wasn't always easy to take that kind of ridicule, but my mum always handled it quite well and knew exactly what to say if I ever got too upset about it: 'Sometimes other people might get a bit jealous of what you're doing. Perhaps it's something they might want to do but they haven't been as lucky as you have. It can be hurtful, but you have to stay grounded and not be cocky or wind people up with it. This might not be something you do forever, so see it for what it is and enjoy it.'

While I enjoyed the modelling, my real obsession was dancing. That was my passion. I still went to a regular class, and I spent any spare time doing extra classes and practising like a maniac. I was never especially academic, but I was always up for working incredibly hard at the things I enjoyed, and, for me, the main thing was dance. It was a brilliant way to expend some of my seemingly boundless energy. I was never diagnosed with ADHD, but having had a daughter that has been diagnosed with it, I can see those same traits in myself. All the characteristics that led to my daughter Betsy's ADHD diagnosis are in me too and have been since I was a child. I wish back then that I'd known what I know now because it would have made life a little bit easier. Most young people with ADHD find it hard to be still or concentrate on one thing, and I certainly found that challenging as a child.

At school, I was a dreamer. Physically, I might be sitting at my desk in the classroom, but, mentally, I was off in my own little world somewhere, daydreaming about all sorts. There were quite a few occasions when I'd be shaken out of a daydream on hearing my name called. Startled and back in the room, I'd see my teacher looking directly at me, asking me my thoughts on, or a question about, the particular topic he or she had been discussing. It was bad enough that I didn't know the answer to the question, but on top of that, I'd be sitting there thinking, *Christ, I haven't even got a clue what the hell you've been talking about for the past thirty minutes! I've been picturing myself floating around on a lilo next to George Michael in Wham!'s 'Club Tropicana' video.* OK, so whoever said daydreams had to be based on reality?

Still, I was lucky that, with dancing, I'd landed on something I loved so much, I was able to throw myself into it, putting all that surplus energy in me to good use, working towards being the best that I could be. I was dedicated. Dancing was the exception to the rule and something that I really could focus on. In many respects, I don't think I've changed all that much. I'm still someone who always seems to be running a mile a minute, always bursting with dozens of ideas simultaneously. The thing I've learned as an adult is that you can't achieve everything on your own. I might be full of ideas, but I also know that I'll generally need a team of people around to help me achieve them. People who can make sense of my mad flashes of inspiration and steer me in the right direction to make them a reality. Or at least try to! Without those carefully chosen collaborators, I find it hard to stay focused on a project – even now.

Many kids back then had jobs when they got to 12 or 13 – paper rounds, maybe a bit of shop work as you got older – but I didn't wait that long. By the time I was about seven, I was already doing modelling jobs and earning some money. I took it very seriously too. If I knew I had a modelling assignment coming up, I was pretty disciplined and strict with myself about what I could and couldn't do in the period leading up to it. While all the other kids were out running around in the streets or tearing around and falling off their BMX bikes, which were very big at the time, I stayed in the sanctuary of my bedroom or my nan's living room. That way, I wasn't going to get any bruises, marks or scratches on me, which might have shown up in photographs. I always wanted to turn up to a job looking pristine and perfect. Oh yes! I saw myself as a professional, even at that age.

I was ten when my dad's sister, Aunt Joy, called to say she had heard about a children's theatrical agent in London looking to audition children to tap dance at Expo '85 in Japan. It goes without saying that I was utterly gung-ho for this opportunity, so Mum and Dad agreed to take me down to London on a Sunday afternoon to the Sylvia Young Theatre School in Marylebone to try for the audition. I don't remember much about it; just that I wanted it badly. Meanwhile, Mum and Dad waited nervously in an adjoining room. While they were there, the school matron – who we later discovered was the mum of actress Letitia Dean (Sharon from *EastEnders*) – came out to collect some paperwork from a drawer. As she was heading back into the audition room, she turned to Mum and Dad, smiled and said, 'She really is good, you know.' Mum told me that at that moment, her heart started racing at the thought that her little girl was going to end up dancing in Japan. A few minutes later, she and Dad were called in to Sylvia Young's office to meet the lady herself.

'Denise did exceptionally well, and she's just what we were looking for,' Sylvia told them. 'But she's too tall.'

At that point, my mum experienced her very first pushy-stage-mum moment. 'The heels on her tap shoes are quite high,' she piped up.

Sylvia let out a little laugh, then explained she had three boys and two girls, so she was now on the hunt for a third girl who had to be shorter than the tallest of the three boys. The day wasn't a complete loss, however. The paperwork that the school matron had collected from the drawer turned out to be a draft agreement and an offer to sign me up to Sylvia's agency. Mum and Dad weren't all that keen initially. I was still on the Tiny Tots books, still getting plenty of photographic jobs, modelling for knitting patterns, clothes catalogues and the like. The only problem with Tiny Tots was that the agent would sometimes get a bit stroppy if

I had a friend's birthday party or was going to the cinema with friends and couldn't make an audition. I might have been keen, but there was the odd time I wanted to be a normal kid, and I've never been one to miss a good party. Sylvia promised us it wouldn't be a problem if I couldn't attend the odd casting, so when my parents asked my opinion, I knew which way I wanted to go. I ended up leaving Tiny Tots and signing with Sylvia's agency.

After that Sunday afternoon, life would never be the same again.

CHAPTER THREE

'Can you do the splits both ways?'

It all started with me joining the Saturday drama and singing classes at Sylvia Young. It wasn't long before I started to get auditions and got cast in several TV commercials and a pop video through the agency. For some reason, a lot of the commercials were shot in Holland. Ad companies over there seemed to use quite a lot of British kids. I often went with my nan, and it became a fairly regular thing, particularly with Mum and Dad having my brother and sister to take care of. It's funny; it was an unusual thing for a kid of my age to be working, let alone travelling abroad for work, but, somehow, I took it all in my stride. I was lucky to have such a supportive family, who were happy to indulge all my mad artiness and passion for performing. Working and being busy was perfect for keeping my active mind occupied, too, that's for sure. I did ads for Dutch cheese, Colgate toothpaste, an American ad for Kool-Aid; I was even in a Milky Bar TV commercial. That was quite exciting. There was an article in a local Essex newspaper at the time, proclaiming that the new Milky Bar Kid was from Essex and two local girls were to appear in the advert too – one of them being me. I knew the boy who'd got the part of 'the kid', his name was Wayne, so you can imagine my confusion when everyone on set started to call him David.

'Why is everyone calling that boy David when his name's Wayne?' I asked my mum.

It turned out that it was the makers of Milky Bar, Nestlé, who suggested that with all the press around a brand-new Milky Bar Kid, the boy might be wise to switch to a stage name of David King, rather than his original name, Wayne King. When I thought very carefully about it, I agreed it was probably for the best. Of course, I found the whole thing hysterical and continued to call him Wayne King anyway.

When the time came, I went to the same secondary school that my sister went to, Grays Convent High School, in Essex. It was the best state school in the area, all girls, but it wasn't a good fit for me right from the start. It was run by nuns and, academically, extremely competitive, which wasn't me. I wasn't unpopular – in fact, I made some good friends at the school – but my passion for the arts and theatre is not what the other girls or the school were about. I'd realised by then that I was a creative person rather than an academic one, and that creativity was never going to flourish at Grays Convent. I felt stifled and hemmed in, with no outlet for the things I enjoyed or felt passionate about.

On top of that, the school was pretty strict. Like many girls of the same age, I was at the stage when I liked to experiment with my hair and a bit of make-up. That was a definite no-no as far as the nuns were concerned. I tried out a new style with my hair once, which required a bit of hairspray. Any kind of hair product was forbidden at Grays Convent, and that day I ended up with a suspicious nun dragging a comb through my hair to check whether or not I had hairspray in it.

It wasn't that it was in any way a terrible school, and, despite its strict rules, there were several nuns there that I liked very much – a big shout-out to Sister Campion: you were my favourite! It just wasn't the right place for me, but, for a while, there didn't seem to be an alternative.

That changed after I went up for an audition for the musical *Annie* at the Richmond Theatre. It was an open audition, and I remember being slightly in awe of all the other kids around me, who were even more stagey than I was. We all queued up for ages, waiting for our big chance. It's funny, thinking about it now. I remember standing on the stage in a row of other kids while the auditioning panel went along the line, asking each auditioning child in turn: 'What's your name and who are you with?'

The answers went something like, 'I'm Sally Smith, and I'm with Sylvia Young,' followed by, 'I'm Jenny Jones, and I'm with Anna Scher.'

Each child called out their full name, followed by the name of their agent or their theatre school. That was until they got to me.

'I'm Denise and I'm with my mum,' I said.

God knows why I didn't mention Sylvia's. I guess it was all a bit overwhelming. Still, everyone on the panel laughed.

I was one of the lucky few to get a part, as it turned out. I was offered the role of Tessie, one of the orphans, whose catchphrase is 'Oh my goodness! Oh my goodness!' Of course, I was thrilled to have bagged the role, but the strict rules of Grays Convent meant that I couldn't take time off to be in the show. For me, this felt like the final straw. How was I ever going to flourish as a performer when I wasn't allowed to perform?

Compared to Grays Convent, Sylvia's was a relatively small school, housed in an old church in Marylebone. It had around 150 pupils in the entire school, from aged seven right through to school-leaving age. I'd fallen in love with the place as soon as I saw it, and desperately wanted to go there full-time. Back then, I was into the eighties TV show *Fame*. I was glued to it every Thursday night. I loved the idea of attending a school where all the kids were singers, dancers and performers. I was also rather smitten with Leroy's character and fascinated by some of his more prominent physical attributes – perfectly highlighted by his Lycra unitard – but that's another story!

The idea of going to Sylvia Young's and being just like one of the kids from *Fame* became everything to me; it was all-consuming. I pictured myself and my future classmates tearing into the streets, clad in Lycra and leg warmers, and dancing on cars, just like in the music video for the hit song 'Fame' by Irene Cara.

I recall sitting on the kitchen floor by the washing machine one day while Mum was trying to get on with the weekly wash. There she was, loading clothes into the machine, while 11-year-old me sat there crying and pleading.

'Please, Mum! Please let me go to Sylvia's school full-time.'

'We just can't afford it,' she said. 'And also, it's not fair on your brother and sister.'

I was devastated, but in my heart I knew she'd have let me go there if she could have. She knew that Grays Convent wasn't a good fit for me, and she'd also seen how much my sister had struggled when she went there. Jackie's struggle was different to mine. She was a shy girl in a school full of outgoing, competitive pupils. Although it was known as a good school, Mum knew I wasn't all that happy, but what could she do? My parents didn't come from money or from a theatrical background; they were just hard-working people with regular jobs. As much as Mum would have loved to have allowed me to go to Sylvia's, it was just beyond what my parents could manage.

Then, once again, Sylvia Young showed faith in me and came to the rescue. Her feeling was that I'd be able to pay my school fees using the money I earned from all the work I was getting and would hopefully continue to accumulate. This was the deciding factor. Finally, Mum and Dad agreed that I could leave my school and attend Sylvia's full-time.

On my first day at my new school, I walked into a room and spotted the girl who would eventually become one of my best friends for life. Costandia, or Cossi as she was known, was in the splits when I first set eyes on her.

'Can you do the splits both ways?' she asked me.

We were inseparable from that very moment.

Cossi was a Greek Cypriot girl who lived in Hackney, and, as time went on, I'd often stay over at her house so I didn't have to endure the long coach journey to and from Essex every day of the week. The estate she lived on was famously quite tough, and the first time I rocked up there to stay, I felt like I'd stepped into another world. These days, parts of Hackney are quite gentrified and trendy, but back then, being a young girl from the quiet of Essex, I felt like I was on the set of some TV crime drama. In fact, the first night I stayed with Cossi, we heard gunfire outside, which terrified the life out of us. I'd grown used to living on a street where my nan and my aunt lived close by and where everyone was in and out of everybody else's houses. In Cossi's world, people were bolting their doors to keep out undesirables. That said, I grew to love staying at Cossi's house, and I was grateful to have somewhere in London to stay, and such a good friend in her. Her mum, Iris, was always wonderful to me; I used to think of her as my 'London mum'.

It wasn't exactly an easy commute to Sylvia's from my home in Corringham. For a while, I travelled to Marylebone by coach every day, smack bang in the middle of rush hour. It took me three hours to get to school most days, so I'd set my alarm for 5am, be on the coach at six and sometimes just about reach the school by nine. There was often an audition after school, so it wasn't unusual for me to arrive home as late as 9.30pm. It was fine for a while, all very exciting, but as time went on, this ridiculous schedule started to take its toll. I was constantly tired. I began to look pale and always had dark circles under my eyes.

Eventually, I felt confident enough to travel by train, which would reduce my travelling time significantly. That worked well for a while, but then came the IRA terrorist attacks in London when trains were a possible target. This made Mum and Dad nervous, especially when I had to call them from a telephone box one day to tell them that all the passengers on my train had to get off the train at King's Cross because of a security alert. We were supposed to travel to the next station on foot, so Mum told me to look for someone who had children with them and stay close, so it looked as if I was part of a family.

In the end, Mum decided to look for a job in London so she could accompany me to and from school. As well as putting her mind at rest, it meant she could make the extra income to pay towards school fees and sundries. For a while, she worked for a London-based charity, but eventually, Sylvia offered her a job working at the agency. By that time, I'd also appeared in several TV commercials and done a few voice-overs, not just for the UK but also for the USA and Holland. Between that and Mum's job, we managed to pay for my school fees, plus pull together the money I needed for school uniforms and show costumes.

It's funny to think back at how self-sufficient I was at such a young age. Betsy is 11 now, but she still seems so young to me. I sometimes wonder if it was just that I was so in love with the idea of performing, or that I was perhaps in too much of a hurry to grow up.

CHAPTER FOUR

Just like the kids from *Fame*

I loved the madness of Sylvia's; the chaos and creativity. I loved the fact that you could walk into the canteen and there'd be three people harmonising in the corner or practising a scene – yes, just like the kids from *Fame*. It was a fantastic place, a little pot of talent where every room seemed to be brimming with creative talent. You only have to scroll down a list of the school's alumni to see just how many famous and renowned faces it has produced. Mel Blatt and the Appleton sisters went there, as did Emma Bunton, Frances Ruffelle (who's Sylvia's daughter), Letitia Dean, Samantha Womack, Adam Woodyatt and Perry Fenwick of *EastEnders* fame, Leona Lewis, Tamzin Outhwaite, Rita Ora, Nicholas Hoult, Billie Piper, Keeley Hawes and, of course, Amy Winehouse too. Danniella Westbrook was in my class, and we were really good friends. I often used to stay over at Danni's mum and dad's place in Essex.

The schedule at Sylvia's was three days of regular classes – Monday to Wednesday; then, it was all performing arts on Thursday and Friday. No prizes for guessing which part of the week we kids looked forward to the most. As far as the regular classes went – English, maths, science, etc. – I was in with other children in my age group, but when it came to the performing arts classes, it was all about ability. I may have only been 11 years old, but as far as dance went, I found myself in an advanced class of 15- and 16-year-olds. Other kids might have been further along with music or singing, so it all balanced out in the end.

Whenever one of the matrons came into a class to interrupt a lesson, we knew there was an audition in the offing. She'd call out the relevant names and say, 'You have an audition at three o'clock. Don't be late!'

It could be anything; an advert for Dutch cheese was one I remember. Once the lesson was over, the kids with the audition would excitedly rush out and get themselves ready, then find somewhere quiet to sit and learn any lines they might have. It was quite mad, really, but it all seemed very natural to us. We all looked out for and encouraged one another too. If one student returned with the announcement that they'd been successful, everyone would be congratulating and cheering for them; even the kids who hadn't been successful. That was the kind of camaraderie Sylvia's encouraged.

The fact that I was paying for most of my school fees from whatever work I got meant that every potential job was hugely important. For most kids doing an audition, it was, of course, a disappointment if they didn't get a call-back or ultimately get cast. However, for me, it could mean the difference between continuing my education at the school I loved or having to leave because we couldn't afford it. I remember going to quite a few castings with a girl who came from her beautiful home to school each day in a chauffeur-driven Rolls-Royce. She was always very blasé about auditions and never seemed to mind whether or not she was successful. I longed to have that laid-back air about me, but for me, it was often do or die when it came to getting a job – or at least that's how it felt. I had a responsibility to myself. Even at such a young age, I was acutely aware that I had to work hard and earn money to be able to keep doing the things I loved and keep learning.

I had a knack of always finding myself in the centre of whatever was going on at school, one of them being a school food strike when all of the students at Sylvia's downed their cutlery and boycotted the school canteen.

Cossi's mum, Iris, was at the heart of the disruption; she ran the canteen and oversaw the cleaning of the school. Everybody loved Iris and her perfectly made jacket potatoes, and being Cossi's best friend meant that Iris would always pile mine high with extra cheese, knowing how much I loved it. The mini revolution happened when, during a rejig of the canteen staff, new people were brought in and Iris's services were no longer required. I'm not sure why. She kept her cleaning job, but the canteen was under new management with a new, streamlined staff. The students were devastated and angered by this news, and we collectively decided that we would not buy or eat any of the canteen food. Instead, we would just sit there at the canteen tables and eat packed lunches until sanity was restored and Iris was reinstated. It wasn't exactly on a par with the miners' strike, but, of course, I was right there in the thick of it all. Iris did eventually get her job back too. Long live the jacket potato!

Remember the OXO family from the eighties TV adverts? Well, the girl who played the daughter in the family was a pupil at Sylvia's, called Alison Reynolds. I came up with the idea of celebrating a 'National Day' every so often, where a pupil who'd done exceptionally well should be honoured with a special day. I'm not sure why this thought occurred to me; any excuse for a celebration, I guess. On 'National Day', everyone, and I mean everyone, including the teachers, would dress up or adopt a visual characteristic of the celebrated individual. Alison wasn't exactly a household name, but she was undoubtedly someone everyone recognised from the famous TV stock cube adverts, which ran from the early eighties to the late nineties. When it was her turn to be honoured – on National Alison Reynolds Day – everyone, including the boys, wore their hair in bunches, just like she always did. Even Maggie, our headmistress, joined in the fun and turned up to school with bunches. I was so lucky to have come up through a school that gave you that kind of freedom. It was no walk in the park, though. When it came to working, we were all expected to buckle down and get on with it.

My strong suit at Sylvia's was dancing – that's why I'd gone there in the first place. As for singing, I was still quite a shy singer back then. It wasn't something I considered myself all that good at, so I never really gave it my all. Sylvia's had an amazing singing teacher called Peter Roberts, who I believe is still teaching there now. He tried to bring out my voice, encouraging me to sing solos when I preferred blending into a group. I always got embarrassed at that kind of exposure. Weirdly,

I was OK if I played a character who had to sing, but whenever I had to sing as me, I'd struggle to muster the confidence. It's something I carried over into my adult performing life. For a long time, I was always a more confident singer when I was behind the mask of a character. I felt exposed otherwise, and it's taken me 40 years to get over that. I suppose that's why the singing part of my career came much later. I didn't even know I had a voice for a long while, and I still don't really know where it came from. I certainly didn't come from a musical or a singing family. My nan used to sing around the house, but that was about it. Like most kids back then, I always had the radio on, but I wouldn't say I was particularly interested in music or learned much about it. Not like my daughter, Betsy, who knows the lyrics to loads of songs, old and new. All I knew was that I loved Wham!, but I think that had more to do with the fact that my childhood crush was George Michael.

The thing I enjoyed most was making people laugh. I was the clown, the joker, always trying to do something a bit rude or naughty that might prove hilarious for others and that I could hopefully get away with. Auditioning for a pantomime with school friends once, I decided to sing 'Think of Me', from *The Phantom of the Opera*, purely so I could see if it was possible to change the phrase 'think of me' to 'finger me' without the auditioning panel noticing. I sang the song in such a sweet and innocent voice: *'Finger me, finger me fondly, when we've said goodbye'.* The people auditioning me didn't twig on; meanwhile, all my mates were giggling in the wings.

Meanwhile, the audition tricks I'd learned when I was young came into play in a big way when I auditioned for the original West End production of *Les Misérables*. This was my first really big theatrical audition. Back then, *Les Mis* was a brand-new show, opening at the Palace Theatre in London. It was a big deal, and I wanted to be a part of it.

For this show, there was a height restriction for auditioning children. When I first got the call to go for the part of young Éponine, I could have just about made the cut, but I'd shot up over the summer, so by the time my audition was due to happen, Mum delivered the devastating news that I was now too tall for the part. Down but not out, I thought long and hard about how I might get around this unexpected and highly annoying obstacle. Then it came to me: I would simply make myself shorter. Easy. First, I went to Laura Ashley and bought myself a long dress, which I would wear for the audition. I was at an age where I was getting into fashion and clothes a bit more, but this wasn't the kind of thing I'd have chosen to wear. It was ruffled and fussy, almost Victorian-looking. Still, I thought it would help me look the part, so that's what I would wear.

The second part of my ingenious plan was to do the entire audition with my knees slightly bent so I'd appear shorter than I was. I walked into the audition space with my knees bent, I sang with my knees bent; they even measured me while I subtly angled my knees under the flowery camouflage of my Laura Ashley. I wasn't particularly nervous about the audition itself, more about getting rumbled. My overriding concern was that the audition might go on for too long because it was bloody uncomfortable. And guess what? I got the part! My plan was a triumph, and I was over the moon. My mum, meanwhile, was a bit more practical and forward-thinking.

'What are you going to do now?' she asked. 'Are you going to do the whole run of the show with your knees bent?'

'Don't worry,' I said. 'I've got the job now; they're not going to take it away from me, are they?'

When the students at Sylvia's found out that I'd got the part, they all clapped and cheered for me. It was such a big thing. Being so young, I did alternate nights with two other children, so we each did two or three performances a week over several months.

Even then, on my first big West End job, I was mischievous. As children, we always had a chaperone at the theatre. Our chaperone was called Anne, and, although she was pretty strict, on matinee days, if we'd been well behaved, she'd take us to Fortnum & Mason, and we'd eat honeycomb ice cream, which was our real treat. The trouble was, we weren't always well behaved. All the kids' dressing rooms were at the top of the building, probably to stop annoying the adults with all the noise we made. Sometimes, we'd hang out of the windows and throw cups of water on people who were passing on the street below. There were quite a few occasions when some unfortunate person who got soaked would march into the theatre and complain. Of course, being kids, we were the prime suspects, but when the company manager or someone from the theatre came upstairs to confront us, we'd all be sitting innocently in our dressing rooms like butter wouldn't melt.

'Oh no, it wasn't us. We'd never do anything like that.'

Once the coast was clear, we'd kill ourselves laughing at having got away with it.

Going from modelling for knitting patterns and Dutch cheese commercials to performing on a West End stage in front of a huge, enthusiastic live audience was a turning point for me. It threw up all kinds of possibilities. It was also what led to my appreciation of musical theatre, although that would take a while to blossom fully. Who could fail to be moved by the score of *Les Mis*? To me, it was gorgeous. It was the first time I'd heard orchestral music played live; I'd never experienced anything like it. In fact, the first night I stepped out onstage to perform in the show, I was blown away by it.

At the end of the show, the sight and sound of the audience cheering and applauding was incredible. I couldn't have imagined experiencing such love and joy for something happening on a stage; something make-believe brought to life. Sometimes, the applause would go on for 15 or 20 minutes. The curtain would come down and go up again, then come down and go up again. It was as if it might never end. It was during one of those seemingly endless encores that I came to a decision: I wanted to be a live performer. I wanted to do everything in front of an audience. Being in front of a camera was all well and good – I was happy and grateful for that kind of work – but this was what it was all about for me. Performing for a camera didn't give me the same high and the buzz that being in front of an audience did, and that hasn't ever changed. Being in *Les Mis* did that for me.

Even now, that score and that show still has such a special place in my heart.

Sylvia Young put on a big show every year in a proper West End theatre. All the students were involved, part-time as well as full-time. Sylvia's shows were a vehicle to showcase all the wonderfully diverse talent she had in her school. They were always a very glitzy affair, with dazzling costumes and an abundance of showstopping numbers. All the top casting directors, producers etc., would come to watch, and *The Stage* always gave them rave reviews. Back then, my Nanny Mary was a professional dressmaker, so it wasn't long before she became part of Sylvia's costume-making team. Nanny Mary also chaperoned me on lots of auditions and jobs once Mum started work in the agency. It was a proper family affair. Spending so much time with my nan made our bond even more special and lasting.

Aged 15, I went with a group of other girls to audition for Anthony Newley, who was casting for his musical *Stop the World – I Want to Get Off*, which was playing at the Lyric Theatre in London. I was cast as Anthony's daughter, Jane, while Martine McCutcheon, aged 13, was cast as my sister, Susan.

During the opening-night party, a glamorous affair held at the Savoy, I went off into the throng, mingling and having my photograph taken by the press. Of course, Mum and Dad were there, and when I eventually made it back to them, Mum asked me if anyone had commented on my performance.

I discreetly pointed out one older man who'd told me how good I was and that I reminded him of his daughter. 'Goodness, that's John Mills', Mum said. 'Both his daughters are very famous actresses.'

It was all very well receiving praise, but I also learned about rejection and how to deal with it. When half your young life is taken up with castings and auditions, there's no avoiding it. It's served me well over the years. It upsets me to see how many young people in the entertainment industry are so affected by negative comments on social media or, worse, trolling. It's not just people in the industry either; we're all constantly bombarded by other people's opinions every time we turn on our smartphones or computers. I think my exposure to a certain amount of scrutiny and rejection at a young age has given me armour. As an adult, when people criticise or pick holes in me publicly – in the press or on social media – I don't take it on board. I try not to let it touch the sides. It doesn't work one hundred per cent of the time – nobody's indestructible – but, as a rule, I'm able to shake it off and move on. It's just somebody else's opinion and nothing to do with me.

I changed my surname from Outen to Van Outen when I was in my teens. It came about because of what Dad told me about the probable origins of the Outen name. When Mum worked for a Dutch pharmaceutical company, all the staff and their partners were invited to attend a Christmas meal. At the dinner, the managing director commented to my parents that Outen was a name of Dutch origin and would originally have been Van Outen. Dad wasn't aware of any family history connected to Holland; his grandparents lived in Wapping, which had many Irish immigrants, including my ancestors on my mother's side. After a bit of research, Dad found out that Dutch settlers had started reclaiming land from the Thames to enable Wapping Marsh to become inhabitable. In return, they got a percentage of that land to keep as their own. Dad thinks he is probably a descendant of those original Dutch settlers, and, funnily enough, as a young child, my dad had light-blond hair and was nicknamed 'the little Dutch boy'. When it came to choosing a stage name, I decided it would be nice to include a bit of the old Dutch in my name. And so Denise Outen became Denise Van Outen.

CHAPTER FIVE

'Isn't that Denise dancing behind those boys on the telly?'

It's funny that people think of me as an Essex girl because, in truth, I spent most of my young life in London: Marylebone, where the school was, or Hackney, Islington and Ladbroke Grove, West London, which was where various friends lived. Because I lived so far from the school, I was forever staying at the house of one friend or another. This was especially true when I had an after-school audition or an extra drama class, or rehearsals for a school show. When I got to the age when I started going out in the evenings, there was no way I was going all the way back to Essex on a late-night train. Instead, I became the princess of sofa-surfing.

Being in certain classes with older girls meant that some of my friends were older than me. Consequently, I started going out in London at a reasonably young age. God, I think I went to my first nightclub at the age of 14, but my parents certainly didn't know what I was up to. Eventually, it became a bit of a regular thing when I was staying up in London. I'd go to Rage, which was at Heaven, under the arches at Charing Cross, or the Limelight on Charing Cross Road. This was about 1989/90 when I was 15 or 16, so I was raving at a very early age.

I would take my clubbing outfit to school in my bag and tell Mum and Dad that I was going out and then staying at a friend's. I stayed at friends' houses so much that they wouldn't have thought twice about it. That said, Mum and Dad were pretty relaxed anyway. I'd been away from home plenty of times for filming and various commercials, and I'd never got myself into any grief. I think they knew they could trust me to be sensible.

After school, I'd go to the house of whichever friend I was staying with – often it was Danniella Westbrook – and then we'd head out to the Limelight, all dressed up to the nines. There was a bouncer called Neville on the door there who always let us in, just because he liked us. From the first time I stepped into the Limelight, I fell in love with it. Housed in an old church, it seemed like a magical place to be, with this amazing music and the most fabulous people everywhere. I'd been to a few clubs before, which, on certain nights, catered towards a young crowd, but this felt so grown-up. When it became a more regular thing, either my dad or Danniella's would pick us up when we came out at 3am, making sure we got home safely. God, we were lucky to have such amazing parents. How many do you know who'd sit outside a club, waiting for their kids at that time in the morning?

Sometimes we'd stay at Danni's, and sometimes we'd go back to mine. We were never drunk or on anything illicit; we simply loved being out and dancing.

By then, it was hard to imagine going out in my home town with other people my age. How could I possibly hang around the local community centre drinking cider when I'd had a taste of a real West End club? I guess I'd grown up in an adult world because of the people I mixed with at school and the jobs I'd done. There was certainly no going back now.

Around this time, I started my earliest pop-singing gig, which was doing backup vocals for a band called Dreadzone. I did this alongside Mel Blatt, who later became one of All Saints. We gigged all over the place, including the London Astoria on Charing Cross Road, always for cash. Despite Mum and Dad being reasonably easy-going, I didn't tell them I was out gigging with a band of blokes at all hours of the night, thinking it might be a step too far. Instead, I'd take my chosen stage outfit to school with me in a plastic bag, as did Mel, so we could get changed when we needed to without detection.

The boys in Dreadzone were so sweet to Mel and me, and we loved performing with them. We'd go round to the place in Ladbroke Grove where they rehearsed, sit there all afternoon and then come out stinking of weed. Not that I smoked it – I've never been able to stand the stuff – but there was always plenty of people lighting up during those rehearsals. I remember going home sometimes reeking of the stuff. God knows how my mum and dad didn't cotton on, although it was a close call at times.

'What's that smell?' my dad would say, flaring his nostrils.

I'd just rush upstairs as fast as I could and douse myself with my Nina Ricci, just to get rid of the terrible smell. Once I'd showered and changed, I'd descend from my bedroom smelling fresh and looking like butter wouldn't melt. If only my folks knew that I'd spent the afternoon in a West London room full of dreadlocked stoners.

Of course, Mum and Dad knew I was doing bits and pieces of singing and that I was getting paid for it, but I don't think I laid on the line what I was really getting up to and with who a lot of the time. What teenager does? Besides, I wasn't doing anything wrong, and this was a paying job. When we played the Astoria with the boys, we might get paid 150 quid, or, for smaller gigs, 50. When you're 15 years old, that's a lot of money, especially back then. Plus, the boys really looked after us. I never once felt threatened or uncomfortable.

At the same time, as well as earning money, I was also learning more and more about performing, about the immediacy of live shows and audience reaction. I recall getting the same buzz going to those gigs as when I'd stood on a West End stage doing *Les Mis*. There was something wonderful about being in front of actual faces, with eyes staring up at me.

As I said, Mum and Dad had no idea that I was singing in a band until one evening when Dreadzone appeared on Gary Crowley's TV show *The Beat*. I'm not entirely sure why they watched the show, and I probably didn't expect them to be watching, but it turns out they were. Mel and I were very excited about the prospect of being on the telly with the boys, but I suppose I still didn't feel like it was news I needed to share with my parents. The story goes that while the show was flickering away on the TV and Mum and Dad tucked into their tea, Dad suddenly looked up, squinting at the screen.

''Ere, Kath, isn't that Denise dancing behind those boys on the telly?'

'What? Don't be daft,' Mum said. 'Why would she be doing that?'

When Mum took a closer look, she said, 'I think you're right. I think that is Denise.'

They never minded, though. It was the sort of thing they'd come to expect from me, and I suppose they trusted me. I think Mum just thought that as long as I was earning money in the field I wanted to be in, and being safe and responsible, then why not?

The TV show I really wanted to get onto was *Grange Hill*. Some of my classmates had got parts in it, but I never got picked, even though I auditioned several times.

Eventually, aged 15, I got my first proper TV acting job: a series regular in a teen sci-fi drama called *Kappatoo*. This meant that I had to relocate to Newcastle. It was something else I simply accepted because it was work. I lived in a house in an upmarket area called Jesmond with several other cast members – a couple of whom were also from Sylvia's. We also had a chaperone and a tutor, so we didn't miss out on our academic studies.

The show was about a time-travelling boy from the future and his doppelgänger, a nineties schoolboy footballer, who swapped places. I played Tracy Cotton, one of the main character's classmates, and was thrilled to discover that I had a budget for my costumes. As it was a sci-fi drama, I went to contemporary designers of the day, like Pam Hogg, and most of my costumes were inspired by the looks I wore for clubbing. I also loved

Gaultier and John Richmond, and I ended up spending all my money on just a couple of great pieces.

It's funny, with all the work I'd done as a child, I should have left school with a nice big chunk of money in the bank, but I pretty much spent it all on my school fees. And clubbing! As far as I was concerned, it was worth every penny. Sylvia's had been the best experience and the best start I could have hoped for. If I could go back now, I would. I loved the freedom we had, the creative community around me, the buzz of getting a job. I even loved prepping for the auditions.

I have to be honest, as big an event as it was, moving away from my home, family and school at such a young age didn't faze me too much. I'm not sure why I was such an independent soul, but that was the truth of it. It was a job, something I loved doing, into which I threw myself. I didn't dwell on what I might be missing back home. This line of thought became a bone of contention in some of my relationships over the years. Much to the annoyance of some of my former boyfriends, I don't really miss people when I'm away. I remember one of my exes once complaining to me, 'You don't ring me much when you're away.'

If I'm going away to do a job, I focus on what I'm doing, and that's that. I suppose it's been both a positive and a negative thing. On the positive side, I can concentrate on the job at hand and crack on with it, but on the other hand, it impacts the people around me and my loved ones. In the past, people I'm close to have mistakenly thought I don't care enough about them or that I'm not bothered about us being apart. That's not the truth of it at all; I just have to concentrate on what I'm doing. It's the way I've always been.

While I was working on *Kappatoo*, I spoke to my parents on the phone regularly, but I wasn't pining for home. On the contrary, I was having the time of my life. Can you imagine, at the age of 15, living in a house with your mates – all earning a decent bit of money? In the day, we'd be on a film set, getting to do what we loved – performing – as well as learning new things every single day. At night, we'd all hang out together, ordering take-out with our food allowances. Of course, most nights, we'd be larking about when we were supposed to be sleeping: chatting late into the night or sneaking off to the kitchen for midnight feasts. Honestly, I was living my best life, set up in an apartment full of cute boys and girlfriends on tap. I was lucky enough to be doing all the things that most kids don't get to do, and I knew it.

The other thing was, I really should have been sitting my exams during my time on the show, but I wasn't interested in academia. I suppose because I'd worked from a young age, the idea of not being able to get a job once I left school was somewhat alien to me. The only exam I remember sitting was biology, but I never took it seriously. I remember my science teacher, Dr Kang, being furious when he spotted my answer to the opening question, 'What is biology?' I'd jokingly written, 'It's a rave', in reference to the big illegal rave of the same name. Dr Kang only saw it because I flashed my paper to a couple of my mates, who started giggling. In the end, I was asked to leave the room for disrupting the exam.

Mum and Dad had slightly differing opinions on the fact that I was missing these critical milestones.

'It's not right; she should be in school taking her exams,' Dad told Mum.

Like all dads, he wanted me to get a good education, and I think he felt I was growing up too quickly. Mum thought a bit more like me when it came to me going to Newcastle to work.

'It's an amazing opportunity for Denise,' she said. 'Think about all the people she'll get to meet and the things she'll learn. This is what she's chosen as a career, after all; she can always go back and resit her exams.'

That's what ended up being the plan. I would go back and sit my exams the following year. It never happened, though. At the time, I just didn't think exams and academic qualifications were what I needed. By the time I left school, I had quite the CV, and the upside of working from a young age was that my experience meant that I landed a fair few jobs. The downside was that I couldn't add up for toffee. Luckily, my English was OK, but I was rotten in anything like history and geography.

Looking back, I wish I had concentrated on my studies more. These days, I'm pretty business-minded, but there have been times when I could have saved myself a lot of upset and grief if I'd been a bit more book-smart. There are specific contracts and situations I could have felt better about if I'd had a clearer understanding of them. I've tended to shy away from too much information and let other people sort things out for me, which hasn't always been the best way forward.

With my daughter, Betsy, I take a different view. I suppose I'm halfway between my mum and my dad on that front. I encourage her creativity as much as possible, but I also want her to concentrate on her studies. I try to be honest with her when it comes to the importance of learning.

'Not concentrating on my lessons is where I went wrong, and now I wish I had,' I told her.

It's not something I dwell on, but it does affect me now and again. Just today, my agent Rebecca called asking if I'd like to be on the celebrity version of *Who Wants to Be a Millionaire?* Now, I'd love to have gone on the show, but how?

'Can I not go on with Eddie?' I asked her. 'We could go on as a *Gogglebox* couple. He's good with the answers, and I'm quite good at sitting there, going, "Ooh it could be B, or then again it might be D – what do you think?"'

That idea wasn't going to fly, unfortunately. I don't know, would that situation have been any different if I'd have sat my geography exam? I'd have probably have forgotten it all by now anyway.

CHAPTER SIX

I was a bit of a late bloomer

I was a bit of a late bloomer as far as boys were concerned. To me, boys were mates rather than crushes. I laughed and joked with the lads, and they seemed to accept me like that, almost like I was one of them. I think it was probably because I was unfazed by some of their brashness and smutty conversation, unlike some of the other girls. I was happy to join in the fun. Down the line in the nineties, of course, I was one of a group of young entertainment industry women who were labelled the 'ladettes', which I'll be talking about later in the book. Perhaps this was where it started, always having a laugh and a joke with the lads when I was 15.

The trouble with that was, none of them ever really fancied me. I just wasn't the kind of girl that the teenage boys mooned over back then. While most of my friends were well on the way to young womanhood, I was a relatively late developer. Many of my girlfriends started their periods when they were 11 or 12; they were growing boobs and pubes. I didn't have my first period until I was 14, and by then, I was tall and a bit gangly, which didn't exactly add to my confidence. I think that's where a lot of my shyness with boys came from. All the other girls had boobs, something for the boys to play with. Meanwhile, I was all legs, with no bum and nothing up top.

I went through a few awkward phases back then. During my Sun-In phase, I sprayed hair-lightening product into my hair with abandon, turning it an orange-ginger. I also had a slightly spotty stage, which was difficult but, I suppose, not uncommon for a teenager. I was also obsessed with having a massive fringe, so I never went anywhere without a Braun Independent gas curler about my person so that I could embellish my fringe at any given moment.

I just wasn't aware of myself as someone who might be appealing to boys, and I certainly wasn't any good at flirting. I was convinced that my forte was making people laugh, so that was what I decided to stick to. On the rare occasion that a friend suggested that one of the boys fancied me, I dismissed it. I didn't believe it because that's not how I saw myself.

I did have one big crush on a boy called Nick Pickard. Nick had two brothers, and his mum and dad owned a pub. We also shared the same birthday, which I thought was a sign we should be together. He was in the year below me at Sylvia's, and eventually became the longest-serving cast member on *Hollyoaks*, playing the character Tony Hutchinson right from episode one. The trouble was, whenever Nick paid me even the slightest bit of attention, I'd go straight into larking about and joking mode. It was, I suppose, a defence mechanism of sorts. I had plenty of confidence when it came to performing or playing a part, but very little when it came to the real me. It's something I didn't think about much at the time and something that never bothered me that much either. My friends just seemed more comfortable and natural around boys, so I sort of accepted that's how it was.

There was one night, however, when I made a real effort. I got all dressed up for a party, and I thought, *Tonight's the night. Tonight, I'm going to get a snog from Nick Pickard.* However, my dreams were shattered when one of my mates informed me during that party that Nick was in the cupboard, snogging somebody called Claire. It turned out to be true, and when Claire emerged from the cupboard, she looked at me with pity.

'Oh, sorry, are you upset?' she said.

'No,' I said stubbornly.

Nick could see what was going on and tried to make amends. 'It's you I like, not her,' he said. 'She just came on to me.'

Of course, he was just a teenage boy doing what most teenage boys do at parties, but at the time I was devastated.

It wasn't until my clubbing days that I got into dating and boys a bit more seriously, and then I always tended to go for the wrong'uns! I'd also get bored quite quickly; possibly my self-diagnosed ADHD kicking in again. I'd start seeing someone, and my friends would say, 'She'll get bored in a month,' and they were often right. I could never seem to settle.

My first proper boyfriend was definitely a wrong'un, although it took me several years to find out just how 'wrong' he'd turn out to be. In my later school years, I had a good friend who lived locally to me. Sam was a year older than me but also went to Sylvia's. The two of us often travelled to school on the train together. She lived in Grays in Essex, so we'd generally meet up en route, with Sam joining the train at her stop. Whenever I was in Essex, Sam and I would hang out, venturing onto the local scene, despite the fact we were both far too young to be out at bars and clubs. Our favourite places were Pzaz, a nightclub in Grays, and the iconic Hollywood's in Romford. I was still only 15 when I first went to these places, but, somehow, we always managed to blag our way in.

Pzaz felt like such a glamorous place, back in the day; one of those clubs with sophisticated laser lights and state-of-the-art sound systems. At 10pm each night, the lighting would change and go all moody while laser lights fired around the room. It was like some kind of opening ceremony, and if you happened to get caught up in it, walking through the doors and descending the stairs into the club at that moment, everyone would stare up at you, lit up like some kind of Hollywood star, making a grand entrance. The entire staircase would light up.

Rather than feeling like a star, I always dreaded people gawping up at me on the staircase. I felt like it increased the chances that I'd get spotted and therefore rumbled for being too young. Generally, we tried to time it exactly right, and the best time was just before ten when there were enough people inside to offer a bit of camouflage, but no grand entrance. Leaving it till after ten meant there was a risk you might not get in at all because there was always a long queue outside.

One night, Sam and I strolled into Pzaz just in time to beat the lights, but just as we got to the bottom couple of steps, it all kicked off, and we were right in the firing line.

On this occasion, we were spotted by two well-dressed guys – smart casual as was required – and, of course, we were looking pretty glam too. It was the done thing. Going out in Essex has always been a dressy affair. You may well have marvelled at all the young people dolled up to the absolute nines on shows like *The Only Way Is Essex*; well, it's always been like that. In some parts of Essex, they power dress just to pop out for a loaf of bread.

That night, the boys, who for legal reasons we'll call Mike and Andy, started chatting to us the second we landed. Mike was blond, blue-eyed and handsome, and I must have thought it was my lucky night, meeting such a hunk, mere seconds after descending the magic stairs. It was the start of my first real relationship, and Sam dated Andy for a while, too, although that didn't last long.

Mike was 23 at the time, and I kept up the lie that I was 18 while in truth I was two and a half years younger than I was letting on. While we dated, we did all things young Essex couples did at that time: cinema dates; hanging out at one another's houses; a few nights out in Pzaz. I hadn't slept with him at this point because I was pretty nervous about sex, especially given the difference in our age. Thinking about it, I suppose I was in awe of Mike, which is probably a reflection of how naive I was, despite, at the time, thinking otherwise. Still, it was all fine and dandy between us for a while until his mate Andy told him how old I was. I assumed he must have found out from Sam, but I couldn't be sure. Mike confronted me one night, insisting I come clean. The funny thing was, once I did tell him my actual age, he was all right about it. He said the age gap didn't bother him because we got on and enjoyed one another's company. We carried on dating for over a year, and in the end, Mike was the boy I lost my virginity to. There was no pressure on his part, it was a mutual thing, but the fact was, he was aware of my age. At the time, I didn't think much about it. Quite a few girls I knew went out with older guys, and though Mum wasn't at all keen on me dating an older boy, she thought I was sensible enough to know my own mind. I'd been independent and mixing with people much older than me throughout my childhood, and there was no getting away from it; I did come across as older than my years. I also think she knew I'd have talked to her if I'd felt like I was out of my depth.

With the benefit of hindsight, I now realise how manipulative Mike could sometimes be; cruel, even. He knew that many of my friends from Sylvia's had done well and currently featured in various TV shows and was also aware that I had the potential to achieve the same success. He seemed to like the idea of that for a while – the idea that he could go out with someone who was on TV. When that success didn't come quickly, Mike never missed an opportunity to remind me of the fact I wasn't doing as well as Danniella Westbrook or one of my other, more famous school friends. It was hurtful, of course, but then the next minute he'd be all lovey-dovey and I'd forget about it until the next time. In the days before mobile phones, Mike and I used to write little notes and letters to one another, but, looking back, I now see that even that was something he wanted to control. Instead of letting me compose my notes in my own way, he started almost dictating what I should write.

'Tell me how much you love me,' he'd say. 'Tell me you can't stand not being with me and how much you miss me when we're not together.'

Eventually, he started to lose interest in me. I guess the novelty wore off, and that was when our relationship broke down.

I was upset at the time, but you tend to bounce back at that age, don't you? Plus, I had plenty of things to keep me occupied. Despite not reaching the level of success of some of my contemporaries, I still had plenty of goals and ambitions. There was still work to do.

I had no idea at the time, but this wasn't going to be the last I heard of Mike, and when he did surface again a few years later, it threatened to turn my world upside down.

CHAPTER SEVEN

Working by day and partying by night

I'd fallen in love with dance music and clubs, going from Wham! to hardcore rave in a single bound. When I wasn't out clubbing, I'd sit in my bedroom listening to pirate radio stations, like Centreforce, which broadcast from Newham in East London. Centreforce was a rave station that became a major part of the scene, promoting all of the big raves around the M25, like Genesis, Sunrise and Biology. Even when I was in school, I'd grab every chance I could to disappear into my own private rave. I often sat next to a boy called Aaron, who was as much into the rave scene as I was. We'd sit there in class, sharing a pair of headphones coming from his Walkman, our heads nodding through a biology class, not listening to a single word the teacher was saying.

Once school was over, I made a whole new group of clubbing friends, many of whom lived in Islington, where I spent more and more time. I was always in London, either working or clubbing, so the commute back to Essex just felt more and more pointless. I think if you asked my mum about that moment in time, she'd say that it was the point I began to drift away from the family. There was no conscious or deliberate attempt to do that on my part, but I guess she'd be right. I certainly wasn't what you might call the model daughter, going out on girly shopping outings and spa days with Mum. I was now completely caught up in the world outside my family, a world of working by day and partying by night. I seemed to have achieved the perfect balance between those two things, but there wasn't much time for anything else. Over the years, Mum and I talked about this. She's been honest that my not being around very much upset her; she would have liked to have seen more of me. At the time, I didn't consider the fact that my mum and dad might have been sitting down at mealtimes, missing me and wondering what I might be doing. The thought that they might be upset because their 17-year-old daughter hadn't been home to see them in three months didn't cross my mind. Now that I'm a mum, I completely get it, but I suppose when you're young, you think differently. Back then, I considered myself a grown-up, existing in an adult world, doing my own thing and making my own money. I was still incredibly young, though. As much as my parents trusted me and knew I had a pretty good head on my shoulders, they must have worried. I know I would if Betsy was out in the world at such a young age, especially getting up to some of the capers I was.

One of the things I loved was making my own clubbing outfits. My nan had taught me to sew when I was about ten. She had a box bedroom, which she'd converted into her machining room. I loved watching her work, and it was there that she taught me to hand-sew. By the time I was a teenager, I was very handy with a needle and cotton, forever sewing buttons on or fixing rips and tears in my mates' clothes, on holidays and trips away.

I was always pretty good at putting together an original look for a night out. Nowadays, I wish I'd kept up with sewing and making clothes because it's something I loved doing back in the day. There was barely an item of clothing I didn't customise in some way, and, in the end, my original take on clubbing gear became popular among my mates, who would ask me to make things for them. I made little frou-frou bikini tops, or I'd buy a T-shirt and customise it with sequins and feathers, knotting it under my bust and pairing it with spray-on PVC trousers. Sometimes I'd go out wearing angel wings, and I always wore a bindi.

Pushca parties were a favourite night out for us; they had a reputation for excitement and glamour. Their nights were always big-budget affairs with specially constructed sets, fantastic lighting and fantastic sound systems.

At the other end of the spectrum, there were the more underground raves around the M25, where we'd all meet at South Mimms service station in Potters Bar. Service stations were always a great place to meet before an illegal rave because they were easy to find and big enough for large groups of keen ravers to congregate.

One particular Pushca party I recall was the 'Fun Furry Fakes Party', where I transformed myself into a glamorous furry club cat with a little skirt, ears and a tail. When the party was over, a few of us went back to my friend Tamara's flat and stayed up all night, which, as you can imagine, wasn't unusual. Tamara must have forgotten that her mum was due to pop round the following day, probably just around the time when we might have been thinking of getting a few hours of shut-eye. When it suddenly hit her that her mum would be there at any minute, she flipped out. She knew her mum would go mad at the sight of all the cans, bottles and ashtrays everywhere, not to mention the various bodies in fun-fur get-ups draped over chairs, while someone threw their guts up in the bathroom. She demanded we all hide immediately, which wasn't what I wanted to hear in my delicate state, at that hour of the morning. I managed to find what I thought was a perfect hiding place in the bedroom wardrobe, but my friend's horrified mother ended up searching the entire place. I'm not sure what she must have thought when she opened the wardrobe door to discover me dressed as a cat.

'Hello, Christine,' I said, like this was all perfectly normal.

'What are you doing in there?' she said. 'Get out!'

These were the years of wild partying and experimenting for so many young people, me included. It was like this craving for fun freedom had swept across the youth of the country. I suppose most generations have their time of rebellion, like rock and roll in the fifties and punk in the seventies. This one was ours, and I feel fortunate to have grown up during the era of raves and house music. I did all of the clubs: the Cross, Bagley's, Ministry of Sound. I lived for the weekends, out every Thursday, Friday and Saturday, and often Sunday as well.

I remember one Sunday morning, after being up all night, my friend Lucy and I were sad to realise that we'd run out of alcohol.

'Where the hell would be open on a Sunday morning that we could get some wine?' Lucy said.

I thought for a moment, and then it hit me. 'Church!'

As a Roman Catholic, I knew that there was Communion wine for sipping, plus there was always a little reception and mingle after the service in the little church in Kensington, where we could get a bevvy. God knows what I was thinking, but I'm ashamed to say it wasn't a one-time thing either.

As well as Tamara, who I'm still very close to, another of my new friends was actress Sheree Murphy. I practically lived with her and her family from the age of about 16. I was about 17 when I started dating a friend of Sheree's brothers, a DJ called Darren, and it wasn't long before we'd moved in together. There was no real forethought or planning that went into our cohabitation; it just sort of happened. This story saddens me a bit because Sheree and I were good friends, and I suppose it was my relationship with Darren and the way it came about that came between us for a long time.

On the night I first got together with Darren, Sheree and I had gone for a night out at the Gardening Club in Covent Garden. Sometime during the evening, Darren asked me if I wanted to go back to his flat, which I thought sounded very exciting and grown-up. I mean, most of my mates still lived with their parents, so when you made your way home from a club, you had to behave yourself and be quiet. You all know what teenagers are like; happy to stay up all night and sleep the day away. Yes, I was bang up for going back to Darren's for a bit of an after-party. The only problem was, Sheree had told her mum that we would be going home after the club, so she didn't want to go to Darren's flat.

'You go, I don't mind,' she told me, but I wasn't sure I should be leaving her to go home alone.

'It's fine, honestly,' she said.

As Darren's place was only around the corner from Sheree's mum's, I decided to take the plunge and carry on partying. The next day, however, I had to do the walk of shame from Darren's place round to Sheree's to get my clothes and bags, which I'd left there. When I arrived at the house, Sheree's mum Heather opened the door, not looking terribly happy.

'Sheree doesn't want to see you, Denise,' she said.

'What? Why not?'

'You don't go out to a club with a girlfriend and then go off with a boy and leave her. It's not the done thing.'

I was a bit confused. 'Sheree told me I should go; she said it was fine. I asked her more than once.'

'It doesn't matter. You just don't do it,' Heather said. 'I'll get your things for you, but you're not seeing Sheree.'

Heather disappeared back into the house while I waited on the doorstep. When she reappeared, she handed me my bags, said her goodbyes and closed the front door. I was left slightly bewildered. Again, it's one of those things that, as a mum, I now understand entirely, but back then, I was a teenage girl, determined to follow the party wherever it went. I didn't stop to think about much else.

Feeling a bit lost, I headed to the nearest phone box and called Darren.

'I'm not sure what to do,' I said. 'I'm supposed to be at Sheree's for the weekend, but her mum won't let me go in.'

I certainly didn't fancy calling my dad at that point. The last thing I wanted, after all that, was him rocking up to take me home with me still wearing my frou-frou bra and him going mad because I'd been up all night. The other option was public transport, but with a choice of the Sunday skeleton service or an X1 coach from Embankment being the only options, that didn't appeal either.

'You'll have to come back round here,' Darren said.

So that's what I did. Within 20 minutes, I was back sitting in Darren's bed with a mug of tea. I guess you could say we were thrown together, and things just developed from there. We went out for a bite later that day, and he asked me what I was doing the following weekend. From then on, I was there more and more until I'd practically moved in. Darren was chuffed because the rent was 40 quid a week, and, with me living there, we could split it and pay 20 each. It was hardly Kate and Leo in *Titanic*, but bloody hell, my own flat in Islington! As far as I was concerned, it was a done deal.

Sheree and I were never close after that, which made me sad. We've since talked about that night, both acknowledging it was a silly thing to have come between us for all those years. At the end of the day, I know Sheree's mum was right: I shouldn't have gone off and left her. I was wrong, and I lost a good friend for a lot of years because of it. I guess the worst part about it is that I have always considered myself a girl's girl – someone who looks after her mates, supports her friends. It's always stuck in my mind that I chose to go off with a guy on that occasion, leaving my friend to get home from a nightclub on her own at the age of 17. I was brought up Roman Catholic, which means that I tend to hold on to guilt when I feel like I've done something wrong. I find it hard to let go of those thoughts and feelings. I guess those things are all part of growing up. They're things that you've done which you learn from.

Darren lived in a housing association flat, passed on to him by his mum. It was a nice place, and quite large. Most of our friends still lived with their mums and dads, so Darren's flat had become the Mecca for after-parties and post-clubbing hang-outs. My mum and dad seemed to accept that I'd flown the coop, although, if I'm honest, they probably weren't over the moon about it. I think by then Mum had gotten used to the idea that I had a huge independent streak and that I was going to go off and do my own thing as soon as I could. She's since told me that one of the reasons she allowed me so much freedom was because it was something she never had. Mum's parents were quite strict with her, and there are lots of things she'd have liked to have done, given half the chance. She's a naturally funny person and probably could have been a performer herself. I've heard people say that Mum should have been on the stage, and I know she would have loved to have done many of the things I have. I believe that's why she was so determined to give me those opportunities and the freedom that went with them. I can't say I'd be happy about my daughter having that sort of free rein at such a young age. The thought of her staying up all night and partying or heading off into the night with friends of friends to unfamiliar places makes me very uncomfortable. It would frighten me.

Times have changed. I think we're more aware of all the pitfalls and dangers out there than we were 30 years ago; the internet, social media and 24-hour news see to that. I don't think there's necessarily more bad things and evil people out there than before; we just hear more about them. We can't help but hear about them.

With all that said, I was, on the whole, sensible and responsible through all of it. I had my wits about me, especially where work was concerned. I never missed a day of work, an audition or a casting call because I'd been out clubbing. Not once. Even if, on occasion, I only managed to get my head down for an hour, I never missed a job. How could I? The money I earned from working often went on the entry fee to a club and a cab home. Despite the odd Sunday-morning trek to church mingles to pilfer the odd glass of wine, we weren't big drinkers; it was too expensive in some of the clubs. For us, it was all about the music, the dancing and the whole club scene, with all its crazy variants. I might find myself at a glitzy West End dance party one night and a dive in Dalston the next, and I loved them all.

● ● ●

With rent and nights out to pay for, I couldn't simply rely on my acting work, so I took a job working in the fashion store Stirling Cooper, on Oxford Street. Diana, a friend of mine from Sylvia

Young's, worked there and managed to get a couple of other girls and me a job. Although I had my sights firmly set on making it in the entertainment industry, as we all did, I also needed to pay my 20-quid rent every week. Also, I quite liked working there, although at times I found it frustrating. My manager at Stirling Cooper was Andrea. She was pretty strict, and I think the fact that we were a bunch of ex-stage school kids, only there until something better came along, annoyed the hell out of her. You can imagine the sort of tricks we all got up to when there were no eyes on us.

One day, our task was to dress all the store's window mannequins, which we decided needed a bit of a revamp, style-wise. It was a time when Björk had just hit it big, so we thought it would be a fabulous idea to give all the mannequins buns in their hair, just like the ones sported by the hip Icelandic singer. Björk-buns, we called them. Not only that, but we then decided that we should have Björk-buns too – all the sales staff.

Andrea was not best pleased when she came into the store to check on our progress. She went mad, shouting at us and insisting we put it all right and de-bun the dummies immediately. It wasn't just the re-styling she was fuming about either. She always insisted that the music we play in-store should be easy on the ear. Pop music was fine, as long as it was middle of the road, easy-going and not too frantic or loud. Well, that day, we'd all been dancing around the store, bobbing our buns to loud banging house music. It's what we always did when Andrea wasn't around.

I have to say she was usually pretty good with a flexible rota, was Andrea, allowing us to swap shifts or make up time if someone had a dentist appointment or a funeral to attend. Yes, she was strict, but she also wanted people to like her. In fact, she often went out of her way to stay popular with her staff.

However, when I landed a part in a Thomas Cooke commercial, Andrea wasn't quite so generous. Doing the commercial meant that I'd need to be away for three days' filming in Gran Canaria, which sounded amazing. I asked Andrea if I could swap a few shifts with my co-workers to accommodate the filming schedule. Andrea told me that I could not, which culminated in a bit of row, during which Andrea practically laughed in my face.

'Why are you chasing this silly dream that you're never going to achieve?' she asked me. 'It's never going to happen.'

That afternoon, I told Andrea that she could stick her job, before marching out of Stirling Cooper onto a bustling Oxford Street. Bloody hell, what had I done? I'd walked out on a job that I relied on. Bits and bobs of commercial work were all well and good, but I needed regular money to pay my half of the rent, not to mention my spends for clothes and going out.

I told myself I'd get by, but I won't pretend I wasn't worried. Was Andrea right? Was this simply some impossible dream I was chasing? I thought about some of my friends and contemporaries from Sylvia's. Many of them were already establishing themselves on various TV shows. Danniella Westbrook, for instance, was now a regular in *EastEnders*, playing Sam Mitchell. By then, whenever we went out, she'd be decked out head-to-toe in John Richmond while I was still upcycling T-shirts with sequins and feathers. What money I did make, I was being increasingly careful with. I knew what I needed to live on, and the rest I tried to save. I knew that all I needed was a lucky break; then, it would be my turn to shine.

Still, I sometimes wondered if I was brilliant enough at any one thing to make that happen. It was something Sylvia had made me consider during a career advice session we had one day.

'The good thing about you, Denise, is that you can do a little bit of everything, so you'll always work,' she said. 'Still, that comes with a downside. Because you don't focus on one thing, you might not flourish in any one field and not achieve the pinnacle of fame and success. Flitting from one thing to another can have both a positive and negative side.'

Sylvia was right. I have always been someone who's known for lots of different things throughout my career but not renowned for one particular thing. I believe it's worked in my favour because, as Sylvia suggested that day, I have always worked. However, back then, with so many of my contemporaries seemingly racing ahead and making names for themselves, I did have a few wobbles. There were many times when I remember thinking, *When is it going to be my turn?*

CHAPTER EIGHT

'Do you fancy being in a pop band?'

I fell into the pop scene by accident. It was one of those things you hear about, you know, being in the right place at the right time, much like the girls from the Human League who were plucked off a dance floor by the band's frontman, Phil Oakey. Sometime in late 1993, aged 19, I was out in a bar somewhere – for the life of me, I can't remember where – when a stocky bloke with blond hair strolled up and said to me, 'Do you fancy being in a pop band?' It was that simple.

This man turned out to be pop music impresario Denis Ingoldsby, who'd already managed some major UK pop acts like Dina Carroll and Eternal. The thing was, he looked nothing like I imagined a successful music mogul might look. In fact, he looked and sounded a bit like he should be selling used motors from a car lot forecourt in East London.

That evening, Denis filled me in on the details of the duo he was looking to form, and we got chatting. Of course, I was intrigued when he said he thought I'd be a great fit in the group. The funny thing was, at no point did he ask me if I could sing. That didn't seem to bother him in the slightest. He just thought I looked like a pop star. Whether or not I sounded like one seems to be immaterial. I guess that's been the case throughout vocal pop group history, and it certainly was around that time. You have your stand-out singers, then the ones who were passable, and then the ones who were just there to up the ante – the ones with the looks and personalities rather than cracking voices. It's the way it's always been. Anyway, I guess that's the way Denis viewed me. I looked all right, and he could see I had confidence, so he wasn't all that fussed about whether I could carry a tune or not.

The following week, I headed to the First Avenue offices in Hammersmith, insisting that a friend come along with me. It was only then that Denis asked me to sing something, and, of course, having auditioned hundreds of times for hundreds of different jobs, I was all ready for action. I performed 'Le Jazz Hot!', the big jazz-hands Julie Andrews musical number from the movie *Victor/Victoria*. It was one of my tried and trusted audition songs, and I knew I could do it well. Once I'd finished singing, Denis just laughed at me.

'Can you sing something more pop or current?' he said.

I was a little bit shocked, thinking I'd done something wrong.

'Not really,' I said. 'I only know rave music.'

Still, Denis didn't seem all that bothered that I wasn't really into pop music and offered me the gig anyway. The band was to be called Those 2 Girls, although, at that point, I'd not even met the other girl, who'd been on board with the project for some time. I was signed by Denis Ingoldsby and Oliver Smallman's First Avenue Management, and, being the successful management team they were, it wasn't long before we were cracking open the champagne at the offices of Arista Records, signing a deal.

It was something I hadn't even considered before. I was an actor, not a pop singer, but this was an opportunity I wasn't about to pass up. The weirdest part about it was, I barely knew Cathy Warwick, the girl I'd been thrust into a pop band with, and vice versa. Nobody seemed to have thought about chemistry or whether we might get on together; we were suddenly this musical entity with a major record deal.

At the time, Cathy was considered the singer. I think I'd only been brought in because Denis thought I looked the part. Cathy had a great voice, but my impression was that Denis didn't know if she was strong enough to make it as a solo artist. Like me, she came from a stage school background. She'd gone to Italia Conti, along with Louise Redknapp (née Nurding), who at the time was part of another one of Denis and Oliver's big acts, Eternal.

With our debut single 'Wanna Make You Go . . . Uuh!' about to hit the shops, we were booked onto the Radio One Massive Music Tour, along with huge chart acts like Boyzone, Take That and Peter Andre. It was all very exciting, of course, but not exactly what I was hoping for. I'd come from a background of performing and acting – it's what I loved – so, for me, this was a bit of a turnaround and not exactly in my comfort zone. They didn't even expect me to do any actual singing. Cathy handling the vocals was seemingly a foregone conclusion, so it fast became apparent, as far as Those 2 Girls was concerned, Denis had brought me in to be 'the pretty one'. Other than turning up at the right place at the right time and learning a few moves, not much else was required of me.

Meanwhile, at one of our early recording sessions, one of the producers asked me to sing something and was pleasantly surprised at the results.

'Oh, you can sing,' he said, as if somebody had previously warned him that I couldn't.

I stood at the microphone feeling happy, but at the same time awkward – although I shouldn't have. The problem was, me singing lead vocals on one of our tracks was not the status quo, and the idea of it put Cathy's nose out of joint somewhat. She was the singer. I was there to look pretty, pout and do a bit of dancing, so when the producers suggested that I sing a bridge or middle 8 of a song, it didn't go down well. That wasn't the deal as far as she was concerned, and she made her feelings clear.

After that, there was friction between the two of us. I don't think it was anyone's fault, really; it was more the way that whole thing had come about. We'd both been thrown in at the deep end with our prospective roles, and we were just expected to get on with it. I could see her side of it: Cathy was a nice girl and what she'd initially been sold when she'd signed up wasn't what she'd ended up with. She was originally going to be a solo artist, but Denis thought she'd have a better shot at success in a duo – hence my presence. Still, there were times on the Radio One tour when Cathy barely spoke to me, and the whole thing felt toxic. It was the absolute opposite to the experience I'd had singing backing vocals for Dreadzone with Mel. Then, we could wear whatever we wanted, dance around, sing and revel in the camaraderie of performing together. This situation was something else entirely. It was all, 'You can't say this, you can't wear that? We weren't even supposed to have boyfriends, so male fans could see us as available. After everything I'd done by that point, it was stifling. In all honesty, the most exciting thing for me was when Todd Terry remixed one of our tracks. I was at Culture Shock one evening, which was a club night at Hollywood's in Romford. The Sharp Boys were playing that night, and when they dropped the Todd Terry remix of 'Wanna Make You Go . . . Uuh!', I screamed out, 'IT'S MEEEE!' It was the highlight of my short-lived pop career.

At the same time as we were on the scene, another girl-pop duo came up through the ranks. Shampoo was a duo doing a more kooky pop version of what we were, and they were having a fair bit of success. It got to the point where we were being compared to them at every turn. Whenever Cathy and I did an interview with the pop bible *Smash Hits* or *Fast Forward* magazine, the journalist would ask what we thought of Shampoo and somehow attempt to pit us against them. I hated all that rivalry. I didn't want to be a part of that synthetic world of manufactured pop, vying for my rightful place as a serious performer against pop stars who wore giant sweets in their hair. Darling, I'd done *Les Misérables*, don't you know!

I was unhappy in the band. Deep down, I knew it wasn't what I wanted to do, but it's not easy to walk away from a situation like that with no other prospects in the offing.

Who'd have thought that something as ordinary as getting on a number 73 bus with a broken heel would change all that and lead me to the start of a whole new phase of my life?

• • •

I'd recently bought a pair of high wooden mules, which I called my 'Sandy shoes' as they were just like the ones Olivia Newton-John wore in the final scenes of *Grease* – you know, the ones she puts the cigarette out with on the fairground floor, just before she urges Danny to 'Tell me about it, stud' and bursts into 'You're the One That I Want'. Anyway, I'd got on the number 73, having just broken one of the heels on my fabulous mules. I ended up laughing and joking with some of the other passengers about my predicament.

At one point, one guy in particular, who I'd been bantering with during the journey, asked me, 'Have you ever thought about being a TV presenter?'

'I haven't,' I said, 'although I have got an agent.'

I'd left Sylvia's by then, having gotten a bit long in the tooth for her agency, which was more child- and teenager-specific. Now, aged 20, I had a new acting agent called Marylin, but I hadn't been doing any acting because of the band.

The guy I was bantering with was called Ben, and, as it turned out, he was a TV producer.

'Look, we're holding some auditions for a new Saturday-morning TV show; you should come in,' he said.

It was a bit of an odd way to find out about a job, but who was I to argue? A few days later, I turned up at a film studio on Wardour Street, where I was asked to do a simple screen test and leave my agent's details. Not long afterwards, I received a phone call from Marylin to say I'd got the job. It was as simple as that. If I took the job, I'd be presenting a show on ITV. Crikey, this was big, not to mention a way out of the unhappy work situation I'd found myself in.

I can remember as clear as anything delivering the bad news to Denis and his business partner Oliver. By then, we'd had a second single, 'All I Want', which had done better than our first single but had hardly set the charts alight. Denis was about to send us off on another Radio One summer tour. There were plans to discuss and a contract to sign, but as I sat there nervously in the First Avenue offices, I had other ideas.

'Denis, I've been offered a TV presenting job, and I really want to do it,' I told him.

He looked horrified. 'Oh, Den! Don't do that, for God's sake – it'll be the biggest mistake you'll ever make. You're a singer in a band signed to a major record label. The last thing you want to do is TV presenting.'

'Denis, I'm not a singer; I don't sing.' My voice was shaking. 'I'm a puppet. I don't do anything.'

'Look, I'll make sure the songs are split a bit more fairly,' he said. 'I'll make sure you get to sing a couple of lines on the songs.'

'I don't want a couple of lines on a song, Denis, and I don't want to be there just to make it all look good.'

'You won't last five minutes doing that,' Oliver said. 'What experience have you had TV presenting? You're not exactly going to make a career of it, are you?'

It was a daunting moment, making my feelings known to these two very successful music business managers: Oliver in his sharp suit and Denis in his tracksuit. They both seemed aggrieved at my suggestion that I could be doing something better than what they were offering. There was literally a contract on the table in front of me, and they were telling me I was mad if I didn't sign it . . . that we were guaranteed to get on the Radio One A-list if we signed and did the tour. What if they were right? What if I was making a massive mistake? I knew both Oliver and Denis were great at what they did and incredibly successful, but that didn't necessarily make it right for me, did it? Besides that, I just wasn't happy.

In the end, I walked out of that office that day, sure that I'd done the right thing. Even if the band was successful and we'd got on the Radio One playlist, *Top of the Pops* or whatever, what would be the point if it made me miserable? How could I be a performer in a band where I couldn't perform, with a bandmate who resented me being there?

I stuck to my guns and left the band, and, as it turned out, that presenting job – a spin-off section of the kids' TV show *Scratchy & Co.* – was the thing that would lead me to the job that would change my whole life: a job that would ultimately afford me the career I have today. That's something that has always stuck in my mind. Suppose I'd listened to Oliver and Denis that day; I'd have ended up on another Radio One tour miming to records I hadn't even sung on and possibly having another minor hit before disappearing into pop obscurity.

Massive! was the section of *Scratchy & Co.* which was aimed at a slightly older audience than the rest of the show. It was a magazine show, I suppose – a real mixed bag, with teen-relevant features, interviews and silly skits, but I wasn't the only presenter. The idea was to team with a model called Malcolm Jeffries, someone I knew by his modelling name, Cassius. He was gorgeous: olive-skinned with long hair and piercing eyes. He was always in the teen girls' mags, like *Just Seventeen*, and exactly my cup of tea looks-wise. I couldn't believe my luck.

Presenting the show allowed me to dip my toe into the world of celebrity culture for the very first time. I got to interview big stars like Lenny Kravitz, who was my first big interview. Up until that point, Malcolm, who was something of a teen heartthrob, handled most of the celebrity interviews, while I did bits and pieces, like wakeboarding on location or being sawn in half by a magician in the studio.

I interviewed Lenny Kravitz at the Portobello Hotel, and, once we'd finished, he told me that he was playing a gig that evening.

'Why don't you come along, and we can have a drink after?' he said.

'I'm not sure I can,' I said, knowing full well that I would.

I mean, if Lenny Kravitz asks you out, you don't say no, do you?

When I arrived at the after-show drinks, the first person I spotted was Lenny's then-girlfriend Vanessa Paradis. He'd been quite flirty during the interview, so I assumed he'd probably just invited me in case she didn't turn up – a Basildon backup, so to speak! Consequently, I didn't stay for long.

The interview with Lenny seemed to go down well, though, and after that, I found myself interviewing Take That, Boyzone; I even interviewed Peter Andre in Prague.

One I'd rather forget was the interview I did with Matt Goss backstage at Wembley Arena. I'd grown up listening to Matt's band, Bros, who were huge in the eighties. This was undoubtedly an important interview, but I was generally quite relaxed when talking to big stars, never feeling particularly starstruck.

When I walked into Matt's dressing room, there was a massive bunch of red roses waiting for me on the chair next to him. My first thought was, *Oh, here we go! Matt's going to ask me out.* I made my way over to the chair and picked up the roses so that we could start the interview.

'They're lovely, Matt, thank you,' I said. 'It's sweet of you to do that.'

'They're not for you; a fan just gave them to me,' he said.

I literally could have died. I'd made an absolute fool of myself, and now I had to sit there and interview him on camera. I couldn't get out of there quick enough.

The show producers seemed to like me, probably because, more often than not, I was able to get things done in one take. I've no clue why; presenting was just something that seemed to come naturally to me. I'd get my script, learn it quickly, then I'd get it done. Coming from the world of modelling, Malcolm was used to being in front of a camera, but I think he found the presenting side a bit harder. As time went on, I started to feel like he was slightly resentful that I was breezing through it while he was struggling, which caused a certain amount of dissent between us. It wasn't the most comfortable working relationship in the end, and after all the bad feeling with Cathy in Those 2 Girls, I couldn't help but wonder if I was doing something wrong. Maybe I was just someone who needed to work solo instead of in a pair. Still, it wasn't like I was going out of my way to be difficult or disagreeable. All I wanted was to do my job as well as I could, whatever that job might be. The other problem was, I was at a bit of a loss as to what I wanted to do. Was I a pop artist? A presenter? An actor? Sylvia Young's words about never achieving a pinnacle of fame because I was doing a bit of everything rang in my ears regularly. However, things were about to change in a big way.

CHAPTER NINE

All about the gimmicks

When it came to going for jobs, I hadn't lost my creative streak when it came to asserting my suitability for a particular role. I wasn't shy about that. Sometimes I'd even add things to my CV that I hadn't done. There were times back in the day when I thought, *Right! What's been shot in the last couple of years that I might feasibly have been in?* I remember going up for a part in a film once, and adding a Roman Polanski film to my CV ... one that I was never in. Of course, with Google and the internet, you can't get away with that sort of thing any more, but back then I was pretty comfortable bolstering my credentials where necessary.

During my time on *Massive!* I was spotted by the producers of *The Big Breakfast* and asked to go up for a screen test to be the weather girl – yet another curveball. What did I know about reading a weather report? Didn't you have to have the right sort of meteorological knowledge for that? What I did know was that this was a fantastic opportunity. It was the summer of 1996, and *The Big Breakfast* had already been going for about four years by then. It had been an enormous success, although it had slipped in popularity a bit since the glory days of 1993, when it was presented by Chris Evans, Gaby Roslin and Paula Yates and got daily viewing figures of around two million. Back then, it was the highest-rated breakfast TV show in the country. Now, Channel 4 was doing a big relaunch of the show, and that's where I came in.

At the screen test, I met the show's creator, Charlie Parsons, and his partner Waheed Alli. As per, I went all out, fibbing about having taken a meteorological course and assuring them that I'd be able to write my own weather report. No one could ever accuse me of not being a trier! Charlie and Waheed later told me that they'd looked at one another when I'd walked out of the room, both slightly stunned.

'Look, she's full of shit, but I love her,' Charlie had said. 'Let's get her on board.'

Waheed told me they knew full well I was making it all up, but if I could sit there brazenly delivering that level of bullshit, I was definitely the girl for the job.

I started on the show in September 1996, and, back in the nineties, it was all about the gimmicks. Do you remember the cable channel Live TV, where the man reading the weather dressed up as a giant rabbit? The original idea was for me to read the weather in a bikini, but I said no to that straight off the bat. The next idea was to take the weather report out of *The Big Breakfast* house and into the air. They wanted me up in a chopper flying around the UK, delivering the weather and the traffic news, and that's what I did. On my first appearance, I hovered over Newcastle, speaking in my best TV presenting voice. It started quite straight, but I ended up with more bantering than weather-watching as time went on.

'If you want to know what the weather's like, have a look out of the window,' became one of my catchphrases. And I was always larking about with the pilot, playing instruments and doing anything else we could think of to liven up the weather slot.

As much as I loved working on the show, it was all-consuming. Now my entire lifestyle had to shift to accommodate work. I was up at 3.45am every morning, so I had to be in bed by eight or half past. The *EastEnders* theme tune was often my cue to get my head down. Everything had changed. I'd gone from being a proper little crazy club chick to an early-to-bed/early-to-rise good girl in a matter of a couple of months. The fact that my boyfriend Darren was still in that clubbing world, out DJing several nights a week, meant that our lives started moving in entirely different directions. Eventually, our relationship came to an end, and I moved out of the flat. By that time, I was away a lot, doing my high-in-the-sky chopper thing all around the country, but I still needed a base in London. A girlfriend called Kerry, who I knew from the club scene, offered me a room in a house in Kilburn. It was a tiny box-room and cost 50 quid a week, which was extortionate compared to what I'd been paying at Darren's. Still, I had to live somewhere, and now I had a decent job so I could just about manage what I saw as the bloody steep hike in rent. I was only going to be there at weekends anyway. From Monday to Friday, I was off in various parts of the country, delivering the weather report to a bleary-eyed nation.

Moving into that room felt quite grim. There was condensation dripping down the walls, causing a musty smell, and, with my bed jammed up against the window, my duvet and mattress often felt damp when I climbed into bed on a Friday night. After a week away working, staying in cosy hotels, it wasn't ideal. The house was a small ex-council property, and several girls were sharing. The bathroom was about as basic as you could get, with mould all around the shower. I knew I wasn't going to be able to put up with the place for long. I remember sitting there on my soggy bed one night thinking, Sod this! The minute I get a bit of decent money, I'm going to get a place of my own; no more sharing or living at a boyfriend or friend's place. For years I'd been living the life of a nomad, staying over at mates' houses when I was a kid to avoid the long commute from Essex to school, and then, when I was older, out clubbing in London all the time. It was finally time for me to have my own space.

CHAPTER TEN

The Daily Denise

My role on the show changed suddenly when I took over as a leading presenter while the show's regular host, Sharron Davies, went on holiday. There had been something of a campaign, championed by the *Sun* newspaper columnist Garry Bushell, to get me off the chopper and into *The Big Breakfast* house, because he felt I had the self-assured approach the show needed. I didn't give it much attention at the time, although, after my time on *Massive!*, I knew it was something I'd be good at. When I eventually landed the temporary role, I was happy to throw myself into it entirely. What I didn't know was that Sharron wouldn't be coming back, and instead of covering her slot for a week or so, I was suddenly a permanent fixture.

Right away, I loved it. *The Big Breakfast* was so much fun to work on, and there was a wonderful family atmosphere in the East London house where we filmed. Everyone worked really hard, but nobody took themselves too seriously. It was the perfect role for me. Suddenly, I wasn't bothered about singing or acting any more. I was having the time of my life at work. The downside of letting these skills go was that I would ultimately lose confidence in my ability to do them, but, at the time, I didn't think about that. I was simply living in the moment, and what a moment it was!

Secure in my new presenting role, and the pay rise that came with it, I decided to find myself a place to live and get my first mortgage. I bought a one-bedroom flat in Harecourt Road in Islington, which was tiny but mine. It was wonderful that I had a place I could finally call my own, but for a while, I didn't have the funds to furnish it. In fact, for a fair old time, I was basically living with a mattress on the floor, my little telly in the corner and not much else. It wasn't exactly the sort of place you'd invite your mates to, mainly because there was nowhere to bloody sit. I recall being on a rare night out with the model Emma Noble, who, at the time, was going out with Prime Minister John Major's son, James. We were at the Atlantic Bar and Grill, one of the coolest hang-out spots in mid-nineties London. With its fabulous art deco halls and late drinking licence, the place regularly attracted the likes of Madonna, Kate Moss, Robert De Niro and Harvey Keitel. It was one of those places that wasn't easy to get into – more like a swish private members' club than a restaurant – and many of the punters just congregated at the bar, never getting as far as sitting down to eat dinner. Actually, if I remember rightly, nobody really ate much in the nineties.

Anyway, after a fun night out, Emma suggested we head back to my place for a drink.

'The thing is, Emma, I've got no furniture,' I said. 'There's nowhere to sit.'

Emma laughed, not thinking for one second that I was being totally honest.

'Oh, that's all right, it'll be fine,' she said with a giggle.

When we arrived back at my place, Emma's face was a picture.

'Oh my God, you've literally got no furniture,' she said. 'Nothing!'

You have to remember that this was before *The Big Breakfast* took off again. Back then, it was still struggling to reclaim the audience it had pulled in when Chris and Gabby were presenting. Yes, I was a presenter on a mainstream TV show, but I was still finding my feet and not exactly pulling in the big bucks. Buying my own flat was a stretch for me and a massive achievement, but being able to afford furniture to put in it was another matter entirely.

When my co-presenter Rick Adams left the show, I held the fort down on my own for a while, sometimes working with various guest presenters with a view to them becoming permanent if the chemistry between us was right. We had Ant & Dec on, which didn't work out – with two of them and one of me. Then we had Davina McCall, which was fine, but the producers preferred the combination of one boy/one girl rather than two women. One Friday evening, I was sitting in my flat, eating chips on the mattress and flicking through the channels – all four of them – when I landed on a show called *Here's Johnny!* It was a Channel 4 show aimed at the Friday-night post-pub crowd. The show's presenter, Johnny Vaughan, was doing a sketch about the joys of Reebok Classic trainers and how they work in any situation.

He made me laugh – actually he made me cry with laughter – so the following day, I called Waheed.

'I've been watching this guy on TV, Johnny Vaughan. He's hilarious. You've got to get him to try him out on the show.'

It turned out that Johnny was already on the radar of the show's bosses, as he'd screen-tested for them a while back. I just had this feeling that we would work together, and, I'm not going to lie, the fact that I quite fancied him was also a contributing factor in my wanting to work alongside him. Let's face it, it was as good a criteria as any!

After the first sketch we ever did together on the show, the phones went crazy. The two of us just worked together, and everyone could see it. From then on, it felt so easy doing the show. We never really had a script, just a running order, so most of what the viewers saw was simply the two of us bantering and naturally bouncing off one another.

From then on, the show became my social life. I'd go to work in the morning and feel as though I was simply hanging out with my mates for the next few hours. It's funny; quite a few of today's big TV producers started their careers on that show. Back then, they were runners and researchers who have gradually moved up the ranks. At that wonderful moment in time, it was a family that everyone wanted to be a part of. We'd sometimes even get celebrities and pop stars turning up at the house in Bow after a night out, just for the fun of it, or perhaps if they were too wired to sleep!

For a while, during that time, my face seemed to be everywhere. My picture was in the *Daily Star* so often that Johnny started calling it 'The Daily Denise'. It was what was she wearing, what was she doing. The truth of it was, I wasn't doing much of anything apart from working. I had this fantastic elaborate lifestyle from the outside looking in, but in truth, when I wasn't working, I was sitting in my little flat, which now had a few more sticks of furniture, and going to bed early. By that point, I was hardly going out at all because I was just too tired. If I did go out, it was to the local shop to get a pint of milk or a bog roll when I got home at 10.30am, and by that time, most people who watched the show were at work, school or uni. Nobody saw me!

That said, I think some of my neighbours must have thought I was on the game, coming home in some of the outfits I did at that time in the morning. They'd see me getting out of a cab, mid-morning, in PVC trousers, tiny little tops and the occasional feather boa around my neck. I'm sure some of them, who'd never seen the show, must have wondered what on earth I was doing dressed like that.

Johnny was living a similar experience as far as new-found fame went, and, while we both knew that the show was doing well, we didn't have much of a clue about how famous we'd become as a presenting partnership.

When we did the red carpet at the BRIT Awards in February 1998, it really hit home. I was wearing a blue rubber dress, and I'd been gifted a pair of white stilettos by Vivienne Westwood, who'd asked me if I would wear them for the awards. When Johnny and I got out of the car that night, somebody on our team told us that the red carpet was going to be pretty crazy, and that there would be press and paparazzi, all wanting pictures and soundbites from us. Johnny and I looked at one another.

'I don't think they'll want to talk to us,' Johnny said. 'This is a music event, full of pop royalty.'

'Exactly,' I said. 'We're just here to present an award.'

That's how naive we were about the impact we'd made as a pair on the show.

When we got out of the car and headed down the red carpet, it was bedlam. The crowd and the paps went nuts; for a moment, the two of us just stood there like deer in headlights. Before that night, we hadn't really been out anywhere together. We went to the house every day and did our jobs – that was our world. When you're looking down a camera lens, you sometimes forget that there are millions of people watching you from the other side. This madness was something new entirely. People were screaming our names and yelling at us for pictures. Even some of the bands and pop stars attending the awards wanted photos with the two of us. It was weird. If I'd imagined something like this as a kid, I would have loved the idea of it, but now, with all this madness happening around us, I didn't like it; it freaked me out.

As for the 'ladette' label, well, that was an odd thing, really, and I'm not quite sure how I ended up with it. The term 'ladette' was born in the Britpop era of the nineties and used to describe the female equivalent of the typical lad: liberated young women who smashed the femininity mould so they could behave just like men. It was a twist on the old, stereotypical gender roles – where the man went drinking, and the woman waited indoors with the tea on the table. Other so-called ladettes included DJs Zoe Ball and Sara Cox, TV presenters Sarah Cawood and Donna Air, and model-turned-presenter Jayne Middlemiss.

OK, so I liked a night out and a drink, but I didn't feel particularly laddish! Quite the opposite. I didn't like football, and I certainly didn't like drinking pints of beer. I was more of a white wine spritzer girl. The one thing I could point to that might have landed me in the ladette camp was my humour. I certainly wasn't stereotypically girly as far as that went. I always had a fairly bawdy, boisterous sense of humour, which is probably why I found it easy to talk to and get along with men.

During this time, it felt like there were all sorts of exciting things coming my way. I walked the catwalk for the Vivienne Westwood fashion show in London, and I even got to present *Top of the Pops*. In the midst of it all, I started hearing from people I hadn't heard from in a while, people from my past who I hadn't been close with but who now wanted to be best mates. As well as that, there was the press and media who suddenly wanted to know everything about Johnny and me. There was something that felt very different about all this. It wasn't just a case of being in the spotlight or being on television; I'd done that for years and just viewed it as work. The nature of this kind of celebrity was fast and intense, and it didn't feel like it was something we could control. The best part of it, I suppose, was the feeling that I was part of something successful and much loved, that I was doing what I did well and reaping the rewards. The downside was the scrutiny Johnny and I were under all of a sudden. I knew that as many people there were wanting to celebrate our success on the show, there would be those who wanted to bring us down. I started to wonder who might come out of the woodwork with stories about me: disgruntled boyfriends or long-forgotten acquaintances with tales about my wild clubbing days.

I have to give credit to my ex-boyfriend, Darren. I know for a fact that he had journalists knocking on his door offering him £20,000 or more to spill details on my past and what dark secrets might be lurking in the closet, but he never uttered a peep. He never told me this himself, although I have bumped into him from time to time. It was a mutual friend who informed me that Darren had turned down large offers of money from the press on more than one occasion. I've always thought fondly of him for that; what a lovely, decent guy.

By then, I'd come to realise how much everything would have to change. I couldn't be just me for me any more; now I belonged to everyone. Suddenly, I watched what I said and considered my actions, especially when I was out in a public place. I had concerns about saying or doing the wrong thing and being judged. It was hard then, but it's even worse now, with all the various social media platforms. Now it's not just the press and media who have their say about you; literally anyone can chime in with an opinion. *Look what she's wearing. Did you hear what she said about so-and-so?* We've all witnessed the celebrities, actors, politicians, and sportsmen and sportswomen who've voiced an opinion on their Facebook page or Twitter, misjudged or otherwise, and have then been publicly hung out to dry for it. One wrong move, and all of a sudden they're the worst person in the world. Cancelled! Now that's scary.

Back then, I tried to push those niggling thoughts to one side and just enjoy the ride. When all was said and done, I was doing what I'd always wanted to do, and I was having the time of my life doing it.

CHAPTER ELEVEN

My worst nightmare come true

During my heyday on *The Big Breakfast*, the *Sun* newspaper asked me if I'd be up for modelling on Page 3. On the one hand, I was up for it, but on the other, I wasn't getting my boobs out for all and sundry to gawp at over their Rice Krispies, so I had conditions. Consequently, I ended up being the first non-topless Page 3 girl. After that, there was interest from some of the popular men's magazines, requesting my presence on their glossy pages in a few sultry photo shoots. Lad mags, as they were known, were a big thing at the time: *FHM*, *Loaded*, *Maxim*, *Esquire*. Men of all ages seemed to have a magazine of choice, which they could grab at the local newsagents along with their Snickers bar, a bag of Walkers cheese and onion crisps and a can of Diet Coke. I ended up doing many photo shoots for these magazines, some shot by iconic British photographers like Rankin and the late Bob Carlos Clarke.

I'd always felt slightly uncomfortable with the idea of being seductive or sexy, but suddenly people were thinking of me in that way. For me, it was all a bit of a laugh. It wasn't that I didn't enjoy being sexy and glamorous in front of the camera – I did – but I just couldn't take it all that seriously. I'd been modelling since I was seven years old when I stood there in my vest and knickers for an Asda campaign. To me, this wasn't any different. Of course, over the years, I've been alerted to the fact that some of those sexy shoots made quite an impression on some young men at the time. This was brought into sharp focus when I got a message one day from a man casually informing me that I was his very first wank. I mean, how do you answer that? 'Thank you for your kind support' doesn't seem appropriate, really, does it?

The important thing was, I was doing it all on my terms. I never did anything I felt uncomfortable with, and I didn't feel exploited. It was all part and parcel of my career, and I always felt very much in control.

However, looming just around the corner was something very much out of my control; something that both shocked and hurt me deeply.

Revenge porn wasn't a widespread term back in the nineties. At least I don't remember hearing it. It's something that's talked about a lot these days, probably because nobody seems to do anything unless they're armed with a smartphone camera. Every moment is captured and shared: holiday destinations, breakfasts, pets, babies. Of course, this includes some moments that might be better off undocumented and kept private but aren't.

I was at work in *The Big Breakfast* house one day when a friend of mine who worked in the phone room there, Victoria Mills – aka Cockney Vik – came to find me, not long before I was due to go live to the nation.

'Denise, I need to speak to you,' she said. She looked concerned. 'Can we talk privately?'

Vik was one of those people who always looked out for me, and we're close friends to this day.

'What is it? What's the matter?' I said, while she pulled me to one side, out of earshot of the rest of *The Big Breakfast* crew.

'I've had a phone call from this random guy who says he's seen a tape of you having sex,' she said.

It was a bit of a shock, but my first instinct was to laugh it off. 'A sex tape? No way, Vik, I've never made one. It's not me.'

'Well, he's adamant it's you,' she said. 'He told me that he'd seen it in a pub where some bloke had been flashing it around to his mates and various other punters. He was showing off because it was you.'

'Vik, I'm telling you I've never made a sex tape. God, I'm much too prudish. Don't worry about it; it's a hoax.'

I honestly didn't think much more about it, but there were more calls from the same guy over the next day or so, who was insistent.

'I don't want to give my name,' he told Victoria. 'The reason I'm calling is that the guy with the video is still touting it around, and I think what he's doing is disgusting. Someone needs to do something.'

He was also one hundred per cent sure that it was indeed me on the tape and, most worrying of all, that the guy was thinking about taking this tape to the press.

As much as I knew I'd never taken part in anything like that, I started to worry. Was it possible I'd been secretly filmed? Had I been so drunk after a night out that I hadn't realised what was happening? Before I'd even had a chance to process it all, my agent, Jimmy O'Reilly, received a tip-off from one of the big Sunday papers. An editor told Jimmy that they were going to run a story about the tape. It's something the press often did back then; they'd let a public figure know if they were about to run some scandalous or salacious story about them, probably to give the subject a small window of opportunity to make a comment or take any action they saw fit.

Jimmy called to say that the paper had it on good authority that it was me in the tape and that there was an accompanying story from one of my ex-boyfriends, Mike, who'd admitted to being the other person in the video. I couldn't believe what I was hearing. Despite knowing I'd never been a part of anything like that, this was now real. This was something that was going out into the world, and there didn't seem to be anything I could do to stop it.

'Jimmy, if I'm in that tape, it was filmed without my consent,' I said. 'I swear I don't know anything about it.'

'Well, if that's the case, I need to let the editor of the paper know,' he said.

Then something odd happened. Suddenly, the paper told Jimmy they were pulling the story, that they were no longer printing anything about the tape or the ex-boyfriend. Jimmy did some digging and discovered that the journalist who'd bought and paid for the video had since noticed the date at the bottom of the recording. He'd worked out that on that date I'd have only been 15 years old, meaning that the fact he'd even watched it was a criminal offence. When we finally got lawyers involved, we were told that the newspaper had essentially paid money for a recording of an underage girl having sex with an adult.

The whole thing suddenly blew up, which was incredibly distressing. Now it was more than a potential story in the press; it was a legal case.

I was within my rights to take legal action against Mike, but I couldn't face the drama of it all. Things have changed so much in the last 20 or so years. Thank God, people are speaking out more about that kind of abuse and manipulation. At the time, I just felt shocked and mortified by the whole thing. My main concern when I first got wind of a possible newspaper story had been, *Oh God! Dad is going to be so embarrassed! He's going to be so disappointed in me.* The idea of me being splashed across the front of the Sunday papers in that way, humiliating my family, almost destroyed me. Now I just wanted it to be over.

The journalist told Jimmy that Mike had been ready to tell all sorts of stories about me. He saw me as a meal ticket, telling the journalist, 'I've been sitting on this for years; I knew she was going to make it.' He'd even kept all the notes I'd written to him and tried to sell those too. That's how calculated the whole thing was. It was like he'd been gathering what he could when we were together because he had an idea it might be worth something one day. Ultimately, he'd been waiting for me to make it big so he could peddle his grubby tape of us. A video I'd known nothing about.

A tricky legal process began, with everyone treading very carefully, particularly the newspaper that had handed over money for the tape. Where Mike messed up was, having been paid a princely sum for his story, he started being flash with the cash in his local pub and mouthing off about it, and me, to anyone who'd listen. Many of them didn't take kindly to it. I guess they knew me as a local girl, a young woman who had done well and was now on their telly every morning. They didn't like the idea that this guy was trying to take me down at all, and that's when it all started to unravel for him. I heard from my lawyer what was going on, but I buried my head in the sand. I didn't want to think about it. Still, there was one more shock to come.

With the tape's existence now out in the open, Mike was questioned by the police and his home was searched. When police tore up the floorboards of his mother's house, they found more tapes. This hadn't been a one-off; he'd recorded dozens of other girls. He'd set up some dodgy old camcorder in his bedroom and filmed himself having sex with girls without their knowledge.

I wondered how his poor mum must have felt when all this came out. She'd never really liked me when we were together. I always got the impression she never thought I was good enough for her precious son; he was the golden boy who could do no wrong. Well, look how that turned out!

When the case eventually came to court, I couldn't face it. I suppose that was when my worst nightmare came true, with my dad having to watch parts of the tape to identify me. It was awful for him and it's something we've never really spoken about. It all just got buried and forgotten. We moved on. Mike didn't go to prison, but the judge told him that he most definitely would if any of the content on the tapes ever surfaced.

The period from my first hearing about the tape from Vik and the court case spanned a whole year. It was a time when I'd only just cracked it on *The Big Breakfast*, and I was finally finding success. If it hadn't been handled right, I guess it could have damaged my career, but, at the end of the day, I knew I'd done nothing wrong. I wasn't guilty of anything. Still, that didn't stop the sense of shame and embarrassment that I felt throughout that whole time. I was just becoming a household name, and suddenly there was something ugly and sleazy hanging over my head, something out of my control. The last thing I wanted was for something like that to define me when I'd barely even got started.

I didn't realise it at the time, but the impact of those events has been long-lasting and debilitating. The idea that my first sexual experience had been recorded and shown to other people was hard to get over. I'd been a trusting soul when I was younger; I'd always tried to see the good in people. Being taken advantage of in that way changed me. Looking backwards from my forties, I can see some of my relationships have been affected by my issues around trust over the last 20 years. I find it hard to trust people, particularly men, and I have sometimes reacted negatively. Instead of seeing the best in someone, I've often found myself searching for the worst. I was always looking over my shoulder, and I've even, on occasion, checked around rooms, looking for cameras. I was also very wary about having sex after drinking too much. For me, being intoxicated and having sex did not go hand in hand as it seemed to for a lot of people I knew, including some of the guys I dated. While some people find that alcohol loosens them up a bit in the bedroom, I was the opposite. If ever I didn't feel in control of what my mind and body were doing, even in what I considered safe environments, I'd clam up. I would stop a guy in his tracks and tell him, as politely as I could, to back off. It didn't always go down well either. Some guys saw me as a girl who had plenty of chat and bravado and loved to flirt, 'givin' it all that', but who suddenly went cold. Again, it was a trust issue. It started with the notion that if I wasn't in control, I might not be able to stop something that I wasn't happy with. There was also the fear that I would black out and not know what someone was doing to me. These thoughts started small but eventually grew into a giant monster within me.

The experience with Mike paved the way for years of me not allowing myself to truly open up to someone. I wish I'd dealt with all those feelings, had some therapy and faced up to it. It probably would have saved me a lot of grief over the years. Instead, I just buried it. It's only digging deep to write down my experiences in this book that has allowed me to think about it now. I suppose it's been like a therapy of sorts because thinking about one event and how it leads to another is like completing a long-unsolved puzzle. Thoughts, feelings and past events finally all fit together and make sense.

I'm not exactly sure when it changed. Perhaps it came with the realisation that I existed in an adult world doing adult things when I was a kid, but I was still a kid. I thought I knew it all, but, in truth, I was pretty naive. During the years when I should have been doing what other children were – learning, playing, growing, becoming a teenager – I was working and trying to be a grown-up, which meant that I missed out on a lot of the important stuff.

Being a mother has meant that all these things have been brought into sharp focus for me. I'm grateful for all the women who have come forward and spoken out about these issues because it makes it easier for mums like me to talk to their daughters about what is acceptable in a relationship. More importantly, what isn't. I would never want my daughter or any other girl to go through the sort of thing I did. Those early experiences are what shape you. They can define how you see yourself and affect how you behave and who you're drawn to in subsequent relationships.

When I was with Mike, I didn't know anything. As wonderful and supportive as my parents were, we just didn't seem to have those kinds of conversations back then. It wasn't their fault; it was a different time. I knew when I was going out with an older guy that Mum wasn't happy about it. By then, however, I was headstrong and independent and I did my own thing. Perhaps if I had gone and asked her advice about certain things, she'd have felt able to have had those talks with me. Instead, I learned everything I knew from the school playground, where, if word was to be believed, everyone was at it!

It's strange writing about all this now – cathartic even – because as a family we've never really talked about what happened to me back then. It's like it was all just shut away in a box for all eternity.

I'm happy to report that I have now buried the demons from that experience, and I've also overcome my issues around trust – mainly because I'm with someone who I know cares about me, loves me, and has no other agenda.

CHAPTER TWELVE

A bit of a blur

When trying to remember some of my nineties nights out in detail, I realise that some are a bit of a blur – excuse the Britpop pun. I'm sure it's the same for many people that were out and about during that hedonistic decade. I worked hard all week, so I lived for those weekends. I enjoyed that social scene and always wanted to have a good time. Talking of Britpop, the mid-nineties saw it in full swing, and many of those bands were out on the scene. Some of the so-called ladettes ended up dating boys in bands, including me.

I flew over to Bordeaux to interview the band Dodgy while they were over there playing a festival. I'd been out drinking the night before the trip, so I was a tad hungover, and when I stepped off the flight at Bordeaux-Mérignac airport, the weather felt unbearably hot. I have to say, I didn't feel at my best on the way to the interview, and I probably hadn't drunk anywhere near enough water to compensate for my post-alcohol dehydration either.

As we started the interview, I remember saying that I didn't feel all that well, but that's about as much as I remember. Somewhere during the proceedings, I overheated and passed out. When I woke up, I was lying flat out on a bed in a tent, under the supervision of one of the festival medics, wearing a tiny little skirt and my knee-high patent leather boots from Red or Dead. The first thing I saw when I opened my eyes was Dodgy's drummer Mathew, fanning me with a magazine. The band's guitarist, Andy Miller, was also standing over me, and, for a moment, I didn't have a clue what was going on.

'Are you all right?' Andy asked.

'I don't know; what happened?' I said.

'One minute you were talking, and the next you just went down,' Andy said.

'It's just so hot,' I said.

'Have you had any water?' the medic asked, and I shook my head weakly.

'Well, let's get you hydrated; you'll feel better, I'm sure.'

Andy looked down at me, smiling. 'Don't worry; I'll look after you.'

I suppose fainting at a festival isn't the obvious way to meet a new boyfriend, but that's what happened, and Andy and I ended up dating for a while.

As well as me dating Dodgy's Andy, Sarah Cawood dated the Bluetones guitarist, Adam Devlin, and Zoe Ball, of course, dated and went on to marry Norman Cook, aka Fatboy Slim. It wasn't like we all went out on double dates or anything. In fact, the 'ladettes' were more splinter groups than we were one big gang. I was good mates with Jayne Middlemiss, having come from a similar background working on Saturday-morning kids' TV, while Sara Cox and Zoe were close. Jayne and I shared the same agent in Jimmy, so she became my go-to at big events, especially when

I didn't know anyone well, which was often the case. Jayne and I would spot one another across crowded rooms, one of us making a beeline for the other.

I suppose the most memorable event I attended with Jayne was the one at Buckingham Palace, but probably not for the reasons you might imagine. It was 1998, and both Jayne and I were invited to meet the Queen and Prince Charles at an event for a select group of young Brits who'd achieved success in the entertainment and media industry. I was surprised to have received the letter from the palace inviting me to an event for young achievers; I wasn't sure what I'd achieved and couldn't work out why I was on the list. Nonetheless, I was chuffed about it and couldn't wait to share the news with my friends and family.

My nearest and dearest were thrilled for me; everyone, that was, except Johnny, who refused to accept that I'd been invited to the palace while he had not. He thought I was winding him up.

'Why would someone invite you to the palace?' he said, jokingly.

'Because I'm a young achiever, that's why, Johnny.'

'So why not me, then?'

'Because clearly you haven't achieved as much as I have.'

'No way,' he said. 'You're making it up.'

Still, I knew I'd have the last laugh and that he'd be eating his words once it came to the actual day of the event.

I asked Sue Judd, who did the wardrobe for the show, to help sort me a dress for the occasion. There was no way I was going to rock up at Buck House in my customary attire, which was a bit out-there for royalty. I mean, for *The Big Breakfast*, I usually wore the sort of thing most girls would wear to a nightclub. PVC pants and a skinny tube top were not going to cut it.

'I need your help,' I told Sue. 'I need something that's not very me. You know, something demure.'

'There's this great new store in Covent Garden called Koh Samui,' she said. 'I'll get you an appointment there.'

This ended up becoming my favourite place to shop for clothes; certainly a lot more pricey than Topshop or Hennes, but if I ever felt like treating myself to something a bit special, Koh Samui was my go-to. I'd always bump into someone I knew while I was in there: Tamara Beckwith was a regular, as was Tara Palmer-Tomkinson – the shop was never short of an It girl.

Now, I know I ended up with a lovely dress for the event, but for the life of me, I couldn't describe it for you now. There was probably a nice strappy heel involved, too – possibly a Jimmy Choo or a Gina, knowing me. Still, I was all set and thrilled to hear that my mate Jayne would be attending alongside me.

Johnny still wasn't having it. 'I'm sorry, there's just no way the Queen has invited you to Buckingham Palace,' he said.

It's true, we often played jokes on one another on the show, so I guess he thought this was just another prank and that everyone was playing along to wind him up.

On the big day, Jayne and I turned up at the palace; it all felt very grand. On arrival, we were ushered through to a large, beautiful room and offered a glass of champagne. Before heading into another room for the line-up to meet the Queen, Jayne and

I nipped to the toilet together. Once there, I was surprised to see that the Queen had some lace and satin tissue box covers, which looked very familiar.

'Oh my God, my nan's got these in her caravan in Clacton,' I told Jayne. 'I'm going to have to take one, just to prove to Johnny that I've been here.'

Jayne was, quite rightly, a bit nervous about me pilfering bog roll holders from the palace. I probably should have listened, to be honest.

'You might get caught,' she said. 'What then?'

'They're not going to notice something like that,' I said, popping it into my bag. 'When does the Queen come in here anyway?'

Later in the evening, I decided to double-dip and go for an ashtray I'd spotted displaying a royal crest. Bingo, I thought. Johnny likes the occasional cigarette; I'll present him with that in the morning. So, into my little bag that went as well.

That night, I curtsied for the Queen in the line-up, we had a friendly little chat, and I met Prince Charles. I went home feeling proud and also smug that I'd be able to present Johnny with my palace mementoes the following day.

After a bit more mickey-taking about my royal appointment the next morning, I handed over the ashtray and the tissue box cover to Johnny, live on *The Big Breakfast*.

'I picked you up a couple of things to prove I was there,' I said.

Johnny laughed and looked surprised, but I was getting messages from the producers in my earpiece fairly soon after.

'You need to make an apology,' one of the producers was saying frantically. 'You need to apologise.'

We often got instructions from the producers' gallery, making sure they got what they needed to make the show as much fun as it could be. I assumed they were saying that Johnny should make some sort of grand on-air apology for not believing me and told him as much.

'NO! NO!' the producer was now screaming in my ear, but I didn't have a clue why he sounded so crazed.

Johnny was now also getting messages in his ear, and that's when he laid it out for me.

'Apparently, Denise, we've had a call from a royal official about you stealing property from them. It's *you* that has to make an apology. You're not supposed to take stuff from the palace, so now you're in a lot of trouble.'

The entire studio floor erupted in laughter while I'm sitting there thinking, *Oh shit!*

After the show finished, I was ushered into a room and questioned by a member of the show's legal team. They wanted to know exactly what I'd taken and why. Given the nature of our show, I still thought this might all be a wind-up, but if it was, it was a bloody good one because everyone in the room looked deadly serious.

'First and foremost, you were invited to the palace as a young achiever,' one of the team told me. 'You're supposed to be a role model for young people, not encouraging and promoting theft.'

Before I knew it, my agent, Jimmy, was on the phone, wanting to know why his phone was ringing off the hook.

'What's going on, Denise? Is all this true? Have you actually stolen stuff from Buckingham Palace?'

'Not stolen exactly; it was just a bit of a joke,' I said sheepishly. 'I was having a laugh with Jayne, and, you know, I guess I took it too far.'

'Well, Jayne doesn't want anything to do with this,' Jimmy said. 'She's not taking any responsibility whatsoever.'

To be fair, she wasn't the one who'd taken the goods home with her, so I was going to have to take this one on the chin and deal with it myself. I hoped it would be seen for what it was, a daft prank, and be quickly forgotten. By that evening, however, the regular satirical cartoon in the *Evening Standard* depicted me stealing goods from the palace while the Queen sat on the loo. I also made the evening news. 'Pilferer at the palace,' they called me!

Jimmy warned me that the situation was serious and that I would have to make a public apology. When I sat down and considered it, I knew everyone was right; I'd not thought it through. I knew how many kids watched the show, so it was hardly the best example for me to be giving. I decided the best option was to apologise on *The Big Breakfast* the following day and then return the items with a personal note to Her Majesty. As a conciliatory gift, I also decided to pop in a pair of small stuffed camels that I'd bought while on holiday in Tunisia with my boyfriend, Andy. *She'll like them*, I thought.

Of course, *The Big Breakfast* made a massive deal out of me returning my swag, with a courier turning up on-air to collect it and then cameras following the courier right up to the palace gates. The best part was that, after the goods were back safely in their rightful place, an official from the palace phoned up the show, chuckling while informing us that 'the Queen accepts Denise's apology'.

When the on-air announcement came that I'd been forgiven, the entire studio floor cheered.

Still, that wasn't the worst of it. Even more terrifying than facing anger from the palace was facing the wrath of Ted from Basildon. My dad loves the royal family and was absolutely fuming with me for disrespecting them.

'You were invited to that woman's house, and you've taken something; that's disgusting,' he said. 'I'm ashamed.'

Of course, I was horrified at having embarrassed my dad like that, but at the same time couldn't help loving the fact that he'd described Buckingham Palace as 'that woman's house'.

I wish I could tell you that I'd learned my lesson when it came to the royals, but not long afterwards I had another run-in, this time with Prince Charles.

The following year, I was invited to host Party in the Park in Hyde Park, where one of the headliners was my favourite pop band of the moment, Steps. After the show, the prince came backstage to meet the performers, but a member of his security approached me.

'You're not cleared to meet the prince,' she told me.

'Why not?' I asked. 'Is there a specific reason I can't meet him?'

'Yes, the incident last year at the palace,' she said.

'What? The ashtray?'

The security woman nodded solemnly. 'The palace officials think you're too unpredictable and suspect you're up to no good.'

'But I'm not going to do anything.'

Before I could protest any further, I was unceremoniously frogmarched away from the royal line and ushered into one of the marquees, where my friend Natalie was hanging out.

'What's going on?' she asked. 'Are you not meeting the prince?'

'No, I'm not allowed,' I told her.

'That's terrible,' she said.

'I know, and I'm not having it.' I marched over to the clear window of the marquee, and while the prince was shaking hands with the members of Steps, I called out to him, then pulled up my top and flashed my bra. That's right; I flashed the Prince of Wales. I'm not sure what came over me, and it certainly wasn't premeditated. If it had been, I'd have worn one of my posh bras rather than the Marks & Spencer nude one my mum had got me. Of course, the second it happened, cameras went off all over the place, and the incident landed me in the tabloids once again with headlines like 'Oi, Charlie! Check out my crown jewels!' being the order of the day. It was all very cheeky and silly, and nobody took it particularly seriously.

Years later, I was invited to Clarence House to meet the prince. This time, it was because of the charity work I'd done for breast cancer care, but I certainly had no intention of taking any mementoes. When Charles spotted me, he made his way over and shook my hand.

'I trust you're not going to do anything naughty tonight,' he said with a very cheeky grin.

'No, I'm on my best behaviour,' I said.

'That's good,' he said with a wink. 'Let's keep it that way.'

By then, I was older and much wiser, and, when I think about it now, I can hardly believe I had the nerve to do some of the things I did back in the day. They say when you're young, you have no fear; well, that was certainly the case as far as I was concerned. Still, I never had any bad intentions. I was just that little bit too mischievous.

CHAPTER THIRTEEN

What goes on in the Met Bar
stays in the Met Bar

As well as Jayne, I also became good friends with journalist Kate Thornton after she interviewed me for a newspaper. She was one of my few 'media' pals, and we became very close. Having been editor of *Smash Hits*, Kate knew everyone there was to know in the world of pop, including Robbie Williams, who, by then, had left Take That and was already a huge solo star. At the time, Robbie was sharing an apartment in central London with his mate Charlie, and somehow Kate and I ended up there one evening. The two of us were planning to head to the seventies disco night, Carwash, and persuaded the boys that they should come along with us. We ended up sticking a wig on Robbie so he wouldn't get recognised as we went in, and we had the most fantastic time, dancing the night away to disco classics.

Kate and I also shared a rather memorable trip to Ibiza together, one of my favourite places in the world.

My first trip there had been with my friend Tamara, and I'd fallen in love with the place the minute we stepped off the plane. It was the dawn of the super clubs, something we'd never really had in the UK, so nights out there were on another level. I was probably only 18 or 19 years old then, and completely blown away by clubs like Manumission. It was a whole new world of partying, which I enjoyed along with everyone else.

On my holiday there with Kate, we stayed at Pikes, one of the most famous hotels on the island, with a reputation for wild nights and hedonism. From the eighties onwards, it was known to be a playground for the rich and famous and is probably best remembered for being the location for Wham!'s 'Club Tropicana' video. When Kate and I stayed there, the DJ Jeremy Healy had the room next door. Now, I could party and stay up late with the best of them, but there came the point where I needed to sleep, as did Kate.

In contrast, our neighbour Jeremy did not. It didn't matter what time the party at the club ended, there always seemed to be an after-party in Jeremy's suite. It was constant and loud. On one occasion, Kate was fuming because we'd been out till dawn, but by 10am we still hadn't been able to sleep because of the music pumping out from next door. It was unbearable.

'Look, he's going to want to go to sleep eventually,' I told Kate. 'That's when we'll get our revenge.'

About four days into our trip, Jeremy seemed to have hit a wall because all was quiet when he got back from whatever party he'd been playing at. It was about 9am, and Kate and I were feeling nice and fresh, having got ourselves to bed relatively early the night before in preparation for a day relaxing by the pool. With no music coming from Jeremy's room, we knew he must have finally gone to bed. It was time to get our own back.

Part of the noise problem had been an air vent that joined our room to his; this became the foundation of my evil plan. I took the cover off the air vent and grabbed a speaker attached to a portable CD player. Once the speaker was installed in the vent, I selected some suitable music. Don't ask me why I happened to have a CD of Chas & Dave's greatest hits with me on my Ibiza clubbing holiday, but I did. It was perfect. I went to the second track, 'Rabbit', and put it on loop, so the same song would play over and over again, and whacked it up loud. I pushed the speaker as far into the vent as I could, then Kate and I made a fast exit from the room down to the pool, locking the door behind us.

It didn't take long before Jeremy found us at the pool, and he wasn't happy.

'What the fuck are you playing at? I'm trying to sleep!'

'Well, now you know what it's like', I said. 'That's what we've had for the first four nights of our holiday.'

The next thing we knew, the hotel staff were on our case to turn down the noise, but even they could see the funny side.

'He's ruined our trip up until now, so he's getting a taste of his own medicine', I said.

• • •

Back in the UK, I'd pop over to Ireland and hang out at the PoD some weekends, which was a fantastic place to party. It was located underneath an old railway station in the heart of Dublin, started by a guy called John Reynolds, who'd previously managed Ministry of Sound in London. I remember dancing nights away with Boyzone or the Take That boys. Whenever I see any of them now, it strikes me how long we've all known one another. God, we were just kids back then.

During that era, I practically lived at the Met Bar, which was the notorious celebrity hang-out of the day, in the Metropolitan Hotel in Mayfair. The place was in its heyday then, and some nights you couldn't move for famous singers, actors, sportspeople and various other celebs. The Met Bar was like my church, in as much that I went there almost every weekend. Yes, it was pretty exclusive and hard to get into, but the parties there were legendary. I think so many celebrities liked it because it was always a case of the old adage, 'what happens in the Met Bar stays in the Met Bar.' One of the things I enjoyed most about the place was that as well as seeing lots of people I knew, there were always a healthy sprinkling of people you wouldn't necessarily expect to see, doing things you wouldn't expect to see. Members of a world-famous pop band, for instance, who felt comfortable and free enough to be open about their sexuality in the cocoon of the bar, when, at that time, they probably wouldn't have in the public domain. The interesting thing was, those things never got out in the press. It was almost as if there was a code that said, 'if you want to be part of this, you play the game.' There was no selling stories or infringing on another person's privacy, as long as they weren't doing anyone any harm.

Sometimes, I even booked a room at the hotel so I could party till late with friends and then go upstairs to bed without the bother of having to get home. Well, I say go to bed. Usually, the party carried on in someone's room until the early hours. What can I say? We were young, and we had lots of energy. That said, my nights out were strictly limited to Fridays and Saturdays. Youthful or not, there was no way even then I could be up half the night and look and feel fresh for a 3.45am call.

I once shared a room there with the author and former model Sophie Dahl. We hadn't planned on it, but at one point during the night, there she was, banging on the door of my hotel room.

'I can't get home, and I've got nowhere to stay,' she said. 'Can I crash with you?'

We ended up topping and tailing, and I remember her feet hanging over the end of the bed because she was so tall.

When we weren't crashing at the hotel, there was often an 'all back to mine' situation. One memorable occasion was ending up at Noel Gallagher and Meg Mathews's house in Primrose Hill, North London – Supernova Heights. This was the then couple's infamous party house, which hosted more than its fair share of riotous late-night dos, full of supermodels, A-listers, and rock stars. Kate Moss, Gwyneth Paltrow, Jude Law, Sadie Frost, Johnny Depp, Ronnie Wood – they were all there at one time or another.

Meg was always the loveliest of women – always so friendly – and after my first visit there, she invited me back several times. If you believed everything you read in the tabloids, though, Supernova Heights was a non-stop orgy of booze and drugs, and, to be honest, I didn't fit in with the whole celebrity party scene. My abiding memory of being there was meeting Noel's cats, brilliantly called Benson and Hedges. I'd certainly heard all the stories of debauchery, and although I was no stranger to a party, this seemed to be on another level. I felt like I was a bit out of my depth with that crowd, and so I generally stayed away.

I have such good memories of those days; things felt a lot more open and freer in many ways than they do today. It's undoubtedly true that good or bad, people got away with a lot more as far as partying went. When I think about some of the situations I found myself in, and some of the people I was with, it often surprises me what *didn't* find its way out into the public domain. True, in those days, you had to watch out for the Sunday papers, but as long as you could dodge a photographer, you were generally safe to do as you pleased, as long as you weren't harming anyone else. Mind you, I was never a person to go hell for leather as far as all that went. I was very much a dip-your-toe-in-the-water-now-and-again type of girl. I never felt swayed or starstruck enough to feel like I had to do something to fit in, and I was always able to walk away from a party before it turned sour. I can look back on those days with fondness but see them for what they were: a long, glorious party, a time when everything seemed possible, and it was all up for grabs.

The fame and celebrity side of it was secondary for me, which is probably why I never made it big while living in LA a few years later. As much as I loved it there, the entertainment scene felt flaky and fake to me, and I wasn't good at making connections or being friends with somebody because of who they were or what they might be able to do for me. I guess that's why I still have the same mates now as I did 20 or 30 years ago: Tamara, Cockney Vik and Cossi. I love them because I know they'd be just as happy sitting eating a bag of chips in Southend as they would dining at the Ned.

CHAPTER FOURTEEN

I was more of a Lambrini girl

Being on such a successful show afforded me some great opportunities. In my last year of doing the show, I somehow found the time to be part of a new sitcom, *Babes in the Wood*, with Karl Howman, Natalie Walter and Samantha Janus (now Womack). I'd finish my morning job and then spend the rest of the day rehearsing or filming. It was a pretty crazy schedule, but at the time I didn't really think about that; I just got on with it. I'd be up at 3.45am, on the set of *The Big Breakfast* from 7–9am, then out of the building by 10am and over to the studio to rehearse all day. After that, I'd film *Babes* in front of a live studio audience from 7–10pm. Then I'd head home and sleep. Then there were the photo shoots and interviews and any other promotional bits and pieces that might be slotted in between all that. It wasn't the best environment for a relationship to thrive in, mainly when your partner is in a band that's away touring and playing gigs so much. It's no surprise that my relationship with Andy started to break down. We just didn't seem to have the time to dedicate to one another.

When I started going out with Jamiroquai's frontman, Jay Kay, I knew things would be different. I had no intention of letting another relationship fail simply because I didn't have time for it. I put my foot down and told my agent, Jimmy, that I wanted the weekends off. Two days with no work unless it was something absolutely unavoidable.

My first meeting with Jay was a bit of an odd one because, when I look back on it, I suppose it was kind of a blind date orchestrated by *GQ* magazine. I was often asked to do random jobs, so when Jimmy phoned to tell me *GQ* wanted me to go to Silverstone racetrack to interview Jay from Jamiroquai, I didn't overthink it. I have to be honest, I didn't really know much about him or his band at the time. His acid jazz style of music really wasn't my bag at all; if I wasn't listening to banging house music, I'd be relaxing to a bit of Whitney or Dusty Springfield. I certainly wasn't into the whole chilled-out weed-smoking vibe associated with the acid jazz scene. I was more of a Lambrini girl, out dancing with my mates. I suppose that was why I wasn't especially star-struck when we first met.

I was dressed up in racing gear for the interview and headed off to Silverstone – as Jay was famously into fast cars and racing.

Once the interview got underway, it became evident quite quickly that there was a spark between the two of us. It was incredibly flirty. I'm not putting all the blame on him either; I was just as guilty. There was something immediately charming about Jay; I liked him right off. He was funny, larger than life and incredibly cheeky. The way we were together reminded me a little bit of how Johnny and I were together, bouncing off one another very naturally and smiling a lot. It was obvious that Jay liked me as well; he seemed intrigued with how comfortable I was, pushing boundaries and giving as good as I got with the banter. I've always loved an innuendo, and some of mine weren't exactly subtle. I remember Jay's jaw falling open in shock at some of the things I said. This was undoubtedly one of the most fun interviews I'd ever done. We ended up racing in a Ferrari, and he seemed impressed that, as fast as he drove, I didn't appear in the slightest bit nervous. He did his best to push it to the limits and get a reaction out of me, but I was determined to stay calm.

'How do you feel?' he asked me after a few mad laps around Silverstone.

'Yeah, good. Can we do it again?' I said. 'Only this time can we go a bit faster?'

As our time together went on, Jay suggested that I come back to see the house he'd just bought.

'Come on, come back to mine,' he said. 'I really want to show you my mansion.'

He wasn't being flashy, just jovial, but as much as I'd have liked to have gone, my overriding thought was my commitment to work.

'I've got to be up at a quarter to four in the morning, so that won't be happening,' I told him. 'I need to be at home in London, not out in the middle of Buckinghamshire.'

I was always very professional when it came to doing the show. I was never late and only took time off if I absolutely had to. I won't lie, I was tempted, but I knew if I went to Jay's place and we had a drink and stayed up late, I just wouldn't make it to work the following morning. However, he was pretty persuasive, and I was having such a good time with him that in the end, I thought, *Sod it*. After all, he'd promised to get me a car with a driver to make sure I got to the show on time, so why not?

Jay's house was in the middle of nowhere, in among 80 acres of land and surrounded by lakes. Of course, back then, in the early days of mobile phones, the signal was bloody terrible. My agent, Jimmy, was trying to get hold of me all that evening and must have thought I'd disappeared off the face of the earth for a while.

'Where the hell are you?' he said when he eventually got hold of me.

'I'm back at Jay's place,' I said.

There was a gasp at the end of the phone. 'You are not back at his mansion!'

'I am, Jimmy, but don't worry. We've got it all worked out, and I will be at work on time tomorrow as usual.'

After that day, I told Jimmy that although Jay was lovely, he wasn't really my type, and we weren't planning on taking things any further. That wasn't exactly true. Jay and I talked on the phone, and he invited me to spend the weekend with him. I think we both knew that this might be the start of something more than a casual flirtation, but the last thing we wanted was a big press story blowing up. As I said, I seemed to be popping up in the press on an almost daily basis back then, and Jay was incredibly famous. The papers would have had a field day if we'd gone public, and it was much too early for all that. I thought it was best not to tell anyone apart from a couple of very close confidants. Even Jimmy was in the dark about it, as was my entire family.

On our second date after the *GQ* interview, Jay suggested that he pick me up in his car at Highbury Corner. That way, nobody would see me coming out of my flat and getting into his car. I remember being quite nervous about it. As I said, I was very much a white wine spritzer, dolly Essex girl, while Jay had this cool, jazz muso vibe about him. Consequently, I was a little bit apprehensive about how I would come across at that all-important second meeting.

'What am I going to wear?' I asked Tamara, who was the only friend I'd confided in.

'Well, you don't want to look too dressed up,' she said. 'You're not going out for dinner or anything. You're just going to his house. You want to look nice, but cool.'

'Right,' I said. 'Nice but cool. So how do I do that? I mean, what does he wear?'

Tamara and I ended up scouring the pages of a magazine, looking at pictures of Jay to get up on his fashion sense.

'Look, he's really into his retro sportswear,' Tamara said. 'I think you should go down that route.'

At that time, seventies Farah trousers were back in. Everyone was either in Farah's or cargo pants. So, I suggested my Farah trousers with a nice little crop-top with my belly button showing – very nineties. I'd top it off with a parka from Duffer of St George and treat myself to a brand-new pair of retro-style trainers.

'Yeah, wear that, it'll look wicked!' Tamara said.

Sorted.

When it came to the morning of the date, I really thought I looked the part. My choice of clothes looked great together, and I'd done my hair in those trendy little spikes I often sported back then. However, when Tamara checked out my outfit, it was with a look of some concern.

'Oh my God, Den, your trainers look well new. I mean, you're going to look like you've just gone out and bought a brand-new outfit. Go over to Highbury Fields and walk around or something. You're gonna have to muddy them up a bit, or it'll just be embarrassing.'

'Really?'

'Yes, you can't go box-fresh. It's not cool.'

The two of us ended up trudging around Highbury Fields, trying to achieve just the right amount of grubbiness and well-worn credibility for my spanking-new shoes. It seemed insane to me, but Tamara seemed to know what she was talking about, so who was I to argue?

'Let me know how it goes, won't you? I'll be dying to know,' she said before I left.

'Well, you'll know if it's gone badly because I'll be back at my flat, and you'll hear from me,' I said. 'Otherwise, I expect I'll be there for the whole weekend.'

Half an hour later, Jay picked me up in the Rari, and we headed out to Buckinghamshire for a romantic evening together.

After all the effort I'd gone to, I was convinced I looked the dog's bollocks, but when I walked into the house, Jay took one look at me and went nuts.

'Oh my God, look at your shoes!' he yelled. 'I've just had brand-new cream carpets laid, and you've walked mud everywhere, for fuck's sake!'

He was half trying to laugh about it but was clearly horrified at my clomping dirt all over his pristine floors.

'What have you been doing? Where have you even been to get like that,' he said.

God, if only you knew, mate, I thought. These trainers were bloody brand spanking new this morning without a bloody mark on them. Honestly, I didn't know what to say apart from 'Sorry!'

'Well, just take them off,' he said. 'And please, next time, don't wear shoes that are covered in mud.'

Bloody Tamara and her fashion tips; I could've killed her!

Still, that wasn't the only awkward moment of the weekend. After a lovely, relaxing couple of days together, Jay suggested I stay over on Sunday night and travel to *The Big Breakfast* house from his place the following morning.

'You might as well stay. I'll get my driver Mark to take you to work,' he said. 'Look, we were up late Saturday, we'll go to bed early tonight, and you can be fresh and ready for the morning.'

True, this meant getting up mega-early, but it was worth being able to spend one more evening together.

When the alarm went off in the middle of the night, it didn't feel like such a good idea, however, but it was too late by then. So, sometime after 3am on Monday, I was crawling around Jay's bedroom floor, rooting around in the dark for my bits and pieces so as not to wake him up. It was then I remembered that I'd left my knickers somewhere, but for the life of me, I couldn't see them. Of course, I knew I had to locate them. I mean, I couldn't leave 'Jamiroquai's house' knowing I'd left my dirty knickers there, could I? Christ, he hadn't even written 'Deeper Underground' at that point!

My other concern was that Jay had a great big Alsatian guard dog called Luga at the time, who slept outside his bedroom. I was also going to have to get down the stairs without him barking and waking up the whole house.

Peering through the gloom out into the hallway, though, Luga appeared to be entirely preoccupied with some sort of toy or something. As long as I could lay my hands on my discarded knickers, I could get past the hound and out of there without too much bother. As I moved closer to the landing outside the bedroom, however, it became horribly clear exactly what Luga had gotten so involved in. He had my knickers in his mouth. There he was, snuffling and chewing away at them at the top of the landing.

'Luga!' I whispered. 'Drop!'

All I wanted was to get my drawers, get out of there, and get to work. Was that too much to ask? It culminated with the dog and me in a tug of war on the landing, with me pulling on one end of my knickers and him snarling and pulling at the other. Not the ending I'd imagined to my first romantic weekend with Jay.

I somehow managed to get them back in the end, but every time I went to Jay's house after that, Luga always came straight over to me and jammed his nose in my crotch. Then he'd look at me with a face that said, *You're all right! I know you; you've been here before*.

All my early liaisons with Jay were very much under the radar. I would go to his house, but we never went out on dates or out in public together. It wasn't that much of a hardship, to be honest. Jay lived in the middle of beautiful countryside in an amazing home. There, we could have fun, eating, drinking and dancing around like a pair of idiots to our heart's content, without the pressure of being under scrutiny. It was a lovely way to start a relationship. We were simply enjoying being with one another, talking and getting to know each other. This first secret phase of our romance lasted for quite some time, and we kept quiet about it. Looking back, I can't believe certain people didn't twig. I mean, it wasn't exactly low-key whenever he picked me up. There I'd be on a Friday, sitting in my little flat, and I'd hear the roar of his Ferrari from Highbury Corner. Then, while Jay waited outside, I'd be sneaking out of my front door, hidden under the hood of my parka, while I slinked into the passenger side of the car.

'Why the bloody hell do you have to bring the Ferrari?' I'd say to him. 'It's not exactly understated.'

As we drove away, I'd always try to slump down in the seat as low as possible, just in case of any wandering paparazzi.

• • •

If the timing had been different, I might have ended up going out with one of the cast of *Friends*, despite never having seen a single episode of the show.

This was when people still left messages on answer machines, and, on one occasion, I got quite an unexpected one. At the time, *Friends* was at the peak of its popularity. Everyone watched that show; everyone, that was, except me. Despite everyone banging on about how good it was, I'd never seen it. I was either in bed early or out somewhere, dancing around my handbag. In fact, to this day, I've still never watched it! Still, a couple of the show's stars had appeared on *The Big Breakfast*, so I knew who they were and that they were extremely famous. Like most of our guests, they loved being on the show, seeing it as much as a fun place to hang out as it was to promote their latest project. I guess that's why we always had the pick of the bunch as far as big celebrity guests went, and, at that moment in time, the cast of *Friends* were about as big as it got.

One morning after the show, Cockney Vik mentioned that she'd had a couple of calls from someone saying he was Matthew Perry, asking if I might be interested in going on a date with him. Vik wasn't sure if it really was Matthew, and I wasn't sure I'd have known him if I'd fallen over him.

'I've taken his number down anyway,' she said. 'He wants you to give him a call.'

'Right.' I took the number, knowing full well that I had no intention of using it.

I'd just started seeing Jay then, although hardly anyone knew, including Vik. There was no way I would be going on dates with some random actor, no matter who he was or how big his series happened to be. In fact, by the time I'd left the building, I'd all but forgotten about it.

A week or so later, I walked into my flat in Islington, with Jay in tow, and hit the play button on my answer machine.

'Hi, this is Matthew Perry,' came the voice. 'I hope you don't mind. I got your number from your agent.'

I glanced over at Jay, whose jaw practically hit the ground as the message continued.

'I hope you don't think this is too forward or cheeky, but I think you're gorgeous, and I'd love to take you out on a date.'

'Is he for real?' Jay said, clearly unamused.

'Er . . . Vik did mention that he'd called,' I said, trying to be all matter-of-fact about it. 'I've said I'm not interested, but he just keeps calling.'

Even though I barely knew who Matthew was, there was a certain satisfaction involved here. If nothing else, knowing that I was being chased by a prominent American TV star was bound to keep my new rock star boyfriend on his toes. I walked calmly into the kitchen and air-punched. The timing of that answerphone message could not have been more perfect. The weirdest part about it was I'd never even met Mr Perry. He'd simply seen me on the show while he was in London and had obviously liked the look of me.

Of course, I never met him or even called. It was right at the start of my relationship with Jay, and we were in the bliss of that honeymoon period.

CHAPTER FIFTEEN

'Would you mind getting off my fella's lap?'

We'd fallen for one another pretty quickly, and I remember thinking at the time that my life seemed quite exciting and full of hope. I had a great job, a great social life, great friends, and now a wonderful new relationship. Still, we continued with the secrecy around our romance for quite some time. It just felt like a hassle everyone knowing, given the high-profile nature of our respective jobs. On most Fridays, once I'd finished doing the show, my driver would take me out to Buckinghamshire so Jay and I could spend our weekends together. There, we could be carefree and silly, listening to music and having fun.

One day, however, some clever clogs got a picture of the two of us together, and that was it. Suddenly, we were front-page news, and once the cat was out of the bag, the press seemed to follow us everywhere we went. The only saving grace was that Jay's house was pretty remote and on private land, so it became a place where we could hide out of the spotlight if we chose to.

As time went on, we started going out in public together more. I guess we had the teething troubles that any new couple might, but there seemed to be added pressures on us, feeling like we were under scrutiny the whole time. People have always been interested in reading about celebrity couples; it's been the same since the golden age of Hollywood in the thirties and forties. It's something I'd never really considered before I went out with Jay. Still, here we were, a famous couple who many people seemed to be fascinated by. I think it was because we were a bit of an odd match. There I was, the bubbly blonde TV presenter who wore frou-frou tops and loved dancing to house music or a bit of Steps, and there was Jay, the cool king of acid jazz. My success had been quite mainstream, while his, at that time, was a bit more cult-like and underground. I don't think people could quite get their heads around it.

This 'celebrity couple' status meant that a night out was sometimes a lot more convoluted than it should have been. It usually involved having a driver for the evening – we couldn't exactly get on the tube at the time – and sometimes even security, depending on where we were going. We also had to be careful who we invited back to Jay's place when the two of us were together, always mindful of who we could trust to be respectful of our privacy.

Although I knew all this might put pressure on our relationship, I sort of thought everything was all right. It was manageable and all part of the package. On the other hand, Jay did not enjoy the whole celebrity couple thing and made no secret of it. It was odd because he wasn't a shy person and certainly wasn't averse to being the centre of attention at times. The problem is, you can't always pick and choose when you want the attention of the media and when you want privacy. Back then, I already knew that there was give and take. If you liked the support of the media when you had something to say or something to promote, there was a price to pay as far as privacy went. You couldn't just turn it on and off when it suited you – you were out there, or you weren't.

It felt to me that Jay didn't really understand that unspoken rule back then. He was known for having a bit of a short fuse, so sometimes when photographers followed us, they'd purposely wind him up, hoping for an explosion they could capture on their camera. The trouble was, we often went to places where we knew the press would be, and then Jay would get angry at them for being pushy. Don't get me wrong, it was very annoying having cameras shoved in your face as you came out of a bar, looking slightly the worse for wear. Still, there were other, less high-profile places we could have gone.

'Let's not go to the Met Bar or somewhere where all the paps are going to be,' I'd say. 'Let's go somewhere more local and quieter.'

Still, we often ended up going out to those cool celeb hang-outs because I think Jay enjoyed the whole lifestyle associated with it. He just didn't like the pay-off. It was the same when we pulled into petrol stations or service stations, hoping nobody would spot us. Half the time, we were roaring through in a red Ferrari, so the chances of staying incognito were practically zero.

As time went on, I started to feel as though Jay was laying the blame at my feet, as if it was me attracting what he saw as press intrusion into our lives. After all, I was on telly every day and often in the papers. Jay hated the idea of us being branded a celebrity couple. That image didn't fit in with how he saw himself as a serious musician, and, at the time, I thought I understood where he was coming from; I just sort of went along with it.

I remember we once pulled into a petrol station. Some guys in another car recognised him, calling him over to say hello and maybe sign something.

'Oi, Jamiroquai!' one of them called out. 'Where's Denise?'

Jay asked me not to get out. He wanted me to stay in the car while he went over to chat with the guys. I remember thinking, *Why is it OK for him to sign autographs and take pictures while I skulk in the car?* I felt like I was hiding, and that wasn't me at all.

• • •

Despite the odd niggling thought, the two of us had great fun together, and we did some fantastic things. One day, Jay announced that Donatella Versace had called, offering to fly us to Paris on a private jet for the Versace runway show. Of course, there was an after-party too. Before the event, I went to Versace in London where I was given a gorgeous dress to wear for the evening. On the day, we took a car to the airfield where we boarded the jet, only to discover that our fellow passengers were Jon Bon Jovi, Naomi Campbell, and George Michael's publicist, Connie Filippello, who was always lovely to me. Despite interviewing and hanging out with various big-name celebrities over the years, sitting on a private jet opposite Jon Bon Jovi and one of the world's top supermodels felt pretty surreal.

The show and the after-party did not disappoint. Still, after that, a select group of us were invited back to Donatella's hotel

suite, where we partied all night. During the evening, Naomi –
who, like all of us, was really getting into the party spirit – started
getting very flirty with Jay. There were a fair few couples 'sharing
the love' in the nineties, especially while they were partying
hard, but that was never my bag. If I was in a relationship, I was
in it. I was a one-man girl, and that had to work both ways. I
certainly wouldn't have been much fun in the Primrose Hill set,
where – if you were to believe the stories – hedonism was king,
and anything went. I'd have been sitting in the corner – the
Primrose Prude!

That evening in Paris, I felt uncomfortable. Still, I said nothing
at first, but when Naomi sat on Jay's lap, I felt like she'd crossed
the line, supermodel or not. Suddenly, the feisty Essex girl in me
rose up, and I walked over to where Jay was sitting.

'Would you mind getting off my fella's lap?' I said, but Naomi
took no notice, shooing me away.

Without a second thought, I jabbed her in the ribs. Jay was
mortified, but I think Naomi got the message – don't mess with
an Essex bird!

I've hung out with Naomi a few times since, over the years,
and it's all forgotten now. Cut to February 2010, while I was
pregnant with Betsy. Naomi asked me to walk the runway in her
'Fashion for Relief' show, a charity fashion show raising aid for
Haiti's earthquake victims. It was an honour to be asked, and
Naomi was utterly lovely when we met up.

'I'm so sorry about that incident in Paris,' she said. 'Have you
forgiven me?'

Of course I had, but that fashion show turned out to be the scene of yet another altercation with a supermodel.

At the show's after-party, I mingled, pregnant and demure in a long white dress, while chatting away to various people.

At one point, I was talking to David Walliams when Kate Moss appeared.

'David!' she called out and made a beeline for the two of us.

I stood there for a minute or two while Kate chatted away to David while pointedly excluding me from the conversation. A bit rude, I thought, but I didn't know her, so I said nothing. Meanwhile, David must have sensed my discomfort and directed Kate's attention to me.

'Kate, this is Denise. I'm sure you two must have met,' he said.

'Oh, I wondered who the pregnant bride was,' Kate said.

Slightly gobsmacked, I held my hand out and said, 'Hi, Kate, I'm Denise.'

'I know who you are,' she said, pulling her hand away. 'You're the bitch in pigtails.'

'I'm sorry?'

I could tell that Kate had had a couple of drinks, but I couldn't believe what I was hearing.

'We've met before,' she said. 'In Ibiza, when you were with your boyfriend.'

I assumed she meant Jay, but I had absolutely no recollection of meeting Kate Moss back then. I mean, she's hardly the kind of person you'd forget meeting, is she?

'I'm sorry, Kate, but I've never met you before,' I said. 'I know who you are, of course, but we've never met.'

'Yes, we have,' she said.

It was horribly awkward, but in a quiet moment David suggested that I simply say that I do remember meeting and that it was nice to see her again.

'No, I won't,' I said. 'I'm not going to pretend I've met her when I've never met the woman in my life. I don't care who she is.'

For whatever reason, Kate clearly didn't like me, and I came away feeling quite mortified.

When I walked into my living room later that night, I spotted my Kate Moss coffee-table book and thought, *Well, that's going straight in the bin!*

I phoned Tamara, and she asked me how the evening had gone.

'I've had such a horrible night,' I said. 'I met Kate Moss.'

'Oh, did she remember you?' Tamara said.

'What do you mean? We've never met.'

'You have,' she said.

'Have I?'

'Yes, you met her in Ibiza with Jay years ago. I remember you calling to tell me.'

'Did I?'

I searched every bit of my memory, but nothing came. I must have been so drunk when we met; I literally had no recollection of it. I might have spent a whole evening with Kate Moss and not remembered it. It remains an unsolved mystery.

As well as the glam trip to Paris, I also flew on Concorde to New York with Jay once, when he was playing a gig there. He booked it because he wanted to treat me, which was a lovely thing to do. The thought that we'd be in New York in less than three hours was mind-blowing, given that it usually took almost eight. As I got ready for the trip, I imagined this romantic trip across the pond, staying in a beautiful hotel suite, just the two of us. However, just before we left, Jay dropped the bombshell that his live-in PA/chef/housekeeper was going to be coming with us.

'Oh, so our romantic trip for two is actually for three?' I said.

It wasn't the only time this happened. In fact, we seemed to be gathering a growing entourage as time went on.

We stayed in New York for two nights, but the return journey on Concorde was utterly wasted on me because I was so hungover. I slept for virtually the entire trip. Looking back, I'm not even sure I appreciated how lucky I was, doing all these wonderful things: Concorde, private jets, arriving in a helicopter at Glastonbury, where we had our own luxury Winnebago. The nineties was a decade when everything seemed to be happening so fast. There were fabulous, fun things happening all the time. It's only now, with hindsight, that I can sit back and appreciate how incredible they actually were and how lucky I was to have had those experiences. I was young, successful and living the life of a rock star's wife. Mind you, I still hated being picked up from anywhere in a roaring red Ferrari; that was an embarrassment I never got used to.

CHAPTER SIXTEEN

Water under the bridge

I can't pinpoint when I started to make decisions about my career based on what I thought Jay would say, but that's what started to happen. After recording a cover version of Kylie Minogue and Jason Donovan's 'Especially for You' with Johnny, there was talk about me signing a record deal with Simon Cowell. In the end, I let the idea go because I worried how it might affect Jay's career as a serious musician.

As time went on, I changed myself to fit in and keep my relationship on track because I could feel that things between us were shifting. It was as if the things that Jay loved about me when we first met had now become an annoyance. In the early days of our romance, he'd tell me how funny I was on *The Big Breakfast*, and how great my on-screen partnership with Johnny was. As time went on, he questioned me about why I'd done a particular thing on the show or he'd point out when he thought I'd made myself look silly.

I suppose deep down I knew I was trying to change myself to fit in with what Jay wanted, but part of me just started to go with it. I remember asking myself when I was a young teenager how old I thought I'd be when I got married, how old when I had children – the answer was always 'about 28' – and how many children I'd have. I thought that by the time I was 28, I'd be a married mum, with my family all around me. Unlike many people I knew, I'd come from a very secure, loving family whose parents had stayed together and still loved and respected one another. I wanted that for myself, and I guess I thought my relationship with Jay was heading that way. There were signs that might not be the case, but I chose to ignore them. I found myself twisting and turning myself to keep it on track, trying to fit inside the mould that would lead to me becoming the perfect girlfriend. A wife, perhaps, and eventually a mother.

As time went on, I felt that our time apart during the week was bugging Jay. It would have been impossible to travel from Buckinghamshire to Bow every morning, so mostly I stayed at my flat in Islington. Jay missed me when I wasn't there, which was a nice feeling, but he also wanted me to travel with him when he went on tour.

'The rest of the band have their girlfriends on tour with them,' he'd say. 'I'd love it if you could be there with me.'

Again, I was happy he wanted me there, but it was out of the question. I had a job that only allowed a certain amount of time off, like any job. If my time off didn't coincide with the tours or trips away, then I simply couldn't go.

When Jay and I went to Ibiza, it certainly wasn't like the holidays I enjoyed with Kate and Tamara. It was Jay's first time on the island, so he really threw himself into the party scene. We were staying in the most stunning villa, which I could never have afforded at the time. Still, it was the usual thing: an entourage of people, non-stop partying and bodies everywhere.

At one point, Jay went out to Space nightclub, and I didn't see him for two days: he literally disappeared. I knew nothing had happened to him because he'd been spotted at Bora Bora beach. Meanwhile, I was stuck on my own in this glamorous villa in the middle of nowhere with no car. Looking back, I don't entirely blame him for the way things were. By that time, I knew the score, and nobody was forcing me to stay in the relationship. I guess I was just clinging on, and Jay was obviously reacting in his own way to the way things were between us.

When I think back to that time, I remember feeling like I had something to prove. I wasn't exactly a serial dater, but my friends always joked about how I got bored quickly and could never hold down a long-term relationship. I'd so wanted this one to be different, so I kept trying. I held on long after I should have let go. Even when I knew things weren't right, I didn't want everyone to see me fail.

Fear was another factor. I'd witnessed the shitstorm of high-profile couples splitting up under the gaze of the press, where every magazine spins their own take on the whys and the wherefores of a break-up, and every interview ends up being about the split, rather than the careers that made them famous. I just wasn't ready for that; I couldn't face it. Of course, I was just putting off the inevitable, and things got worse rather than better. I just wish I'd had the balls to say, 'this is not working', and walked away.

It was a lesson I only needed to learn once. These days, I would never stay in a situation that I knew wasn't working. When you know, you know.

Over time, things started to change, and by things, I mean me! *I do want to be with him*, I thought, so I should make an effort to try harder. Perhaps it was time to leave *The Big Breakfast* and try out some other things. I'd made a name for myself; surely, there were plenty of jobs I could do that would fit into my life with Jay better than the one I was doing.

My close friendship with Johnny also started to throw up problems, not just for me but for Johnny too. Our TV partnership was quite unique. We laughed a lot together, we had chemistry, and there was a clear but unstated flirtatious electricity between us. For a while, many people assumed we were in a relationship, or that we'd been together, or that we fancied one another. None of that was true, but they were common misconceptions.

When I was first with Jay, he was all for my partnership with Johnny, telling me how good we were together, but down the line, he wasn't so keen on the idea that people thought that Johnny and I might be 'a thing'.

Johnny had similar issues. I remember him telling me of an experience he'd had while on holiday in Spain with his wife, Antonia. They'd been sitting on the beach when a group of British guys started shouting over to them.

'All right, Johnny! Where's Denise? Why aren't you with Denise?'

It made him uncomfortable, especially knowing how it must have made Antonia feel. I knew how he felt. I'd had similar experiences being out with Jay, with people calling out, 'Where's Johnny?' while Jay and I were out together. I could see how much it grated on him. He was a successful rock star, out with his girlfriend, while random strangers made comments about another bloke and me.

Even though there was no truth in it, I guess it couldn't help but affect how Johnny and I interacted with one another. I certainly remember pulling back from the closeness and the banter towards the end, and I think he did too, and we stopped socialising outside the show. Whereas we once might have attended events together, that all fizzled out. I think we both felt that pressure from within our respective relationships.

In the summer of 1998, Jamiroquai released the single 'Deeper Underground', which featured on the movie *Godzilla*'s soundtrack. It was a massive hit, the band's first-ever number-one single. From then on, Jay's career went even higher into the stratosphere, and everything changed. He started going out and partying a lot more. He's since been very open about his cocaine abuse and what it did to him, but I'm sure you can imagine what that does to a relationship.

The thing I found hardest at the time was constantly being surrounded by people, even at his home. Of course, he had the studio there, so his band would often be there recording. I loved all the guys in his band, but having them around so much meant that Jay and I were rarely alone. From then on, after a night out, it was usually a case of 'all back to Jay's house', whatever time of night it was.

I couldn't be a part of that while I was working, but I remember getting up in the morning and stepping over the lines of shoes of people who'd crashed out somewhere in the house. Of course, there were times that I joined in, and there were some memorable nights that I loved, but it sometimes felt relentless. I found myself craving a normal relationship – my boyfriend and me on the sofa, watching a movie and eating a takeaway. Was that too much to ask?

Unfortunately, our jobs and respective lifestyles no longer allowed for those simple pleasures. That side of our relationship faded away to nothing.

We even had an assistant/chef living with us, which often meant I couldn't even go into the kitchen without finding somebody there.

During the summer of 1999, I could feel Jay pulling away from me, which scared me. I'd recently been to Australia to do a TV show, knowing that he didn't want me to go. When I got back from the trip, he was cold and distant, and I felt like I was being punished. I'd also said no to going on tour to Japan with him, which wasn't popular. It's not that I didn't want to – I'd have loved to – but I had a job too.

Jay was recording his next album, *A Funk Odyssey*, at the time; the album that featured the lead single 'Little L', which he later said was about the break-up of our relationship due to his cocaine habit. I think many people assume he wrote that album after our break-up. However, he was actually writing those lyrics while we were still together. It wasn't a break-up song as some people reported; it was more about his unhappiness with the way I was while we were still together.

I knew that if I was going to pull us back from the brink, I had to make a concerted effort. It was probably already too late by then, but at the time I suppose I refused to accept it. On a day when the band were all at Jay's for a day of recording, I wanted to do something nice for him or be helpful or useful in some way. I told Jay that I was going out to the supermarket to buy and prepare lunch for everyone, then went and bought a roast chicken and some salads. It was a beautiful summer's day, and I thought it would be nice for us all to eat lunch together outside. A while later, I returned from the shop and walked into the kitchen with bags full of food. Jay and the band were sitting around the kitchen table, eating, and my heart fell like a stone. While I was gone, he'd asked his live-in chef to prepare food for everyone.

We talked about it later that night, with Jay telling me I didn't need to buy food and cook because he had a chef.

'I know, but sometimes I just want to be like a normal couple,' I said. 'It's not normal for me to have a live-in chef; it's not for the sort of person I am or for the sort of person you used to be.'

Of course, having dinner prepared for you can be fantastic, but not all the time. Suddenly, we were living in a rock star's pad rather than a home. All the sweetness that we'd had together at the start of the relationship had disappeared. However, I was still desperate to get it back. At the time, Jay and I were friends with Ronnie Wood and his wife, Jo.

'They've got it right,' Jay once said to me. 'Jo really looks after Ronnie; she's always there for him.'

Of course, Ronnie and Jo had their own well-documented struggles, but at that time Jay looked up to them, seeing their relationship as a model one. I remember thinking, Maybe he's right. Perhaps I could be more like the 'rock star wife' and look after him. I started to believe that my career was getting in the way of us being happy – that if I pulled back from such a busy work schedule, things would somehow get better between us.

Meanwhile, things had started to go a little sour with *The Big Breakfast* when it was time to negotiate new contracts. Johnny and I had always got on so brilliantly. Still, the news that his agents were negotiating a separate deal from me with Channel 4 made me feel uncomfortable. As far as I was concerned, we were a team. We were in this together. Why, then, was there suddenly to be a difference in our pay grade? Yes, it was the age-old thing about men versus women and a difference in pay. I was upset, of course, and for a long time I blamed Johnny. With hindsight, I realise that he was just doing what his agents and lawyers were advising him to do. There were a lot of other influences in play. What upset me the most was that I was so into the idea of us being a family, a team. I've always considered myself a team player, and suddenly, because of money and status, it was every man – or woman – for themselves. Imagine Ant going off and insisting he deserved more money than Dec. Well, that's kind of how I felt.

Nowadays, when I see Johnny, we usually end up laughing and joking with one another. All that stuff is water under the bridge. Still, it would be nice to sit down with him and talk about what happened back then and how we both felt about it. Cathartic, perhaps. Our partnership was a pretty rare thing in television at its peak, and in the end I left that partnership when we were still smashing it. We were the number-one breakfast show, and the chemistry we had together worked and had made us both household names. The reason I left is that the whole vibe felt different all of a sudden. It was like your best friend going off and doing something behind your back, and suddenly you don't trust them any more. I probably should've stayed a bit longer, but at the time I felt like it might be time to spread my wings and try a few other options.

I can't be sure from Johnny's side of things, but I believe that he felt like I'd deserted him while we were flying high. I wish we'd had a face-to-face and discussed it back then, but we never did. Johnny's not big on confrontation, so I don't know how he'd have reacted to that anyway.

If there was one job in my career I could go back and do all over again, it would be presenting *The Big Breakfast*. I loved every second of it. There was a real family atmosphere to the show. With it being so successful, everyone in front of and behind the camera was sharing that experience.

Once I stepped away from the show, I thought about all the things I'd put on hold for so long, like singing and theatre. I'd missed those things, but I was out of the loop. Now, as far as all that was concerned, I wasn't even sure I had the confidence to sing or act any more.

CHAPTER SEVENTEEN

The loneliest I've ever felt in my life

After I'd left *The Big Breakfast*, I thought I was clearing a path to become that perfect rock star's wife. I'd smile as I told my friends, 'I'm not going to work so much now; I'm going to do a bit less. It's what I want.' Looking back, I wonder who I was trying to convince: my mates or myself.

It's funny, when I tell newer friends about this period now, they comment on how unlike me it all sounds, and I agree. It wasn't just unlike me; it really wasn't me. Looking back, I don't recognise myself at all.

It didn't work anyway. Instead of feeling like I was being a support to Jay, I just felt like I was in the way the whole time. The worst part about it was that all the confidence I'd built up over the years started to slip away. Bit by bit, I was losing myself, but I didn't realise it was happening. As far as I was concerned, I was getting it wrong, trying to be a career woman when I should have been focused on my relationship. I looked around and saw that many of my friends had settled down. They seemed to have happy lives where they went out for dinners, watched movies, and went on days out and holidays with their partners. I started to tell myself that my mistake had been focusing on work for my whole life. That was why I didn't have the everyday life and the happy relationship that many of my friends had. I can't really blame it all on Jay because it was simply what I was telling myself. I was trying to achieve a cosy normal life with a man who wanted the opposite of that. As much as I was changing myself, I was also trying to change him, to tame him, you might say. It didn't come from a place of wanting control; I just wanted us to be happy. I wanted to go back to when we were first dating, when it was always just the two of us. Of course, we couldn't go back. Fame, attention and money had seen to that. Now, the love we once had for one another had turned sour. When I was with him, we were in an 11-bedroom mansion that was always full of people, but it was the loneliest I've ever felt in my life.

Still, there must have been something deep in me that stopped me from giving in and moving in with Jay completely. I still held on to my flat, my little slice of independence, despite virtually throwing in the towel with work. Maybe I knew deep down that I didn't want a life with a chef and housekeeper and rooms full of people the whole time. I still don't. I could be earning millions, and that would never be the life for me. It's just not me. I sometimes wonder if Jay felt like I was being ungrateful because I often found it hard to accept things from him. Like the time when he surprised me with a Volkswagen New Beetle. It was a sweet and generous thing for him to do because he knew I loved them, and somehow he managed to get me the first one in the country, imported from Germany. As kind and as wonderful a gift as it was, I was reticent about taking it at first. I didn't feel comfortable accepting lavish gifts from him or anyone. To be honest, I would have preferred a week away on our own, simply having a nice holiday.

Everywhere we went there were press, and, of course, I was the one who was known for being in the tabloids every other day because of my job on the telly. Sometimes, Jay would suggest that it was my fault, even that I'd tipped them off about where we were going to be. This became a big thing between us, and it hurt. Of course, it wasn't true; I never had control over that kind of thing, and I wouldn't have dreamed of selling stories or pictures to the press. The trouble was, it was happening. The press did seem to know about our every move, and I'd sometimes read stories and titbits that I felt were being leaked by someone in our inner circle.

I started to feel paranoid about certain people around me, and I began to distance myself from friends. When Jay and I were going for a holiday to Antigua, I remember telling a friend who'd asked that we were going to Majorca because I didn't trust them with the information. I started to suspect everyone. When we did finally get away somewhere, the press would invariably find us. The usual story was that Jay would blame me, I'd end up in tears, and the holiday would be ruined.

It was unbearable at the time, and I was so scared of being blamed every time it happened that I felt like there was nobody I could trust. Whenever it happened, Jay would ask me if I'd told anyone, and, by then, the only people I'd said anything to were my mum and dad. Was it possible that *they* were selling stories? I'd got myself in such a state about the situation by that point that my mind was running rampant with crazy theories. Eventually,

I started to distrust my family too. I already had major issues around trust and being spied on after the incident with Mike and the sex tape, which wasn't exactly helping. I kept thinking my flat was bugged, and I'd be looking over my shoulder everywhere I went, in case I was being followed.

The worst thing that happened during this time was the loss of my good friend, journalist Kate Thornton, due to my paranoia. We'd been friends for ages, but when a press story revealed some behind-the-scenes details about Jay and me, I blamed her. I'd had private conversations over the phone with her, and I'd sometimes leave her voice messages if I was upset after a row with Jay. Now, some of the things we'd talked about were there in black and white. Kate was a features editor at the *Sunday Mirror* then, so I jumped to the conclusion that she must have leaked a story about us.

Years later, of course, I discovered I was one of the victims of phone hacking by a national tabloid newspaper. Everything made sense then. Of course they knew where we were and what was going on the whole time; they had access to my whereabouts, phone calls, and voicemails. I've since spoken to other people who were caught up in the phone-hacking scandal who've told me that they went through the same kind of mistrust and paranoia that I had with friends and loved ones. What a horrible thing to have done; every throwaway comment you make to a friend, every whispered word to a loved one, all spied upon. And for what? Some salacious story for people to gasp and giggle about.

Kate and I had once been as thick as thieves, but we didn't speak for ten years. I wish now I'd been a bit more grown-up at the time and sat down and discussed it with her, but I never did. When the true extent of phone hacking became apparent in 2011, it was a revelation to everyone. As time went on, more and more high-profile people and celebrities were revealed to have been victims. In early 2013, I appeared on the *Strictly Come Dancing* live tour, which Kate hosted, and that was when we finally connected again.

'I owe you such a huge apology,' I told her.

Being the person that she is, Kate forgave my mistake, and now we're friends again. Still, we lost ten years of friendship that we can never get back, which I find very sad.

• • •

The approaching new millennium was not shaping up to be the glorious new beginning I'd hoped it might be. I was at a stage in my relationship with Jay where I was doing everything I could to make things better. Somehow, though, whatever I did seemed to make things between us worse. On top of that, I felt like my career was at an all-time low, having just presented a brash, sex-based quiz show called *Something for the Weekend*, which was not at all well received.

On New Year's Eve, Jay threw a party at his house. It was an event that should have been exciting and fun but ultimately highlighted how far Jay and I had drifted from one another. I invited a bunch of my friends, and, of course, all his mates were in attendance, but the party felt fragmented, with two distinct groups. Instead of mingling, both sets of friends stayed in their own bubbles. It felt bizarre. There was one awful moment during the evening when Jay got down on one knee, in front of all my friends, as if he were about to propose. As I looked down at him, somewhat surprised, he jumped to his feet.

'Only joking,' he said.

By that time, I felt uncomfortable in the house I lived in, as if I were perhaps surplus to requirements. It's not surprising, I suppose. The house often seemed full of people, whether it was Jay's staff who worked there or the other members of Jamiroquai who were there to work with Jay in his home studio. It wasn't that I didn't like hanging out with the band. They were lovely guys; we just didn't seem to have any time for the two of us, which made things all the more difficult for me. I was lonely in a house full of people.

It's not that I was living there full-time either. I still had my flat in Islington but spent most of my time living at Jay's because that was what he'd wanted. He liked the security of having me around and to come home to because he was always off travelling and on tour. Of course, it wasn't always possible because of my work, but there were also times I turned jobs down so I could be around for him. One of the reasons I'd left *The Big Breakfast* was so I didn't have to be up and on set at the crack of dawn and could spend more time at home, which seems crazy looking back. In fact, as time went on, I made all sorts of minor changes to try to make our relationship run smoothly. In the end, I was hardly doing anything at all, but that wasn't ideal either.

'What are you doing today?' Jay would say to me.

'Nothing much', I'd say, but then I'd feel guilty for not being busy.

As morning broke on 1 January 2000, we were all still up after the party, so I turned on the TV and tuned into *The Big Breakfast*. My heart sank, seeing everyone having fun on the first show of a new century. Why wasn't I there? That had been my domain, my life. Why had I given it all up?

I remember wishing I'd stayed, but whenever I'd mentioned returning to the show, Jay hadn't been keen on the idea.

'You've done it; you don't need to go backward', he'd say.

I told myself he was right, but a little voice inside kept telling me I'd left too soon.

I remember feeling very lost that New Year's morning. My career was adrift, as was my relationship. I'd even isolated myself from friends and family, still paranoid about all the leaked stories about Jay and me to the tabloids. In the following weeks, I really didn't have much going on at all. I'd lost myself, scared that I was letting a successful career slip away from me. It didn't help that *Something for the Weekend* hadn't gone as well as I'd hoped. True, it was a high-profile TV job, but it certainly didn't do me any favours as far as being a sought-after or respected presenter. In fact, the press went to town on me. As far as the media was concerned, the show was low-rent and vulgar and I'd crossed the line; I was disgusting.

In February 2000, something unexpected happened while Jay and I were out in a restaurant in Islington. It wasn't a particularly romantic or glamorous restaurant. In fact, it was an all-you-can-eat pan-Asian place called Tiger Lil's on Upper Street. Nice enough, but the sort of place you'd go for a mate's birthday or an after-work do rather than a romantic meal. Anyway, sometime during the evening, Jay pulled out a stunning diamond engagement ring and proposed. I was taken aback, but not for the reasons you might think. Rather than feeling excited or happy that Jay had decided to commit to our relationship long-term, I found the whole thing a bit odd. Apart from the fact that we hadn't been getting on particularly well, it just seemed weird that Jay, who set such high value on his privacy, would propose in such a public place. He also seemed very hyper and excited at the time. The fact that all the staff could see what was happening made me feel terribly self-conscious and embarrassed. Looking back, I think I said yes because I didn't know what else to do. I told myself it was what I'd been waiting and hoping for all this time. It was, but there was something that didn't sit right with me about when and how it had happened. It was all a bit of a blur, to be honest. In fact, I didn't even get to finish my noodles.

We went back to my flat after the meal, but Jay decided he wanted to get back home to the recording studio later in the evening. I was disappointed but not surprised. I remember sitting alone on my sofa, thinking, *Why did I say yes? What was I even saying yes to?* My mind was also buzzing about why Jay might have proposed so unexpectedly. Could it have been the handsome pop artist who'd made no secret of the fact that he'd 'had a thing for me' for some time? I was due to fly to Dublin the next day for an event that the pop star mentioned above was also rumoured to be attending. Was Jay in a hurry to get a ring on my finger, just in case? Friends told me later that he'd bought the ring planning on a big romantic gesture, which made a wok 'n' fry on Upper Street seem all the more random. I guess the equivalent now would be someone getting down on one knee in Wagamama.

Later that night, I got a call from my good friend Julian Clary congratulating me on my engagement. The news was out already. I figured that the restaurant must have called someone at a newspaper and told them what had happened. So that was it; we were engaged.

Of course, announcing an intention to marry was never going to make a floundering relationship any better. Still, by then, I think I was just trying to keep everything together. My career, like my love life, was a deep well of uncertainty.

I went back to *The Big Breakfast* for a few months in September 2000, but it felt as though Johnny, my co-host and former partner-in-crime, had moved on. He was upset that I'd left in the first place but had since got used to presenting the show with various new partners. It wasn't the same, and I felt like I was having to work twice as hard to achieve a camaraderie that had come so easily before. On top of that, Jay was unhappy that I'd caved and gone back to the show. It was as if I was jumping through hoops to people-please the whole time, and it wore me out.

Meanwhile, the main TV channels didn't want to touch me any more. I'd presented *Record of the Year* for ITV three years in a row, but I was dropped from that because, after *Something for the*

Weekend, they no longer saw me as 'prime time' material. I had to face up to the fact that it had buried my TV career.

I was utterly lost. I'd had so much going for me, so much potential, and now I felt like it had all slipped away. It was gone.

CHAPTER EIGHTEEN

'I think you should do a musical'

Early in 2001, Jimmy made a suggestion that seemed to come straight out of left field.

'I think you should do a musical,' he said. 'Something completely different to shake things up.'

'A musical? Why would I want to do that?'

I don't know why, but to me, the idea of doing a musical somehow felt like a step backwards. I'd done TV and a couple of films by then, and this was in the days before TV presenters, soap actors and celebrities were getting involved in musical theatre in a big way.

'That's where you came from, isn't it? Singing, dancing and acting at Sylvia Young's,' Jimmy said. 'I've got an idea about something you could go up for.'

Chicago was the big new show in the West End at the time, and Jimmy went to the show's producer, Barry Weissler, with the idea of me playing the role of Roxie Hart. At first, Barry wasn't keen on the idea.

'Why would I put Denise in *Chicago*?' he said. 'It's doing very well because people love the show. It doesn't need a celebrity name to sell it.'

Jimmy asked if I could audition anyway, and Barry agreed.

'No special treatment, though. She'll have to go through the process like every other actress.'

I decided to go for it. It was, after all, just an audition, and if I didn't end up getting it, nobody would be any the wiser. Suddenly, I felt like I had something to be hopeful about, something to try for.

For the first part of the audition, I had to prepare two songs, and there was a scripted section to perform. Deep down, I knew I had it in me to make this happen, but it had been such a long time since I'd dipped my toes into the world of theatre and singing, I was going to have to dig deep.

The night before my audition, I stood in the kitchen at Jay's, excited to tell him my news.

'I've got something to tell you,' I said.

I noticed his face drop. I think he thought I was about to tell him I was pregnant.

'I've got an audition,' I said.

'Cool, what is it?'

'Well, you know the musical *Chicago*, in the West End? I'm auditioning for one of the lead roles in it. Roxie!'

'What, onstage, singing live?' He sounded surprised.

'Yes, it's a big West End show.'

Jay looked at me for a moment, taking in the news, and then he said, 'You can't do that.'

'What do you mean?' I thought he was joking.

'You'll get up there and embarrass yourself. You can't do it,' he said.

To say I was taken aback was an understatement, but Jay wasn't the first person who'd had doubts. A few close friends had also expressed concerns, reminding me how exposed I'd be up there onstage in front of a theatre full of people.

Still, it was hard to hear, especially from Jay. Despite our relationship being pretty much toxic by then, there was a big part of me that still wanted to make it work. I thought perhaps me starting something fresh and new might somehow help, and I honestly thought Jay would see it as good news. No, not good, fantastic.

In the space of a few hours, my whole mood changed. The magic carpet had been pulled out from under me, and with it had gone all my hope of starting something new, which now felt pointless. I called Jimmy, confused and upset.

'I don't think I can do it, Jimmy. I'm not sure it's the right thing for me.'

'You can do it. I know you can,' he said.

Jimmy was smart. He knew pretty much everything that had gone on with me for the last couple of years, professionally and personally.

'Denise, please don't make the same mistake again,' he said. 'Do not put your career on hold or on the back-burner again. You need to do this for you.'

I knew he was right.

The next day, I arrived at the Adelphi Theatre feeling terribly nervous – quite unusual for me, as I'd always been reasonably confident at auditions. Apart from not feeling very good about myself, I also had some big shoes to fill. Ruthie Henshall had played Roxie in the show while Ute Lemper had played Velma Kelly. They were both seasoned stage performers and renowned for their work in musicals. Meanwhile, I was a TV presenter who'd done a bit of acting. Despite my theatrical beginnings at Sylvia Young's, it was TV that I was best known for. That, and gracing the covers of magazines.

As I waited for my turn, Jay's words were ringing in my ears. I could hear some of the other girls doing their auditions, which rattled my nerves even more. I was also aware that I was very thin. Tiny, in fact, having shrunk down to a size six because I hadn't been eating properly. I wondered if I looked as bloody awful as I felt. As I waited for my turn onstage, the negative voices in my head were on overdrive. Who did I think I was, imagining I could step into a musical on a West End stage? If ever there was a moment when I would walk away from something, it was then, but something stopped me from turning around. Maybe it was pride – I don't know. I just knew I had to go out there and prove that Jay and everybody else who'd cast doubts in me were all wrong. I was capable of doing this, more than capable. It's what I'd done since I was a kid, what I'd trained and worked hard to do. Before I could think any more about it, I was called to the stage. This was on!

After all the nerves, I sailed through the acting part of the audition, particularly the American accent, which I'd already perfected. Once that was over, I performed my old favourite 'Le Jazz Hot!' from *Victor/Victoria* and the Richard Rodgers song 'Where or When'.

Taking my first steps at our home on Howell Road in Corringham, aged ten months

In my Christmas dress from Marks & Spencer (my sister Jackie had a matching outfit), aged two years and seven months

Mexican hat night at Highfield
Caravan Park in Clacton-on-Sea!

With Jackie (she is on the left) at the Corringham
and Stanford-le-Hope Carnival, aged five

Before my primary ballet exam, aged six

Before my primary modern dance exam, aged seven

Getting ready for a choreography competition at the Susan Stephens Dance School

My first photo with the
Sylvia Young Agency,
aged eleven

On a family holiday
to Malta, 1989

The best job I ever had! I laughed every day with my mate Johnny Vaughan. *The Big Breakfast*, 1998. Ken McKay/Shutterstock

In happier times with Jay.
Always cheeky and fun

With Johnny Vaughan at the Brit
Awards, 1998. This was at the height
of our *Big Breakfast* fame. We stayed
up pretty much all night and went
straight to the live breakfast show

Opening night of the musical *Stop the World*, at the Savoy in London with Joan Collins

The hoodie says it all. New York is one of my favourite cities in the world. This was taken during my rehearsal period for *Chicago* © Big Pictures

PLAYBILL ®

AMBASSADOR THEATRE

CHICAGO
THE MUSICAL

WWW.PLAYBILL.COM

A programme from my run as Roxie Hart in *Chicago* on Broadway

Flying to Vegas with
David Walliams to
meet Sir Elton John

V Festival at Hylands
Park in Chelmsford.
Betsy's first live event!
We loved it. No
camping though, I
drove there and back.
How life changes after
becoming a mum!

Strictly Come Dancing 2012 with my professional partner, James Jordan. This was taken before my first live dance. I was very nervous

Flying solo on radio at Magic FM, regaining my confidence

Golfing at the Grove in Hertfordshire

Onstage in London's West End
at the Arts Theatre performing
in *Some Girl I Used to Know*

Drunk and smitten! The night I met Eddie on a blind date at Soho House

Cycling from Vietnam
to Cambodia in the
sweltering heat, 2014

Trekking the Himalayas with my partner in crime Lydia
Bright (having kicked off our white Essex stilettos!), 2017

At my cousin's wedding,
with my family

Filming *Gogglebox*
with Eddie!

With the first round in the bag, I was thrown in with choreographer Vanessa Lee Hicks. She put me through my paces, teaching me the choreography for 'Hot Honey Rag', which is the one with the cartwheel in case you don't know it. Vanessa became a good friend and ally to me. As the audition process progressed over the next couple of weeks, she confided in me that she wanted me to get the role. I don't know if she could see how fragile I was or perhaps knew how much I needed it, but Vanessa was backing me all the way. I recall a couple of times when we were rehearsing at Pineapple Dance Studios and only had one precious hour. When our time was up, Vanessa went to the reception desk to ask if a class was coming in straight after our slot. When there wasn't, she'd ask if we could have an extra 30 minutes, just to give me a bit more time to perfect my moves. Vanessa called me Sparrow because of my tiny frame. In fact, she still uses that name for me to this day.

At one stage, it was down to three other actresses and me, then me and one other. When Barry eventually said those magic words, 'Denise, I want you to do the part', I was ecstatic. What made me even happier was the fact that I hadn't been handed it on a plate just because I was a so-called celebrity name. No, I'd worked hard, and for the first time in a long while I felt proud of myself.

Interestingly enough, once I'd played the part of Roxie, Barry employed a string of celebrities on the show, realising it was great for profile as well as ticket sales. Among many others, Ashlee Simpson, Brooke Shields, Tony Hadley, Marti Pellow and Alison Moyet have all appeared in *Chicago*.

I started rehearsals without even mentioning it to Jay; I kept it all quiet. I'd still been spending much of my time at Jay's place in Buckinghamshire. Yet, for various reasons, things were changing. For a start, I was rehearsing every day at Pineapple Dance Studios in Covent Garden or at the Adelphi Theatre on the Strand. It made more sense for me to stay in London. Aside from practicalities, Jay and I weren't getting on at all. Actually, that's an understatement; things between us were pretty awful by then. The only thing I could do was throw myself, body and soul, into rehearsals and try to accept that I would have to move on, however hard that might be. We were still in contact throughout, but it was random and disjointed – a vast difference from living together as a full-time, committed couple. Those days were gone, although I was still holding out this distant, naive hope that if I was a success in *Chicago*, there might be a way back for us. With hindsight, I was still looking for his approval, I suppose.

All this must have been hard for my mum and dad to witness. They knew me better than anyone. I think Mum, in particular, was aware of how much I'd changed during this time. She knew me as bubbly, confident and self-assured, but that was no longer what she saw. I was disappearing before her very eyes, and I knew it, which made me pull away even further. I was embarrassed, I suppose, because I knew I wasn't being authentic. I was known for being ballsy and opinionated, a strong, independent young woman who had a successful career and knew what she wanted. Now, it seemed, I was giving that all up, bending over backwards to make a relationship work with someone who, quite frankly, was no longer interested.

I heard reports come back that Jay had cheated on me in France, but I didn't believe it; I wouldn't. To this day, I don't know if there was any truth in it. All I knew was that I loved him, and I was holding on to this idea that we could go back to how it was at the beginning. I spent so long trying to chase that ideal that I lost myself in it.

I wasn't a person that shouted and argued; I hated that kind of heated confrontation. It's still the same now. In the seven years I've been with Eddie, we've had two arguments that we marked down as fairly big rows but certainly nothing major. Back then, with Jay, however, I found myself arguing and shouting all the time. After one particularly horrible blow-up, I called my mum.

'You don't sound happy,' she said.

'I'm not,' I said, finally admitting it to myself as much as her.

'You're going to destroy yourself if you stay in this,' she told me. 'You need to get out of that house, Denise. You need to find yourself again. Your career is going tits up, and your self-esteem seems to have disappeared. You need to walk away.'

It was a stark warning but I knew she was right. I was still clinging on, even though there was barely anything to cling to. I had to do something, and fast.

On that same day, I calmly packed up my belongings and left Jay's house for good.

At the time, a friend of mine, Joely, had been staying at my flat because I was never there. Now I had to tell her that I needed it back, and she was very understanding and kind. Knowing how upset I was, she asked me if I wanted her to stay with me to help me get through it.

'I just want to be on my own,' I told her.

When I was alone, I just cried, sobbing for hours, feeling as if I'd messed everything up. It was such a raw, empty sadness, something I'd never experienced.

I immersed myself in the part of Roxie, and in the rehearsal process, deeply. It was the only way I could get through the pain of the break-up. It worked most of the time, but there were many nights at my flat in Islington where I just felt hopeless and lonely.

• • •

I'd always had long hair, and before the promotional photo shoot for *Chicago*, I had extensions in. However, not long before the shoot, I found myself alone in my flat, drinking and crying and hand-picking the extensions out of my hair, one by one, like a crazy woman. When I woke up the following day, my head was a fright. I stood at the bathroom mirror, horrified and wondering what on earth I'd been thinking.

I called my friend Jamie, who was Elton John's hairdresser, desperate.

'Jamie, I've destroyed my hair,' I said. 'I've pulled my extensions out, and it looks a nightmare. I don't know what I'm going to do.'

With the promotional photo shoot looming, Jamie reassured me that he could help and get me in somewhere fast. I ended up at Trevor Sorbie, meeting with the man himself. I filled Trevor in on the new job and what I'd done to my hair, and thankfully he took control, only . . .

'I'm going to take it short,' he said. 'Very short.'

'No, Trevor, please don't do that.' I'd never worn my hair short and couldn't even imagine it.

'Trust me, you're going to love it,' he said, and chopped into my hair with abandon.

I suppose if I was going to trust anyone with my hair, Trevor was a perfect choice. A celebrity hairdresser since the late sixties, Trevor invented the iconic wedge haircut.

The photo shoot was a couple of days later. When the resulting photos were released in the press, several articles popped up in various magazines and supplements encouraging women to 'get the Roxie look!' – and I even heard that when Renée Zellweger made the film of *Chicago*, she was inspired to get a similar look after seeing me perform the part of Roxie on Broadway.

On my big opening night, I walked into my dressing room at the Adelphi Theatre to find it filled with red roses. I remember thinking, *Wow! Jay's sent me all these flowers*. I don't know why my mind jumped to that conclusion; I guess it was just habit. It turned out they weren't from Jay but from George Michael. I can't remember what the note said precisely, but the message was something along the lines of, 'I felt like you needed this.'

Of course, I was nervous that night, but I had a fantastic time up there, and the audience was as warm and enthusiastic as I'd hoped. Still, you never know how the critics are going to perceive things. With the way my profile had been for the past year, it was anyone's guess what kind of reviews I'd end up with. Happily, they were more than favourable.

After the show, the producers threw a party for me at the Light Bar in the St Martin's Lane Hotel, with press, media and invited guests. It was even on the news that night that I'd opened in a West End show. However, my triumphant opening didn't end up being the big showbiz story of the following day. That accolade went to Jay, who'd gone out on the town that night. On his way out of a nightclub, he was involved in a fight with a photographer, smashing the guy's camera. He was charged with criminal damage and common assault, so it was front-page news, even though the charges were eventually dropped through lack of evidence. The headlines, however, certainly took some of the shine off my big night.

Appearing in *Chicago* was a huge turning point for me, professionally and emotionally. My success in the show was a wake-up call, reminding me that I could do something on my own and that I was capable. I'll admit it wasn't easy. I spent much of the run feeling sad. It's one thing coping with a break-up, but being a high-profile couple meant that I was also dealing with the various stories leaping off the pages of the tabloids at me several times a week. It was incredibly hard to see and read about Jay hanging out with new women all over the place.

Still, I had my own stab at dating during my run in *Chicago* with the actor Nick Moran, who was in the movie *Lock, Stock and Two Smoking Barrels*. He was a lovely guy, but I was on the rebound big-time.

I remember texting a friend of mine while Nick was staying at my flat one night. The messages went something along the lines of . . .

Me: It's not working with Nick.

Her: Why not?

Me: I don't like his shoes.

Her: What?

Me: I'm really fussy about footwear.

In truth, of course, I was just looking for an 'out'. It probably wouldn't have mattered who I dated or however wonderful he was; I simply wasn't ready.

One day, Barry came to me with an announcement I was in no way expecting.

'I want you to come and do the part in New York,' he said. 'Play Roxie on Broadway. There's an American actress I'd bring over here, so we can do it as an exchange.'

'Are you sure?' I was gobsmacked. 'Of course, I'd love to do it.'

The idea that Barry believed in me enough to take his show, his baby, to Broadway was the massive shot in the arm I needed. This was it: a complete change; a new start. New York City.

I was all ready to pack up, get on that plane and head for the bright lights, but it was early September 2001, and the world was about to change forever.

CHAPTER NINETEEN

I'd fallen in love with New York

After 9/11, everything was uncertain, and the rules changed. Often in theatre, when a British actor performs in a Broadway show, an American actor comes over to appear in the West End version by way of an exchange. This wasn't happening post 9/11 because there was so much extra security in place. As well as that, nobody even knew who I was in America so I would have to get special permission and an O1 visa – a non-resident US visa – where applicants must demonstrate extraordinary ability in their field of work. Through my old boss on *The Big Breakfast*, Waheed Alli – now Baron Alli, a member of the House of Lords – I was able to get a letter from the prime minister, Tony Blair, endorsing me. It was tricky, but in the end we managed to get permission for me to travel out and do the show.

I flew to New York in a haze of excitement, taking Tamara along with me. We stayed in an apartment at the Trump International Tower on Columbus Circle, which overlooked Central Park. It was an incredible place, owned by Barry Wiseler but mine for the duration of my stay in Manhattan. As excited as I was, I was happy that Tamara was with me. Despite my recent success, I was still quite fragile and certainly not back to my old self. I still wasn't eating enough or sleeping particularly well, so

Tamara was kind of like a babysitter for me as well as a friend, sharing in the excitement of the trip. She made sure I looked after myself. I needed it too. I got tonsillitis almost as soon as I arrived, which left me feeling run-down and stressed.

On the first day of rehearsal, I'll admit I was apprehensive. It's one thing holding your own on home turf, but this was Broadway. Surely, every stage actor's dream. It was certainly mine. For the first few days, it's fair to say that some of the cast were slightly wary of me. Not nasty; just a tad frosty. I think it was a case of 'What's she doing here when we have plenty of our own actors who could be doing the role?' Let's face it, most of them had probably never even heard of me. That was going to be my first job, proving myself to my fellow actors. I wasn't even thinking as far ahead as pleasing the critics; I just wanted to show the rest of the cast that I was the right choice for the show and deserved to be there.

On the other side of the coin, the cast not knowing who the hell I was became strangely liberating. I felt like I could really immerse myself in the role, playing it to people who had no preconceived ideas about who I was and what I'd done before. I was playing it in a way that I wished I had when I'd opened in London – without fear.

This feeling went further than just my part in the show. Being in New York opened my eyes and made me see a bigger world. I realised how small everything had felt in the past year. It had all had been a worry: work, my love life, the negativity of the press. Even during my run in *Chicago*, I'd been running on empty. I was desperately sad about the end of a relationship, always fighting to rise above it and keep working. Suddenly, it was like I was in my own movie, wandering the streets of New York where nobody knew me. I was doing my dream job and living in a fabulous apartment. The world was bright and hopeful again.

During rehearsals, I quickly bonded with the cast and made a good friend in one of the young girls from the press office, Julia. She'd also moved from the UK to New York, and we hit it off right away. We'd go out for dinner after work during the rehearsal period, or we'd head for cocktails at the Hudson Hotel, where they had a DJ on the roof terrace. I was very much embracing the New York life and loving it.

I even felt confident about my Broadway debut. On the day of my big opening – press night – knowing I would be reviewed by all the theatre critics of the American press, I was calm. I walked along Broadway toward the Shubert Theatre, and it dawned on me that I wasn't even nervous. I just remember smiling and telling myself to enjoy the night. I hadn't really been able to enjoy the London press night because of all the negativity swirling around me at the time. Now I was fine. I was simply looking forward to giving the best performance I could give and enjoying a wonderful evening.

There was such excitement in the theatre that night. I'd loved performing in the West End, but the audiences are famously more reserved in London than they are in New York. If an audience is enjoying a Broadway show, they really get behind it. It was such a surprise to see people whooping and cheering throughout the performance. Good or bad, I certainly didn't have to wait until the end of the show to find out whether they were enjoying it or not. I was getting an instant reaction, and I was buzzing from it. Once it was over, I told myself that, whatever the reviews were, I'd done my best, and I'd loved every part of it. For once, it hadn't all flashed past in a blur. I'd soaked in every second, and it was something I knew I'd never forget. I certainly wasn't going to let anything ruin that for me, not even the odd shitty review. In fact, I told Barry not to even send me the reviews; I didn't want to see them.

He'd laughed. 'Well, if they're good, I'm going to tell you.'

The first hints of any news about my Broadway debut came from home. I woke up to my phone beeping with congratulatory messages and texts from friends and family in the UK. At the same time, I could hear the phone in the apartment ringing and the whirr of the fax machine. Barry had faxed the reviews over to me, just as he promised he would if they were good. And they were good. Very good. Even Clive Barnes from the *New York Post*, America's most revered theatre critic, gave me a fantastic write-up.

When I checked my messages, I was confused and amazed to discover that my mum had appeared on Lorraine Kelly's show in the UK that morning. Now that was really something. I'd always tried to keep my family out of the limelight, knowing how things can sometimes get twisted in the press; I guess it was my way of protecting them from anything I might get up to. I called Mum straight away to find out how she'd ended up doing an interview with Lorraine – all while I was asleep in New York, five hours behind UK time.

As it turned out, Lorraine had seen the response from the critics and decided to get Sylvia Young on the show to make a comment about her one-time student's Broadway triumph.

'The thing is, Sylvia didn't want to appear on the show,' Mum told me.

'Why ever not?' I asked, somewhat surprised.

'Well, she hadn't had her roots done, so she phoned me and said, "Kath, you'll have to do it." I told her I didn't know if I could, but she said I'd have to because her roots needed doing.'

Eventually, when I was back at home, I watched a video of Mum's interview. Poor Mum had been caught entirely off guard, but the funniest thing about it was the posh voice she put on during the interview. It didn't even sound like her.

'Mum, why are you talking like that?' I asked her.

'Well, it was being on telly,' she said. 'I suddenly just went into my posh telephone voice without thinking.'

• • •

The rest of my time in New York was wonderful. I met amazing people and made many friends. It was after that show one night that the lovely Andy Williams came to see me. We ended up duetting on a new version of the classic Frankie Valli song 'Can't Take My Eyes Off You'. In fact, there were many nights when I'd get a message telling me that there was an actor, singer or celebrity in to watch the show. Andrew Lloyd Webber was one of those people, and that was the start of another story. Even some of my neighbours were famous. Usher lived in an apartment in my building, and I'd often bump into him in the lift where we'd have a friendly little chat.

Once Tamara had gone back home, I was on my own in Manhattan, forced to live like a grown-up for the first time ever. True, I'd always been reasonably self-sufficient, but I'd pretty much flown by the seat of my pants. Now it was just me looking after me. There was no Mum and Dad, no close childhood friends and no boyfriend to lean on. I certainly wasn't partying in New York as I had in London. Broadway is hardcore, with ten shows a week sometimes, so there was no room for late nights and hangovers.

Looking back, I realise that it was the best thing that could have happened to me. Having come out of a painful break-up, I'd flown away to what seemed like another world. It was exactly what I needed. With the rehearsals and then the show's run, I was only there for about three to four months, but that was enough time for some of the wounds to heal. It was the time I needed to re-discover my confidence and start to believe in myself again.

At the end of it, I remember wishing that I could have gone back and redone the London run of the show with this new-found confidence and carefree attitude. I knew I'd have enjoyed it so much more. For the last couple of years in London, I'd spent so much time walking on eggshells, constantly worrying whether I was saying the right thing where the press was concerned. Pretending everything was all right, when it wasn't, just to keep the peace, or so people didn't see me as a failure. Here I didn't care what people thought about me or what a review about my performance might say. I was just living in the moment and enjoying it. I'd fallen in love with New York, and I'd sort of fallen in love with the new me too.

If there's one thing I'd say to young people who find themselves under the constant scrutiny of public comments and social media, it's don't worry so much about what other people think of you! You can waste your life worrying about the opinions of others. It's just not worth it. It's something I learned back then, and I've carried it with me ever since.

CHAPTER TWENTY

Andrew was a huge Avril Lavigne fan

I even got my wish as far as repeating the London run was concerned. After the success of my Broadway performances, Barry asked me to return to the West End for a limited six-week run. I couldn't really say no. Here was my chance to show the UK audiences what I could really do.

In the end, it was a bit of a double-edged sword. While I enjoyed doing the show again on the West End stage, being in London felt like a step back. The minute I landed, it was like I was back in the world of my failed relationship and being judged. The freedom of being in New York seemed to evaporate very quickly. Whenever I saw something written about me, there it was: I was Jay Kay's ex-girlfriend; poor heartbroken Denise. I remember a friend being at my flat when I was feeling particularly upset about it one evening.

'You just have to stop talking to journalists about Jay,' she said. 'Don't mention it, and they'll get bored and talk about something else.'

'That's the thing, I don't talk about him,' I told her. 'I'll do interviews and talk about *Chicago*, and when it comes out, there'll be loads of bits from old interviews thrown in for a bit of drama.'

It was true. Despite avoiding the subject of my love life or Jay in interviews, the thrust of the finished article would generally be along the lines of: 'I mended my broken heart in New York, and now I'm back to show him what I've got!'

It was very frustrating, but by then I knew what to expect. I also knew the kind of stories that sold papers.

• • •

One of the most positive things to come out of my time doing *Chicago* was my friendship and working partnership with Andrew Lloyd Webber. He'd seen me do the show on Broadway and at the Adelphi, and, unbeknown to me, was busy hatching a plan.

It started when I got a call from Jeff Thacker, who was directing the 2001 Royal Variety Performance. He told me he'd love it if I could perform on the show, but he was quite specific about what I should sing.

'I'd love it if you could do "Take That Look Off Your Face" from *Tell Me on a Sunday*,' he said. 'I think the song will be great for you.'

I couldn't disagree. When I perform a song, I always like to tell a story wherever possible. It doesn't all have to sound fantastic as long as I get the feeling and the narrative of the lyrics across. This Lloyd Webber and Don Black song was a number that most definitely had a story.

I didn't know why at the time, but my performing this song had been Andrew's idea. He was basically auditioning me on the biggest stage possible – in front of millions of people.

I'd recently bought a little cottage in Wales, near Abergavenny. A few days before the Royal Variety Performance, I took a couple of girlfriends there for a few days of country air and relaxation. While I was there, I got a throat infection. I don't know if it was stress or that I was run-down, but I just seemed to be susceptible to throat problems around that time. With rehearsals for the Royal Variety at the Dominion Theatre imminent, I told Jeff that I was worried about my voice as my glands were like golf balls. At the dress rehearsal, things weren't much improved. I felt a bit better and thought I could probably belt the song out once for the actual show, but singing it in full beforehand in a sound check wasn't a good idea.

'If I belt this out now, I won't have a voice tonight,' I said.

'You have to rehearse,' one of the crew said. 'Everyone has to do a camera rehearsal.'

I'm sure they all thought I was being a bit of a diva, but I knew what would happen if I let rip before the show; I'd have nothing left!

Jeff knew I wasn't just being difficult but issued a stern warning nonetheless.

'Denise, you cannot let me down on this. If you screw this up, you're doing it on live TV in front of the Queen.'

'I promise I won't mess up,' I said. 'Just let me save my voice for the show.'

When it came to the performance, I sang it with conviction and sold the song as best I could, still unaware that this was all under the watchful gaze of the Lord Lloyd-Webber.

After the show, Jeff came to my dressing room. 'Denise, Andrew's here, and he wants to say hello.'

'Oh, right, of course,' I said, still not knowing what was going on.

Andrew came in and started talking about his big plans for a new version of *Tell Me on a Sunday*. He spoke to me as if I knew all about it and that I was already involved. Meanwhile, this was the first I'd heard about it, so I was more than a little confused.

Andrew assumed that Jeff had told me that he had his sights set on me doing it, which is why he wanted to hear me sing the biggest song from the show, but, of course, Jeff had not told me.

'I didn't tell you because I knew you'd freak out and get all self-conscious,' he confided a little while after. 'Also, I didn't want to build your hopes up in case it was a non-starter.'

After the show that night, I felt a bit giddy. This was turning out to be a brilliant evening, but it wasn't over yet. I relaxed post-show, hobnobbing with some of the big stars on the bill that night: Cilla Black, Tom Jones and Paul O'Grady. At some point during the evening, Julian Clary came over to find me.

'We're all going to the Shadow Lounge, darling. You have to come along!'

Before I knew it, I was in a car on my way to a gay club in a Soho basement, with Julian, Paul, Cilla and Tom in tow. We all ended up in one of the booths at the club, drinking champagne and having a fine old time. At one point, I was pole dancing with Cilla and the boys while Tom Jones cheered us on, which, let's face it, isn't how you would expect an evening to go. That's about as camp as it comes. The only thing was, I had a beautiful long Ben de Lisi dress on loan for the evening, which rather suffered throughout the night. As I'd been dragging my fabulous frock around the Shadow Lounge, I'd collected the odd cigarette butt, and the bottom of the dress was completely sodden. It was a top night, though; one I'll never forget.

Not long after that, Andrew called to invite me over for dinner at his house. I was surprised and flattered that he'd called me personally rather than getting an assistant to do it and, of course, I told him I'd love to go. On the night, he sent a car to pick me up and take me to his house, where I enjoyed a wonderful supper with him and his wife, Madeleine. Afterwards, Andrew started talking about *Tell Me on a Sunday* again. However, I still hadn't been told anything specific, and no offer had been made. I certainly didn't want to just assume that I was definitely doing it. This was Andrew Lloyd Webber, for God's sake! I decided that this was all just probably another audition, a try-out of sorts. We ended up around the piano with me singing another one of the songs from the show, 'Come Back with the Same Look in Your Eyes', while he played.

That was quite a moment; standing around the piano at Andrew's house, singing a song from one of his famous hit shows.

'I'm thinking we could write some new songs for the show,' he said at one point.

'That sounds lovely.' I smiled enthusiastically. 'So who else is in the show?'

Andrew looked at me like I was mad, probably because *Tell Me on a Sunday* is a one-woman show. Originally, though, it had been part of a two-act show called *Song and Dance*, starring Marti Webb and the dancer Wayne Sleep, so I'd assumed it would be the same thing again. Andrew's new plan, however, was to do *Tell Me on a Sunday* as a standalone piece for the first time ever, but how would I have known that? Nobody had told me a bloody thing! I left the house still none the wiser as to whether Andrew was just tossing ideas around or whether he really had plans to put his show on with me in it.

When it was eventually confirmed, I was, of course, over the moon.

• • •

By then, I'd dipped my toe back into the dating pond again. After my run in *Chicago*, I started dating a guy called Richard Travis, who owned Brown's nightclub and the bar Denim in Covent Garden. I'd met Richard at Brown's one night when I'd got hideously drunk and was probably still not in the best frame of mind after my break-up with Jay. I remember him warning me about the paparazzi outside the club that night because I'd had one too many. To be honest, he probably felt a bit sorry for me. I'd actually met Richard some years before. While I was signed to a record label with Those 2 Girls, Richard also had a record deal and was releasing his own music. When his career had fizzled out, he became a successful club promoter. Eventually, he bought a couple of nightclubs of his own.

That evening, I'd ended up sobering up and crashing at Richard's apartment in Camden. I guess I was partying a fair bit at that time. I felt like I'd worked so hard, right from my time on *The Big Breakfast*, so now it was time to let loose. Still, Richard could tell that I wasn't in a good place. The more I went out to forget, the more I fed the press stories.

'I think you should be looking after yourself,' he told me over coffee the following day. 'You're really talented; you need to take care of yourself and cut down on the nights out. Don't go down that path; it's not worth it.'

Now, with *Tell Me on a Sunday* on the horizon, Richard was even more adamant that I needed to keep my focus.

'You've got such a great opportunity here to prove yourself as an actress and a performer. Don't throw it away.'

I knew he was right, and the more time I spent with him, the more his positivity seemed to rub off on me. For instance, I'd got myself into a bit of a rut of staying up into the early hours and then sleeping late, never having much of a day if there was nothing specific to get up for. Now, I was staying home and getting up earlier. There was a certain irony in Richard dissuading me from nightclubs when he owned a couple himself. Before I knew it, I'd had my first taste of sushi, and I was drinking green tea and using a steam inhaler to look after my throat and voice. My new regime of healthy habits paid off. My agent informed me that Andrew had commented on how professional I was, which was nice to hear.

Richard and I managed to stay under the radar as a couple for a while. Still, nothing remains secret forever, and all of a sudden, I was back in the papers with a new man in tow. The spin on the story was that he was seen as this flashy, roguish nightclub owner, and once again, I'd gone for the wrong man. It was a case of poor misguided Denise again, but the truth of it was that Richard was taking care of me. He was encouraging me to look after myself a bit more. Ultimately, I knew there was no point whinging about the press. When you're a person in the public eye, it comes with the territory. The only thing I could do was put my head down and get on with my work.

It was around this time that Andrew called again with another suggestion.

'I think the best thing would be for you to come and stay with us for a few days,' he said. 'The writing process is very hands-on, and it would be nice for Don Black, the show's lyricist, to get to know you.'

The next thing I knew, I was living in Andrew's house in Sydmonton in Hampshire, preparing for my next stage role.

Tell Me on a Sunday is a song cycle telling the story of Emma, a British woman, who journeys to America in search of love. Her romantic misadventures take her from New York City, to Los Angeles, and back to Manhattan again as she realises the road to love is never as simple as it seems.

Just like I had when I was in New York, I found myself in a place where I felt comfortable and at ease with the world. Andrew and his family were the most wonderful hosts, making my stay there quite blissful. I recall gorgeous summer mornings, looking out of my window and seeing rabbits playing on the lawns there.

Incidentally, the location of Andrew's estate is close to the setting for Richard Adams's novel *Watership Down*.

Whilst there, we rehearsed scenes while Andrew and Don wrote songs, allowing me some input. We scrutinised the show, taking out anything that didn't work and workshopping and perfecting the things that did. It's safe to say that I spent the best part of three months working with Andrew almost every day.

During my stay, Andrew and I would often stay up late into the night, talking. Sometimes, we'd even sit down in his wine cellar, drinking beautiful wine and talking about the different kinds of music we enjoyed. Andrew was a huge Avril Lavigne fan at the time, which came as a bit of surprise. After a glass or two, he'd play Avril's music really loud, and the two of us would rock out in the wine cellar, oblivious to the rest of the world.

When Matthew Warchus came on board as director, we transferred from Andrew's house to Pineapple Dance Studios to workshop the show there. Matthew was a bit method as far as acting went, and at one point, he came up with what seemed like a bonkers idea at the time. He felt that I really needed to live the character of Emma – the young woman in the story who moves from London to New York – rather than just playing her.

'I think it would be good for you to go and live in New York for a while,' he said. 'That way, you can really live in Emma's shoes for a while.'

I certainly wasn't going to turn down an opportunity to go back and live in New York, but this time around, I was put up in Andrew's apartment – where I had my own butler!

It was a bit like going home, being back in New York, and Richard came out to join me for a while, which was lovely. We ended up being together for a couple of years in the end, but it was just one of those relationships that ran its course. I think Richard would have liked a bit more commitment from me, but I got itchy feet, which was a bit of a running theme. It's funny; I could never seem to get past three years with any relationship. I remember friends telling me that I needed to give things a chance, but I just wasn't made that way. I'd never want to cheat on someone. To me, it's best to be honest and tell someone when I'm not feeling it any more.

· · ·

Back in London after my stint living as Emma in New York, Andrew took me to the Ivy for dinner one night.

'I want you to feel comfortable doing the show, so I'll take you around to each of my theatres and you can choose which one you'd like to do the show in,' he said over dessert.

Of course, I knew he owned several theatres in the West End, but I certainly wasn't expecting to have my pick.

I knew as soon as I walked into the Gielgud Theatre that it was the one. As grand as it was, with it beautiful curves and ornamental balconies, it was also moderate in size, so there was an intimacy about it that I liked. I finally took to the stage for *Tell Me on a Sunday* at the Gielgud in 2003. I put my whole heart into it, and what started out as a six-week run turned into ten months of sold-out shows. I loved doing the show. I never got tired of the buzz of coming along Shaftesbury Avenue and seeing my name and photo on the billboards of the theatre. I even stopped drinking for ten months, so my focus was entirely on the work.

I'll always be grateful to Richard, because he made me pull myself together and got me to focus on what was important during that time. I guess you could say he put me back on track.

CHAPTER TWENTY-ONE

Flip-flops, bikinis, kaftans and summer dresses?

In 2004, Johnny Vaughan and I reunited for the TV game show *Passport to Paradise*. I suppose it was an attempt by a TV production company to recreate the magic that we'd once had together on *The Big Breakfast*. The show had a team of writers and was all scripted, but Johnny and I always worked much better in the chaos of a show where everything was live and off the cuff. The show wasn't the big hit everyone thought it might be and only lasted one season. Still, it wouldn't be the last time that the two of us would find ourselves thrown together in an attempt to rekindle the glory days of our *Big Breakfast* partnership.

Having enjoyed myself so much doing *Tell Me on a Sunday*, I felt like I wanted to dip my toe back into acting. I auditioned and screen-tested for a recurring role on ITV's *Where the Heart Is*, and I was delighted to get the part of nurse Kim Blakeney. Leslie Ash had recently departed the show, and I think I was brought in to fill the gap she'd left.

The show was filmed in Huddersfield. Some of us in the cast used to call it 'where the arse is' because the location was so remote and out of the way.

We often filmed in real houses, and I remember thinking that it was the coldest place on earth. I mean, so cold that if your nose ran, you could form your own icicle! It certainly wasn't the most glamorous job I'd had, with long shoots in what always seemed to be freezing cold weather. There was a female director on the show who I felt didn't like me. It didn't matter how nice to her I was or how hard I tried; she hardly spoke to me or gave me any encouragement. When she talked to me, it was to tell me to be quiet if I spoke to another cast member on set. I got a bit fed up with it in the end. One day, in an act of defiance, I refused to take my coat off for a scene because it was so cold. There I was, sitting in a living room in my parka. It must have looked completely bizarre to the audience, doing an indoor scene with a coat on. I have to say, I wasn't the most convincing of nurses either, not when it came to the practical side. I remember once having to bandage a man's gangrene-infested foot while holding a conversation. When I looked down at my handiwork, I'd practically mummified the poor actor's leg.

'You'll have to cut that out of shot,' I said sheepishly.

One of the best things about the job was not having to get glammed up all the time, as I had to with my TV presenting roles. It was a nurse's uniform to the knee, black tights and Doc Martens. Done.

I did 13 episodes of *Where the Heart Is* between 2005 and 2006. Despite the long shoots and the cold, I enjoyed my time working on the show. I loved the cast and had a regular cab driver called Jean, the archetypal Yorkshire woman, always making me laugh on my way to and from the set. It was a world away from anything I'd done before, working on a set and filming a drama, but I learned a lot from the other cast members. I take my hat off to actors who appear in soaps and recurring dramas because it's hard work and such long hours.

• • •

Despite feeling like a veteran, having been in the entertainment industry for such a long time by then, I'd never been to Los Angeles or visited Hollywood. That was about to change after a run of terrible events.

I'd recently bought a flat in Hampstead, which I'd purchased on the first viewing, plus it was the only one I'd looked at. I recall the estate agent looking at me like I was mad.

'Don't you want to look at the other ones I've got lined up for you?' he said.

'No, this is the one,' I said.

It was the same with my wedding dress a few years later. I literally bought the first one that I tried on in the shop. I've always been a bit like that. If I see something that I like, I don't see the point in going around the houses to look for something better.

Not long after I'd moved into my new home, I received the terrible news that my nan had been diagnosed with breast cancer. The whole family was devastated. I remember her coming to my flat with Mum while she was ill, hardly able to get down the three steps that led to the door. It was heartbreaking. I knew then that she wasn't going to make it, and it upset me deeply. While she was there, I made up a little bed in the garden for her under a tree so she could be out in the sunshine.

Mum came into the kitchen that day looking so sad.

'I don't think Nanny has long, you know,' she said.

'I think you're right.' I could see how weak she was.

On 9 September 2005, not long after that visit, my nan died. It was one of the saddest times of my life; she'd always meant the world to me. After the funeral, I planted a rose bush under the tree where I'd made up the bed for her that day. Her name was Mary, and this beautiful bloom was called the Mary Rose.

One of the things my nan had always said to me was that I needed to go back and work in America. She'd been over to see me in *Chicago* on Broadway, along with the rest of the family, and had always been so proud. She thought I needed to get back over there and do some more of the same. I'd never been that fussed about making it big across the pond. I loved New York, but as ambitious and driven as I was, I was quite happy carving out a good career for myself on home turf and staying put in the UK. However, that was all about to change.

A little while after my nan died, I went on a girly holiday to Dubai with my good friend Lucy. We'd had a wonderfully relaxing time, and I decided it was time to start afresh and lay my past troubles to rest. As we sat having dinner one night, I was in a reflective but happy mood.

'I've had such a lovely holiday, Lucy. Let's hope that's the end of all the bad stuff and the start of more positive things.'

With that, my phone rang. My upstairs neighbour in Hampstead informed me there was water pouring out of the front door of my flat. I immediately called my dad, who dashed round with his keys to check out the damage.

'Is it bad?' I asked when he called me back.

The fact that I could hear him sloshing through what sounded like a paddling pool told me that it was awful. It turned out that the entire place had flooded after Thames Water had been to remove a disused pipe on the street, taking up paving stones outside my flat. They'd ended up connecting the old line, which had no cap, so now the water was literally pumping into my basement flat, which I'd only just decorated and which was now completely ruined.

'You can't live here,' Dad told me over the phone. 'You're going to be out of here for months.'

'Can you believe this?' I said, turning to Lucy.

'Not after what you just said, no more bad luck,' she said.

Still, I was covered by insurance and managed to find a lovely flat in the area to tide me over. It didn't feel like home, though; I had very little of my own possessions around me. Most of it had been ruined in the flood. I even lost a suitcase of mementoes from under my bed, containing lots of old photos of my nan. I felt pretty low about the situation.

One cold grey morning, I sat in my rented flat thinking, *What am I doing here? I'm not in my home; I've got no major work stuff happening.* What was stopping me from taking myself off to where the sun's shining? That afternoon, a strange thing happened when

I went round to my flat to see how things were progressing. Before my nan died, she'd given me a necklace that my granddad had bought for her. It was a quarter dollar piece, and she'd worn it every day for most of her life – she loved it. When I reached the steps that led down to my flat, I noticed something shining up at me from the floor. When I bent down and picked it up, it was a quarter coin. God knows what it was doing there, but it was a sign from my nan, as far as I was concerned. She's always wanted me to go to America, and I needed a bit of sunshine. I knew what had to be done. I went straight back to the rented flat and booked a flight to LA. God knows what I was going to do once I got there, but I was going!

I booked a room at the famous Sunset Marquis hotel and packed a suitcase. I had no thoughts of work or networking or anything other than getting away and feeling the sun on my face. Initially, I booked my room for two weeks, but I ended up staying for four months. In a hotel suite!

I had the time of my life on that trip. Of course, it was costing a bomb staying in a hotel, but with the pound being so strong against the dollar, I convinced myself it was OK and that I could afford it. I kept telling myself that if something was a hundred dollars, that was really only fifty quid. That wasn't the case at all, but that's what I told myself.

The Sunset Marquis is well known for its celebrity clientele, particularly those from the film and music industries. It has a mix of suites and villas, and is home to the infamous Bar 1200, or the Whiskey Bar as it's also known, where you'll often find more than a smattering of rock stars or TV and movie icons. I loved my time staying there, meeting all sorts of people and getting friendly with many of the staff who worked there. LA was really just like I imagined it. Everyone seemed to be 'in the business'; every waiter, waitress and barman was a budding actor or had a script they were trying to sell. Either that or they were starting work on a film next week, or were a distant cousin of Brad Pitt. I heard it all during my time there.

The weird thing was, I wasn't interested in any of that. Work couldn't have been further from my mind. I was all about getting into my bikini and topping up my tan or hanging out in the hotel bar, having a good old laugh with new mates Jimmy Nesbitt and Steve Coogan. One day, Gerard Butler walked past me at the pool, and we got chatting. He asked me if I wanted to accompany him to the Golden Globes after-party, but when I thought about it, I just couldn't be arsed. I wasn't interested in all the glitz and glamour, and I certainly wasn't interested in dating anyone famous. I just wanted to chill out and have fun.

There didn't seem to be any reason to go home either. My dad had been right; the repairs and renovation of my flat were taking forever. Each job that the builder said would take two weeks took six, and, basically, the whole place had to be gutted. What on earth was there to rush back for?

• • •

One night while I was having drinks at Chateau Marmont, I got chatting to a TV exec called Paul Telegdy, who worked for BBC

Worldwide. He asked me what I'd been up to, and when I told him about my connection with Andrew Lloyd Webber, he looked surprised.

'That's funny; we're just about to start doing a version of his recent BBC TV show over here', he said.

The previous year, Andrew had had huge success with his show *How Do You Solve a Problem Like Maria?*, a singing competition in which the winner would land the role of Maria von Trapp in Andrew's new production of *The Sound of Music*.

'We're doing a similar format, looking for a Danny and Sandy for a new Broadway production of *Grease*', he said.

As the conversation went on, there was talk about me being involved with the new American show, which was called *Grease: You're the One That I Want!* There wasn't much mileage in me being on the judging panel, as nobody there knew really who I was, so he suggested that I co-host the show, along with Billy Bush, who was the cousin of the current president, George Bush. It turned out they'd been auditioning female presenters to co-host for weeks but hadn't managed to find the right fit to work alongside Billy. By the end of the evening, I'd secured myself a TV presenting job in America. I was slightly gobsmacked, to be honest, as it wasn't what I'd planned at all.

'I haven't even got an agent in the US', I said.

'Don't worry', Paul said. 'I'll get you one tonight.'

By the time I left the hotel, I was signed up to Endeavor, which is part of the William Morris Agency. Not only that, but the filming of the show started imminently, so Paul said that I should pack my stuff and be ready to catch a flight to Chicago the next day. *Pack what stuff?* I thought. My flip-flops, bikinis, kaftans and summer dresses? That's about all I had with me; I'd come for a holiday, not to work. The climate in Chicago would surely call for something a bit more substantial than the gear I had, especially in November.

In a crazy whirlwind of two or three days, I'd packed a bag, flown to Chicago, checked into a hotel, shopped for warm clothes, and was now all set to present a major new American TV show. All this, just from sitting in Chateau Marmont having a glass of Pinot Grigio.

Just as I was settling into the swing of doing the show and starting to wonder whether I was ever going to go home, I got a call from a TV producer friend of mine, Suzy Lamb.

'Andrew's doing another BBC show where he'll cast the lead in his next West End musical. It's going to be huge, and he wants you to be on the judging panel.'

My first instinct was to say no. I was extremely grateful for the offer, but the point of coming to LA had been to get away from work and really kick back for the first time in years. Plus, contestant auditions for Andrew's new show would be starting while I was still filming the *Grease* show. How would that work?

Also, I wasn't sure I was ready to go back to the UK. For a while, I tried to talk myself out of it, telling Suzy that I wasn't sure if it was the right show for me or even if I liked the idea of being a judge.

'Look, just come back and talk to us; give it a try,' Suzy said. 'Andrew's quite insistent that he wants you because he trusts you.'

I wasn't so sure. Presenting a singing contest was one thing, but who was I to give advice and judge potential West End stars? Yes, I'd done a couple of shows myself, but I wasn't sure I had the confidence to judge other performers. John Barrowman was to be the other judge, and he was more than qualified. I still didn't really think of myself as a singer, so I wasn't sure this was the right fit for me. Eventually, Andrew called me himself.

'You bring something to a character when you perform,' he told me. 'You can help me find the person who can tell a story. That's what I need from you. You're more than qualified to do this, Denise.'

In the end, I decided to fly back to the UK and do Andrew's show, *Any Dream Will Do* – so-called after the song from one of Andrew's most popular musicals, *Joseph and the Amazing Technicolour Dreamcoat*. The only problem was that my duties on both shows did indeed overlap, so there were occasions where I found myself finishing a live show in LA, then having to fly back to London to film auditions for *Any Dream Will Do* during the week. The UK show aired on Saturday TV, less than a week after the US show finished. I'd gone from kicking back in LA to a full-on whirlwind of work in a matter of weeks.

Still, even that wasn't the most significant part of my new judging role on *Any Dream Will Do*. I mean, who would have ever imagined I'd end up meeting my future husband doing that very show?

CHAPTER TWENTY-TWO

A bit of harmless fun

I think it was apparent to everyone from day one that Lee Mead was a contender to win Andrew's new Saturday-night TV singing contest. The show's idea was to find a new Joseph for the leading role in a new West End production. It was a fantastic prize that also came with a London apartment for the duration of the show's run thrown in for good measure. Lee was fantastic on the show, and that wasn't just my opinion: Andrew loved him; John Barrowman loved him. In fact, one week we all had such positive things to say about him that the producers suggested we say something critical, just to make sure the show had enough balance and would keep the audience guessing. As we all know, there's no fun in watching a competition when you know exactly who the winner is going to be, right from the off. The trouble was, none of us could really think of anything to critique Lee on. That's how much he shone.

Still, aside from joking with John Barrowman that Lee was 'a bit of all right' and being very happy for him when he ultimately won the show, there wasn't much more to our association during the course of the series.

Once the show was done, I flew back to LA, all ready to resume the 'me time' I'd put on hold – just for a month or so. This time,

I decided to be slightly more economical and rent an apartment. I found a lovely little place on Oakhurst Drive, which is in West Hollywood, a stone's throw from the Four Seasons Hotel, and it didn't take me long to slip back into my carefree, relaxed California existence.

There were some hilarious nights out on that trip, and, of course, being out on that scene, I was bound to bump into some interesting and very famous people. One memorable occasion was when David Walliams called me up and casually asked if I fancied nipping over to Vegas.

'What, now?'

'Yes, tonight,' David said. 'It'll be fun.'

Simon Fuller, who, among other things, had managed the Spice Girls and created *American Idol*, had a private jet that would fly us over. We could just go for the night and enjoy a bit of harmless fun. When I turned up at Burbank Airport to catch the jet, I really didn't know what the plan was or who was going. Still, there I was on a private plane with Simon, David and David's *Little Britain* partner, Matt Lucas.

We arrived in Las Vegas and headed to the famous Caesars Palace Hotel on Las Vegas Boulevard, where we all got in the elevator. I assumed we were heading to a room organised by Simon, but David informed me that we were 'just popping in to see Elton.'

'Elton?'

'Yes, he's doing his Vegas residency here at Caesars, so we're popping up to his room to say hello.'

'Oh, right!'

I'd met Elton John before while I was with Jay, but I certainly hadn't been expecting to find myself in his hotel suite that evening. Of course, the suite was huge and fabulous, and Elton was welcoming and absolutely lovely.

'I'm hungry. Why don't we order a Chinese takeaway?' he suggested at one point.

I think it was his day off, so I guess he was in the mood to kick back and relax. So, somebody dutifully called out for a takeaway – not room service . . . a takeaway.

Once the food had arrived, and we were all sitting around eating, I remember thinking, *This is so, so bizarre*. I'm in this amazing hotel, probably housing a few of the world's top chefs, sitting here with megastar Elton John, eating a Chinese. It wasn't even a fancy Chinese from some swanky restaurant along the strip. It was in regular cartons and looked just like the sort of thing you'd order from your local high street takeout. In fact, I recall thinking that the chow mein looked distinctly iffy and wasn't very nice at all.

Afterwards, Elton got us some gambling chips, and we all went downstairs to hit the casino. I'm no gambler, but I had a bit of a go. It turned into an enjoyable night – gambling in Vegas with Elton and the boys from *Little Britain*, full of champagne and quite dodgy Chinese food. The funny thing was, we didn't even stay in Vegas for the night. By 3am, we were back on Simon Fuller's private jet, flying back to LA. Before I knew it, I found myself sitting in my apartment, thinking, *God, that was random*.

I wasn't sure how I could even describe the night I'd just experienced to my friends back home because I was pretty sure they wouldn't have believed me. You'd think that kind of experience would be a one-off, but I had a similar megastar hotel encounter not long afterwards. At the time, I was good friends with an English agent called Ben. He was working and living in LA. We'd first met during my *Big Breakfast* days when Ben had accompanied some of his American clients for interviews. Since I'd been in town, we'd had quite a few fun nights together. On an evening when the Grammys were being held, we'd been hanging out together having dinner when Ben suggested we head to a party. There were Grammy after-parties all over town, and, knowing how successful and well known Ben was, I think he'd probably been invited to a few of them.

'Have you got your passport?' he asked me as we sat in his car.

'No, why? Where are we going?'

'You'll need ID to get into one of these private parties,' Ben said. 'You'll have to go back to your apartment to get it.'

I guessed it was the norm for everyone to have ID in LA.

Once I'd retrieved my passport, we were off. Still, apart from Ben telling me it was a Grammy Awards after-party, I had no idea where to. He was all very secretive as we made our way there. On reaching our destination, we headed into an underground car park where we were met by a security guard standing by the lift leading to the hotel's upper floors. When we came out of the lift, I could see a group of people gathered around the door of a hotel suite, all trying to get inside. Ben and I approached the door and slipped through the small gathering, where I showed my passport before being ushered inside.

The minute I got in, I was dying for the loo, so off I went while Ben toddled off to find us some drinks amidst the bustling noise of the party. Well, this bathroom turned out to be the darkest toilet in the world. After a quick wee, I found myself struggling to get the fiddly poppers done up underneath my tight black bodysuit – 'bodies' as they were known by us girls back then. This tricky task took quite a while, but before I'd had the chance to finish it, someone was hammering impatiently on the bathroom door.

'All right, I'm nearly ready!' I shouted, picturing some poor guy, desperate to burst through the door and relieve himself.

The banging continued, so when I'd finally got myself together, I unlocked the door, yanked it open and snapped, 'For Christ's sake, give me a chance, will you?'

Looking back at me, wide-eyed and slightly alarmed, was Bruce Willis. I'm not sure who I was expecting to see standing outside the toilet with his legs crossed, but it certainly wasn't the bloke from *Die Hard*.

'So sorry, Bruce,' I said. 'I couldn't get my poppers done up.'

The party was in full swing, with people drinking, chatting and dancing around the rather fabulous hotel suite. Ben and I headed over to a high fireplace in the room's lounge area, where, sitting on a throne-like chair, was Prince. This was his party in his hotel suite.

He looked very serene, sitting there like royalty with his cane, and let's face it, he was royalty as far as the music industry went.

I was impressed! As I sipped my drink, my eyes darted around the room, and I realised just how many famous faces there were dotted around the place. Jennifer Lopez was standing just a few feet away from me, and David and Victoria Beckham wafted past me as I stood there, soaking up the atmosphere. After a couple more drinks, I happily danced around the fireplace in the lounge area with some of the other guests when Prince caught my eye. I felt like I wanted to say something; I mean, when else would I get the chance to chat to The Purple One? Only I didn't know what to say. In fact, the best I could come up with was, 'Great party, Prince!'

Prince nodded, and I turned away, cringing to myself. Why on earth did I say that? Why? Needless to say, the conversation ended there.

This was another occasion when I got back to my apartment and wondered, *Did that really just happen?* Of course, I'd met and interviewed so many famous people over the years, some big stars in fact. Still, it's those unexpected funny moments that always stick with me. Those 'I can't believe that just happened' situations.

Like the time Ben tried to set me up with a friend of his at Chateau Marmont. We'd had one drink together, and I was just about to ask him why we were sitting at a table for five when there were only two of us, when he announced that he'd invited a couple of friends and hoped I didn't mind.

'No, that's OK,' I said, although I wasn't mega-keen as we'd just come out for a casual drink, and I wasn't particularly dressed up.

Ben seemed to know absolutely everyone in town, so it was anyone's guess who these 'friends' might be.

My instincts were bang on. Seconds later, Chris Rock breezed through the hotel bar and sat down next to us, closely followed by Courtney Love. They were both friendly, and as we all chatted away, Ben had something else to tell me.

'My friend Anthony is going to be here soon. I'm *really* keen for you to meet him,' he said with a wink. 'I think you guys will get on brilliantly.'

'Anthony,' I said suspiciously. 'OK.'

I suppose I shouldn't have been surprised when Anthony Kiedis from Red Hot Chilli Peppers walked in and sat down, but I was. Anthony went to sit opposite me, but Ben jumped out of his chair.

'No, you guys sit together,' he said, swapping places with his mate. 'I'll sit over there.'

You didn't have to be Poirot to figure out Ben was trying to set the two of us up. Still, he might have warned me. I'd have at least mentally prepared myself, and I'd definitely have glammed up a bit more than I had, knowing I was going to be spending the evening with a table full of music and comedy legends.

'How long are you in town?' Anthony asked as we chatted. 'Are you working or just on vacation?'

I told Anthony a bit about myself, and he suggested we hang out sometime and swap numbers. Me being me, I ended up getting quite drunk and eventually found myself slow dancing around the Chateau Marmont with a Red Hot Chilli Pepper.

It was a fun evening, and Anthony did message me a couple of times afterwards. As I've said, I wasn't really in the market for a relationship at the time, especially with someone as famous as Anthony Kiedis, as lovely as he was. I'd gone to LA to put the past behind me, to have fun and enjoy myself, staying as low-key as one could in West Hollywood. That definitely meant no high-profile dating situations.

CHAPTER TWENTY-THREE

The do's and don'ts of dealing with the media

In the autumn of 2007, I was back on the West End stage in a new production of Jonathan Larson's *Rent*. The production was to be a 'remixed' version of the original show, with big pop productions instead of the gritty rock of the original. Behind it was the team behind Kylie Minogue's slick, lavish pop concerts: director William Baker; choreographer Ashley Wallen, who went on to choreograph some big movies, including *The Greatest Showman*; and musical director Steve Anderson. I played outrageous bisexual performance artist Maureen Johnson. My co-stars were actor Luke Evans and Siobhán Donaghy, one of the founding members of the girl group, Sugababes, with whom I became very close friends. Rehearsals happened throughout the summer of 2007, with the show opening at the Duke of York's Theatre in the autumn. I loved doing the show, but it was hardly stress-free. During the rehearsal period, there was drama with the show's producers and the creative team disagreeing about various things. When the show did open, the reviews weren't quite as glowing as everyone had hoped. That said, *Rent* had a decent run, and the audiences seemed to love it. In fact, it developed a bit of a cult following with people coming back to see it multiple times.

At the same time as *Rent* was running at the Duke of York's Theatre, the winner of *Any Dream Will Do*, Lee Mead, was over at the Adelphi in *Joseph*. I remember someone who knew Lee telling me that he'd been struggling with dealing with his new-found fame. He was a regular guy who'd been thrust into the spotlight without any guidance on how to deal with such a massive change in his life. I suggested that Lee might give me a call so I could have a chat with him. There was no romantic plan on my part; it was merely to offer a helping hand. Let's face it: if anyone could advise someone on the dos and don'ts of dealing with the media, I was that girl!

When we eventually spoke, it transpired that it wasn't just the press and media attention he was having a hard time with: he also had a couple of female fans who had been slightly more enthusiastic than they perhaps should have been. He'd ended up with people following him when he came out of the theatre and even hanging around outside his apartment on the South Bank. The truth of it was, Lee was now hugely famous. The final of the show where he was crowned winner and given the lead role in *Joseph* had been watched by millions, so he was a celebrity before he'd even set foot on the stage. It had all happened so fast, though, which was why he was finding it hard.

I chatted to Lee over the next week or so, giving him the best advice I could, and even putting him in touch with a guy I knew who could organise some security for him if he felt like he needed it. It's funny, people often thought that Lee and I were complete opposites, but as we got talking, I realised that we actually had quite a lot in common. Like me, Lee was from Essex; we were familiar with many of the same areas and hang-outs, and our family backgrounds were also quite similar.

After several friendly chats, Lee asked me if I fancied going out for a drink, so after our respective shows had finished one night, we went to the Light Bar, which was in the St Martin's Lane Hotel.

I suppose this was our first date, but I wouldn't exactly say there were fireworks. In fact, Lee was quite nervous. I thought he might be worried about the press spotting us and jumping to the wrong conclusion. I know I was. I'd been a judge on the TV competition he'd won, and although the show had ended several months before, I certainly didn't want anyone to think there was something dodgy going on behind the scenes.

After that night, we went on a few more dates. They were simple affairs, nothing extravagant, which is the way we both preferred things. Inevitably, news got out that we were seeing one another, and there was the odd suggestion that the show had been a fix, which was hard on Lee. He'd won it fair and square, having been the front runner from very early on in the series. Mercifully, that line of thinking didn't carry on for too long.

The thing I liked most about my early relationship with Lee was that we managed to stay low-key, despite both being in the entertainment industry. We kept everything simple, staying pretty much under the radar, which felt lovely. It was a world away from some of the experiences I'd had in the past. Lee was a straight-up guy who never messed me around or let me down, and I just felt like we fitted. Whenever I was going a mile a minute with all my ideas, Lee was a great, level-headed sounding board and a calming influence. On the flip side, he'd be encouraging to give things a go when I was reticent about trying new things. Lee loved acting, and, although he enjoyed musical theatre, he wanted to spread his wings and get into some more character-based acting.

'You should try some drama or a film,' I told him.

An agent called Lindy King, who was also my acting agent at the time, was helpful to Lee. Lindy looked after actors like Keira Knightley and Ewan McGregor, so she knew what she was doing. She saw potential in Lee as a serious actor and encouraged him to pursue it, as had I. I was aware of how hard it was to be considered for the acting role once you'd become a celebrity. If Lee was going to be an actor, he would have to really commit to it. He did, too, taking an intensive course at the Lee Strasberg acting school in New York. Lindy wrote the introductory letter that helped him get a place on the much-coveted course.

I'd seen how good his performances were, even in the realms of a musical. I knew he could do it. Lee's determination and his time at Lee Strasberg helped him carve out the successful TV career he has today.

My relationship with Lee remained refreshingly straight-forward, with no dramas and no games. It felt good between us. When we weren't working, we'd spend quiet times together, having dinner or watching movies. Looking back, I guess it was what I considered to be 'proper dating' and a world away from what I'd been used to in past relationships.

After a while, it dawned on me that I hadn't moaned or complained to any of my friends about Lee. Of course, knowing myself as well as I did, this was quite a big thing.

Sitting with Mum one day, she made an observation.

'You seem really happy.'

'I am. Very happy.'

At that moment, I think I realised just how true it was. Of course, I'd been happy in the past, but there was something different about how I felt now; there was no stress, no anxiety about what may or may not happen. I felt centred.

It was clear that Lee felt the same, only that he was one step ahead of me. Unbeknown to me, he was planning a proposal and had bought an engagement ring, all ready to do the deed on an upcoming holiday in Antigua. He'd told Mum and Dad and a couple of my closest friends, but, other than that, he'd kept it all very close to his chest.

Before we left, however, Lee got quite nervous about transporting the ring through the airports on the way to Antigua. He didn't want to risk putting it in the hold in a suitcase that might go missing, as cases sometimes do. He also didn't want to risk the ring setting off any alarms if he put it in his hand luggage. So, in the end, he plumped for proposing the night before we went.

We were at the house in Kent that evening when Lee got down on one knee, told me how he felt, and asked me to marry him. I'm sure being proposed to on a beautiful night in a hot country would have been fantastic, but there was something lovely about him doing it this way. It was natural and heartfelt. What was really lovely was the two of us going to the airport the following day, knowing that we were engaged, without having let on to anyone else. It felt like a wonderful little secret that we would share once we'd reached our holiday destination after the perfect romantic celebration dinner.

Our wedding was as beautifully simple and private as our relationship had been. We got married in the Seychelles and only took close family. The last thing we wanted was a big fanfare and a celebrity wedding with an accompanying magazine spread. We didn't even tell that many people we were getting hitched.

I think the media and even certain people who knew me found my marriage to Lee a bit hard to get their heads around. In the past, I'd dated rock stars and nightclub owners, and now here I was with Joseph! I don't think some of them could get past the loincloth and the dreamcoat, to be honest. The truth is, they were all going by what they'd seen on the show, where Lee came over as quiet and a bit shy – yes, very unlike me! That wasn't really him at all. Lee had a lot to say for himself and was always very chatty in private. My close friends all loved him, as did my mum and dad.

I went into marriage with Lee genuinely believing he was the person I could spend my life with and have children with. That was something I'd been asked about a lot around the time Lee and I got together. At almost every interview I did, the question of motherhood would arise. Had I thought about kids? Was I planning on becoming a mum anytime soon? It was something I'd thought long and hard about. Many of my close friends had children by then, and although I laughed off the good-humoured comments about me 'not getting any younger', inside I was starting to panic.

I was 34 when Lee and I started dating, so I decided if we were going to start a family, it was time for me to get a check-up on all my bits and pieces. You know, just to make sure everything was in working order. Actually, I do love a full-body MOT. As I've gotten older, I feel as though if something is going south, I like to know way in advance so I can do everything I can to put it right, rather than getting sick. Of course, you can't be a hundred per cent sure of anything, but I do like to keep on top of things.

While my lady bits were being given the once-over, I had my fertility checked. As terrifying as it sounds, having kids over the age of 35 puts you in the category of a geriatric mum. I know, shocking, right? So, fertility was one of the things I thought I should check on. To my surprise, the news wasn't encouraging. It turned out that my fertility was very low, and the advice from the clinic was that if I wanted to have children, we needed to crack on with the baby-making.

Broaching this with Lee, who's seven years younger than I am, wasn't the easiest thing in the world. Still, when I voiced my concerns about my low fertility, he was honest and understanding.

'I guess I wasn't planning on children just yet, but if that's the situation, we should get on with it,' he said.

So off we went!

My doctor at the clinic told me that I might need to take my foot off the gas as far as work was concerned. Too much pressure and stress certainly weren't going to be conducive to me getting pregnant. It was true; I'd done a hell of a lot of TV work in the previous months: *Who Dares, Sings!* for ITV, *I'd Do Anything* for BBC, and *Hairspray: The School Musical* for Sky TV. As far as TV shows about musicals were concerned, I just about had it covered. I'd also recently started a big new job, which was something I'd never done before, and despite everything the doctor had said, that one really did end up becoming a major source of stress.

CHAPTER TWENTY-FOUR

'I see you've brought the circus with you'

In 2008, Johnny Vaughan and I were reunited for one final time, on the radio rather than television. It was strange how it came about, and, in many ways, I wish I'd trusted my original instinct. It might have saved a lot of sleepless nights and anxiety if I had.

It all started when I was a guest on Johnny's regular Capital Radio breakfast show. I'd called into the show for a phone chat, and we'd ended up having a really good laugh. It had felt just like the old days, with the banter flying between us and an easy flow of humour. The audience obviously agreed, as there was a flurry of messages after the show saying how great it was to hear the two of us back together and how perfect a team we made. There were even a few suggestions that I should join Johnny as a regular presenter on the show. Still, I'd never even thought about doing radio. I suppose I liked the glamour of TV, putting your lippy on and getting into a lovely frock, ready for the camera. For the most part, I enjoyed that transformation.

Not long after that, my agent got a call from the boss of Capital Radio, Richard Park, saying that he'd love me to be a part of the breakfast show. I was pretty taken aback when I heard. Where had this come from? I was pretty sure that if Johnny had wanted me on the show, he'd have called and asked me himself. As well as that, I knew Johnny loved doing the show. He'd built it up on his own, and he was bloody good at it. Why would he suddenly need a sidekick?

I asked my agent if he was sure that Johnny wanted this.

'As far as I know, he's a hundred per cent behind it,' he said.

The next thing I knew, a lunch had been arranged for me with Richard and Johnny, to discuss plans to introduce me to the show. When Richard and I arrived at the restaurant, however, we found out that Johnny wasn't going to be there after all; he was on holiday with his wife.

Sitting there picking over my salad, I still felt a bit uneasy about the whole thing, especially as Johnny wasn't even there to say his piece.

'Johnny's so up for this,' Richard told me. 'We all think it's going to be amazing.'

The thinking behind it was that Johnny's version of the show was great but quite laddish, with him and a bunch of blokes in the studio. The idea was to redress the balance and throw a bit of a female perspective into the mix. After all, plenty of women were getting the kids ready for school or going to work with the radio on in the car.

I was offered a really great financial deal from Capital. To be honest, it was far beyond what I thought it might be for radio, which I took to be a measure of how much they all wanted to make it work. By then, I was really excited about the idea, especially knowing that everyone, including Johnny, was behind it.

It all happened very quickly. Before I knew it, Capital was recording new jingles for the *Johnny and Denise Breakfast Show*, and a press shoot was organised. Johnny was OK on the day of the shoot – a little grumpy, perhaps, but he didn't always like photo shoots – so I put it down to that. On my very first morning doing the show, I arrived to find a bunch of paparazzi waiting to get pictures. I hadn't been expecting that at five in the morning. Still, there were quite often pictures of the more well-known DJs coming in and out of the building online, so I didn't overthink it.

When I walked into the studio, Johnny grunted under his breath.

'I see you've brought the circus with you.'

I made light of it, brushing it off and asking Johnny to show me the ropes. I mean, this was a whole new world for me. There were knobs and faders all over the place; I didn't know where to start. Johnny told me that he'd be behind the desk at the controls, and I'd be on the other side of it. That was all well and good, but, as the days went on, I felt like I was there to read the weather and the traffic news and chip in on the odd newspaper story when I was asked. There was no actual hosting involved for me at all. I was a spare part. I also noted that although the jingle announced the '*Johnny and Denise Breakfast Show*', Johnny would often come out of the jingle saying, 'Welcome to the "Johnny Vaughan Breakfast Show".' I wasn't all that bothered at first. In fact, he would sometimes apologise for missing out my name.

'I've been announcing it one way for so long, I sometimes forget,' he'd say.

I agreed it must have been an easy mistake to make, but it went on for weeks. Other things irked me too. Sometimes there'd be an item or a whole portion of the show where Johnny wouldn't include me or ask my opinion at all. He'd even hold his hand up sometimes if I went to speak, as if to stop me.

It was very frustrating, and it wasn't getting any better. He wasn't just shutting me out; he was making me feel bad about turning up for work.

During Wimbledon, we both went to interview Annabel Croft. Now I'll admit, I don't know an awful lot about tennis. I always enjoy it, and, of course, I love the strawberries and champagne, but I'm not an expert on all the players or the ins and outs of the rules. We arrived at Wimbledon and met up with Annabel, who was due to give us a bit of a rundown of what was happening at the tournament that year. Just as we were about to start the interview, Johnny said, 'Let me drive this one, Den. It's probably better if you don't speak.'

I stood there feeling humiliated. It was so demoralising, imagining all the people around us thinking I had nothing to say, that I had nothing to bring to the party. I remember thinking right then and there, *Why am I here? Why am I doing this job?* I'd gone into it wanting to learn about radio and how it all worked, but my confidence had been well and truly knocked sideways.

On my way home in the back of a taxi, the driver chatted away happily to me while I did my best to hide behind my phone because I was in tears. Did I really not have the intelligence to speak? Is that what people thought of me? Back home, I told Lee what had happened.

'Den, why are you doing the job?' he asked me. 'It's making you miserable, and you just feel rubbish all the time.'

I knew he was right. Yes, I was being paid extremely good money, and I knew how lucky I was, but was that enough to feel so unappreciated and stressed? In my heart, I knew that Johnny was no monster, and he hadn't meant to hurt me, but this was his territory, and I guess he was used to being in control. I respected the fact that he'd done the show on his own for several years and that he was finding the adjustment hard. At the end of the day, it wasn't his choice to bring me in as a sidekick, but the network's. I understood that. Still, the way he dealt with the situation made me feel worthless, and no amount of money can make up for that.

The saddest thing was, almost all of the memories I had of the two of us on *The Big Breakfast* were of us laughing and joking, but now it was as if we were two strangers who'd been thrown together.

It didn't help that my workload was getting ridiculous. I was getting up in the middle of the night to start the breakfast show at six, and once we'd finished at nine, I'd head off to a TV studio where I'd be filming all day, sometimes getting home at ten at night. Still, I could have dealt with that if the situation hadn't been as it was; I'd done it before, after all.

Cut to the doctor telling me to take my foot off the gas with work, and it was becoming more and more apparent that something had to give. By this time, I'd looked into all kinds of options as far as becoming a mum was concerned. These included the possibility of having some of my eggs frozen, just in case. When it was clear that Johnny would never accept me as an equal on the show, I decided to sit down and think about what was really important to me. Was it the big paycheque, or was it my physical and mental well-being? At that point, there was no question about it: contract or not, I was going to have to throw in the towel at the breakfast show.

Ashley Tabor-King, the founder of the Global Media & Entertainment group, had recently taken over Capital, giving the station a much-needed boost and making a massive success of it. Ashley didn't want me to leave my job on the breakfast show, so I knew I had to convince him it was best for everyone. I turned up for a meeting at his penthouse apartment with all my medical information, citing stress and my doctor's advice about becoming a mother as a reason for my departure. It probably sounded like madness to him, something that could have been overcome. What I didn't do, however, was tell him how sidelined I felt and how difficult things had become between my co-host and me. I didn't want Johnny to be blamed for pushing me out. As far as I was concerned, this was something the two of us would eventually work out. As bad as things were between us, I've always loved Johnny, and the last thing I wanted was for him to lose his job or be on the end of bad press because of me. If I walked away now, there was a chance we could still be friends. I even offered to help find them someone to replace me, suggesting Lisa Snowdon, who I knew Johnny would get on with.

After six months in the job, I was due a two-week holiday anyway, so before any decision was final, Lee and I went off to Greece for a much-needed break. Lisa stepped in to fill the gap while I was away. She was great, and the tone of the show changed immediately. It was actually hard for me to listen to it; Johnny was completely different with Lisa than he'd been with me. It was clear that he was making her very much part of the show, and she was made to feel welcome. It was a world away from the show we'd been doing together. I remember listening while lying around the pool in Greece, knowing what was about to go down.

'I don't think I'll be going back to the breakfast show,' I said to Lee, and that's precisely what happened.

A few days later, I received a message telling me that Lisa had worked out really well and that they wouldn't need me to come back to work. I suppose I was relieved. I didn't care about the money and told the powers at Capital that I was happy for them to say that I'd walked away because of other commitments and a heavy workload. That wasn't the case, but what the hell? I was out of there. As it turned out, that line didn't go well for me. A close friend of mine was one of the heads of PR at Capital. She phoned to tell me that the spin on the story was to imply that I was having some kind of nervous breakdown and that I couldn't cope, so they'd had to get rid of me. Luckily, she was able to shut that particular story down. Still, the general feeling was that I was this whinging, crazy woman who couldn't cope with the work: God, the irony of that. I might not be perfect, but if there's one thing

I pride myself on, it's not being afraid to roll up my sleeves and work hard.

The spokesperson for Capital said: 'It takes a special kind of person to consistently rise early and give the public the level of entertainment they expect each morning. Denise requested the opportunity to break her contract immediately, and we obliged. Johnny was an integral part of the initial decision to bring Denise into the show. I think he was surprised to learn she couldn't cope with the early starts.'

I remember seeing one of the daytime TV shows where the topic was people caving under the pressures of a job. My situation was cited. The inference was that nurses and firefighters worked for much less money doing much more pressured jobs. Shame on me for not being able to hack a morning radio show. It made me feel sick. People had no idea what I'd gone through with that job, and it was several years before I spoke about just a little of what had gone down.

After that, my relationship with Johnny completely soured, and it was a very long time before we spoke again. The whole thing made me very sad, but even then I thought it was just another one of our spats. Johnny and I have a lot of history. There was a connection borne out of living through such a significant and unique experience together, both starting our careers and finding fame at the same time. In my heart, I knew that one day we'd somehow make things up between us. Just like with the contracts issue on *The Big Breakfast*, I've still never sat down and had a conversation with him about it, and I probably never will.

Having been permanently banned from working for Global – seriously, I was banished – I was thrilled when I was offered my own show for the Bauer network, on Magic FM, a few years later. When I was offered the chance to do a show there, my first question was, 'Who will I do the show with?' I guess because of what had happened at Capital, I assumed I'd be paired with someone else.

'We want you to have your own show,' they told me, but I wasn't convinced I could do it.

In the end, I took the job gratefully, and the station put me with a fantastic producer called Louise Maloney, who took the time to teach me how to do radio properly. She was nurturing and kind, and she taught me all the things that I'd hoped to learn when I was at Capital. It was a wonderful, supportive atmosphere, and I thoroughly enjoyed my time there.

CHAPTER TWENTY-FIVE

I do love a glass of rosé in the sunshine

Once I'd stepped away from the job at Capital, there was more time to spend with Lee, which was exactly what I needed. I did a bit of self-healing, got over myself and decided it was time to move forward. By that time, we'd spent a fair amount of time trying to get pregnant, and I'd started to wonder whether it was ever going to happen.

In the summer of 2009, I went to the Edinburgh Fringe to perform in a one-woman show called *Blondes*, which wasn't one of my most outstanding stage performances. The show was a celebration of some of the iconic blondes who'd influenced me from childhood and helped shape my life: Dusty Springfield, Marilyn Monroe, Madonna. It was written by my friend, Jackie Clune, who'd written some of the additional material for *Tell Me on a Sunday*. Still, looking back, we cobbled it together without the care it deserved. The guy who produced the show assured me that the Fringe was the perfect place to try it out.

'You can be very low-key, and people are quite forgiving,' he told me.

I imagined that I'd be playing in a tiny venue with a bar in front of 20 people, which is what I wanted if I was to dip my toe into the water with my own show, but oh no! I ended up at the Underbelly, where Joan Rivers had played the previous year. Not a tiny pub at all, and not under the radar.

On opening night, the theatre was full of critics, and none of them liked our little show. I was sort of all right with that, really, because I didn't really like it myself that much, if I'm honest. I'd had a great writer in Jackie and a great director in Clarke Peters, but we should have spent longer developing it. The problem was that there was no real cohesion between the stories – it was a bit of a mishmash. Clarke is a fantastic director, but even he didn't know what to do with it. I mean, when you're Diana Dors one minute and Britney Spears the next ... well, that's enough to confuse anyone, I suppose.

Anyway, I'd committed to doing the run, so I was stuck with it. It was a long way from my triumph on Broadway doing *Chicago*, I can tell you. Still, I went into it with the same commitment because that's what you do when you have a paying audience in front of you. Meanwhile, I was feeling as sick as a dog the whole time I was there and knackered as well. Every night, I'd get messages from other performers and friends working on shows, inviting me along to a bar or a show whenever I wasn't onstage.

'There's this fabulous interactive play,' someone would say. 'It's at a hotel, and it starts at midnight!'

'Midnight? You're joking, right?'

By 10.30pm every night, I was back in my rented apartment in slippers, chomping away on cheese and onion crisps. For some reason, I couldn't seem to get enough cheese, and I went through bag upon bag of fried salty snacks. Sick, tired, craving cheese; you'd think I might have put two and two together and at least considered the possibility that I might be pregnant. I didn't, though. I think by that time, I'd been trying for so long, I'd almost given up. I just carried on doing my show, sneaking out of the theatre each night in my parka with the hood up, shamed because every critic in every newspaper had given *Blondes* a one-star review.

After four weeks, I headed back to London, where I got together with Cockney Vik and another old friend from *The Big Breakfast*, known as Rough Bird. Her real name is Anna, but she was known as Rough Bird because of the way she'd always looked when she arrived for work at four in the morning. It was toward the end of the summer, and we were all sitting in Rough Bird's Surrey garden, sipping glasses of rosé. Now, I'm certainly no wine connoisseur, but mine tasted distinctly weird. To be honest, Cockney did tend to love a cheap bottle of wine from Asda, so I just put it down to that. In the end, though, I just couldn't drink it, which is very unlike me, because I do love a glass of rosé in the sunshine.

Cockney said, ''Ere, you're not pregnant, are you? When I was pregnant with Annabel, that's what happened to me. I had a glass of wine, not knowing I was pregnant, and it made me feel sick.'

'No, I can't be,' I said.

'Maybe you should do a test,' Rough Bird suggested.

I had plenty of pregnancy tests back at home, bags of them in fact, but when I got back to our flat in Hampstead, I was so tired I went straight to bed. At three o'clock the next morning I woke up feeling like my hormones were going crazy, racing around my body. *I am pregnant*, I thought. I feel different. Lee was fast asleep, but I got out of bed, grabbed a test kit and went to the bathroom. It dawned on me then that I hadn't done a test for a while; I'd sort of been putting it off. As much as I wanted a baby, the reality of having one made me feel nervous. I wondered, had I been looking after myself properly? I had been eating a lot of crisps.

When the test was positive, I rushed back into the bedroom to tell Lee, who was so excited. We both ended up in tears.

'How did I not know?' I said. 'How have I not realised this?'

It all made sense now: the tiredness, the feeling sick, the endless bags of crisps. Suddenly, it all fell into place, and I was so happy. The one-star reviews of the Edinburgh Fringe show meant nothing now. I was going to be a new mum.

My pregnancy was generally relatively smooth, and I enjoyed the experience. My craving for cheese never diminished, and as it turns out Betsy absolutely loves the stuff. The only fly in the ointment was that Lee was on a UK tour with a play, so he felt like he was missing out on the pregnancy. When you're an actor on tour, you generally get one day a week off, and rushing back to see me and then back off somewhere up north all in one day was very hard for him. I guess that was one of the main reasons we decided to find out the gender of our baby upfront, to give him something to be excited about. These days, gender reveal events are all the rage, but that wasn't the case back then. Most of my friends only discovered what they were having once the baby had popped out. I'd been convinced it was a boy, but we were both over the moon to find we were having a little girl. Lee was thrilled because it made him feel a part of the experience despite not always being there. It meant that he could go out shopping while he was away and buy Babygros and blankets for his new daughter and then bring them back to London on his day off.

Meanwhile, I was busy nesting, messaging my friends who were already mums for advice, and watching episodes of *One Born Every Minute*. As with most things in my life, I wanted to make sure I was organised and ready for the new arrival. As usual, though, I couldn't just sit there waiting. I started sketching ideas for maternity dresses, which ended up as my own range of maternity wear for Very, quite a new company at the time. All in all, it was a wonderful time for me, and I couldn't wait to become a mum.

CHAPTER TWENTY-SIX

Why wasn't I allowed to say I was upset?

After my difficult time at Capital Radio, I seriously could have done without more drama on my next big television job. Unfortunately, that wasn't to be.

Following the success of *Any Dream Will Do* and *I'd Do Anything*, there was a buzz about Andrew Lloyd Webber's new BBC show, *Over the Rainbow*. This was a similar format, aiming to find a new Dorothy for a new production of *The Wizard of Oz*.

In late 2009, Andrew called and invited me to a dinner at his house. It was an informal affair, but he asked a couple of key members of the press, including Sara Nathan, the show business editor at the *Daily Mail*. It was basically a bit of a schmoozing dinner, where Andrew would announce that he was about to embark on another of what had been very successful musical TV shows. Most nights at Andrew's were laid-back and informal, and, I have to say, he's a wonderful host. So, as well as looking forward to the evening of finding out more about the show, I was also excited to share the news of my pregnancy with Andrew and his wife, Madeleine.

During the evening, I was chatting with Sara when Madeleine offered me a drink.

'I'm not drinking at the moment,' I said, smiling.

'Oh, have you got something you want to tell us?' Madeleine said.

'Yes, I'm pregnant!'

'Oh, this is wonderful news, absolutely wonderful,' Sara said, calling Andrew over to join us.

I didn't mind everyone knowing. We were on the verge of making an official announcement anyway, and I was already past the 12-week mark. Of course, everyone was pleased and congratulated me. Still, as we continued our conversation, Sara posed the question of how my pregnancy might fit in with the schedule for the new show.

'How's it going to work with you being pregnant?' she asked.

'Oh, it's fine,' I said.

My agent had already been sent the schedule of the filming. As I was having a planned caesarean, it was something I knew I could work around. I'd be pregnant during the auditions and would have given birth by the time the live Saturday-night shows kicked off. It actually worked out well.

Madeleine suggested that a caesarean would be hard to get over quickly and that it was a significant operation. Meanwhile, I'd spoken to enough people who'd had one, so I felt confident that I'd be more than OK. Besides, I only had to sit in a chair and critique performers. It's not like I'd have to do anything particularly strenuous or physical.

From that moment on, though, the conversation didn't appear to be going my way; it was all worried frowns and whispering.

Andrew seemed flustered, convinced that I wouldn't be able to do the show any more.

'Of course I can do it,' I tried to reassure him. 'I'm pregnant; I'm not ill.'

There suddenly seemed to be a lot of negatives being thrown at me, and it was left on a note of 'we'll have to discuss it.'

I remember getting a taxi home that night, thinking, *I'm not going to end up doing this show*. It was a sinking feeling in my stomach that I just couldn't shake. The worst part about it was that we'd gone from 'congratulations on your happy news' to 'you can't possibly function on a TV show' in a very short space of time. This was all in front of the show business editor of the *Daily Mail*.

I couldn't help thinking about women from other cultures in developing countries. Women who have children and then get up and walk ten miles to collect water for their families. Christ, I'd only have to sit in a swivel chair in a bit of make-up. What was the big deal? Also, I loved Andrew's shows and always had such a great time doing them. The thought of not doing it was gutting.

For a while, I thought things might have settled down. I asked my agent if she'd had any news about me being replaced, but she hadn't. I assumed Andrew had had a rethink. I mean, we were good friends, and he certainly knew how capable I was under pressure. My agent had even received a draft contract from the BBC.

A couple of days later, however, my PR, Simon Jones, got a call from Sara Nathan asking him, 'How does Denise feel about being replaced by Charlotte Church on the new show?' Simon called me right away, and I told him that I hadn't heard a bloody thing about it.

'The BBC is putting out a statement to say that Charlotte is doing the show in your place,' he said.

As much as I'd worried something like that might happen, I was gobsmacked. As well as the fact I'd received my contract, Andrew hadn't said a word to me about any of this. I was so upset, particularly seeing Dannii Minogue, who was pregnant while she was on the judging panel of *The X Factor*, who appeared to have a much more supportive team running the show.

Not long after the official announcement, I did a press conference for a charity walk I was doing with Natasha Kaplinsky. The walk was for Sports Relief. Before the press conference, I was advised by both the charity and the Beeb that if anyone asked about me being replaced on *Over the Rainbow*, I should go with a 'no comment' approach.

Why? Why wasn't I allowed to say that I was upset? I was there talking about doing a charity walk as a heavily pregnant woman but seemingly incapable of being a TV judge. There was absolutely no reason for any of it.

Inevitably, the question did arise. A journalist asked me how I felt about being replaced by Charlotte.

'I feel disappointed and let down,' I said. 'Being pregnant is not an issue for me, and I feel fit and healthy.'

Andrew and the BBC received quite a bit of negative press after that. Andrew said it was the BBC's decision and that he'd wanted me to do the show. The BBC denied it was anything to do with my pregnancy. Of course, I had no idea what conversations had gone on between them. Jay Hunt, who was controller of the BBC at the time, even called my agent, keen for me not to talk about it publicly. I ended up going in for a meeting with Jay, which didn't go brilliantly. I think my agent would have liked me to say what Jay wanted to hear: 'Oh, it's all fine; I haven't got any issue with it.' Something that wasn't likely to jeopardise future projects with the channel.

I remember feeling like I was walking through customs at that meeting; like I was guilty even though I had nothing to hide. It was a proper 'head down in the headmistress's office' moment: *'Tell us what you've done and what you've said.'*

Meanwhile, I was sitting there pregnant, thinking, *Where's the support here?* I've just lost my job with no explanation whatsoever.

I just couldn't bring myself to sit there and play the game. I told Jay that I felt let down and that I was upset. The truth was that the entire discussion about me not doing the show because of my pregnancy happened in front of me and in front of a showbiz journalist. Of course it was going to get out, and of course they were going to get negative press. Sure, I could accept that people sometimes get replaced, but where they'd messed up was sending a first draft of a contract, including schedules and dates, and then going into discussions with my agent – all before my pregnancy was announced.

'If you'd have just picked someone else from the off, I could have dealt with it, but up until last Monday, I was still doing it,' I told her.

It was hard for me to watch Charlotte do the show at first, although I had no bad feelings towards her. I was a fan of Charlotte, and I thought she did a great job. Strangely, as the series went on, I really enjoyed watching *Over the Rainbow* as a punter. In the end, I even let go of any bad feelings I had. I suppose I had a choice: I could either get all bitter and twisted about what had happened, or move forward. Of course, I had to choose the latter because, in truth, I had so much to look forward to.

In many ways, I think my experience as a woman in the entertainment industry and in the public eye has been different from that of a man doing a similar job. Why is it that men seem to be able to get away with so much more than a woman can?

Things are changing for the better, which gives me hope and makes me happy, but let's be honest, it really needed to happen, and it's been a long time coming. When I spoke out about how I felt let down as a pregnant woman, it really went against me. Yes, things ultimately worked out, but it was a long time before the BBC employed me again after dropping me from *Over the Rainbow*.

At the time, I felt like there was no value in having me on the show because of my 'condition'. It's something I thought about when I spoke to other friends around that time. Some women wanted children but were afraid to take the plunge, so to speak, because they were worried about 'work'. How would being pregnant and taking time out to have a baby affect their careers? This was particularly relevant to friends of mine in entertainment at one point. However, I'm sure it's something women worried about across the board. Two very good friends of mine both confided in me their concerns about how their careers might change once they became mums. We shouldn't have had to have those conversations. Thankfully, though, that's also changing. There are so many branding opportunities now, too, with Instagram and other social sites. These days, celebs seem to be popping out babies all over the shop, and it can be pretty lucrative. Good luck to them, I say!

Even going back to my early days in TV, despite being celebrated for having this ballsy, no-nonsense way about me, some TV executives saw it negatively. I was a guest on a live TV show once. Although I can't for the life of me remember what it was, I certainly remember the cringeworthy experience I had just before we went on air. There's usually some manner of briefing before you appear on a chat show. Someone will remind you not to mention a specific brand or to promote anything you're not supposed to be promoting, or not to swear if it's not that kind of show. On the show in question, I was pulled to one side and given a very specific type of briefing by a producer. It was along the lines of 'don't do or say anything outrageous, or anything shocking, or naughty'. In other words, behave yourself.

'I do know how to act on a TV show', I said, taken aback.

I felt like I was being treated like a naughty child going to visit their posh aunt for tea: *Don't put your dirty hands on the clean tablecloth, Denise! Be polite! Don't scoff all the custard creams!*

OK, so I hold my hands up to the fact that I'd flashed my bra at Prince Charles a couple of years before, but that was a jokey couple of seconds at a music festival when I was young, not on a live TV show in front of millions of viewers. Also, I don't think that conversation would have happened with a man. Can you imagine someone telling Leigh Francis or Jimmy Carr to stay in their box while they were on telly? Or someone telling David Walliams off for straddling Simon Cowell and grinding him in a lap dance on the judging panel of *Britain's Got Talent*? I doubt Amanda Holden or Alesha Dixon would have got away with that, and I'd probably never work again if I did it! Men are, on the whole, trusted to know how far they can take things on any given occasion, but there were many times I wasn't afforded that courtesy. Whatever I did in my early days had tarred me with a reputation that was hard to shake off. It was as if I wasn't allowed to grow up or evolve as an entertainer, and that was sometimes hard to take.

Happily, I feel like I'm starting to leave all that behind me now. With the changing environment in TV, theatre and film, with bosses finally addressing equal pay among all genders, things will hopefully get even better for women. I wonder if everything has changed, though. I still believe there are double standards at play. Women are often judged more harshly than men. It's as if certain types of behaviour are almost expected of men, so they get away with it, but when a woman does something similar, the knives are out. Of course, social media has been a bloody great magnifying glass for this kind of thing. Anyone can have their say about everything, which can be exhausting – especially when you're the one who's on the end of it. Thankfully, that's one thing I try to let wash over me. Blocking out and ignoring negativity is the best way to combat it. Just don't give it oxygen.

I'm glad to say that ultimately my experience on *Over the Rainbow* did not destroy my relationship with the BBC or with Andrew. How could I let that happen? I have always had a lot of love for Andrew, and I'm happy to say that hasn't changed. This was a hiccup. Whatever the thinking behind my departure from the show was, we have all moved on from it now. That's why I can write about how I felt at the time without feeling angry or hurt. It's all an experience.

When the BBC called my agent and asked me to be a contestant on *Strictly Come Dancing* a couple of years later, they said as much themselves. What was past was past; there was no bad feeling. Looking back, I see it as one of those things that happen in life that hopefully I've learned from. They're the experiences that hopefully make us stronger, better people. That said, it's also been quite cathartic to get my thoughts down on paper and set the record straight. That's never a bad thing, is it?

CHAPTER TWENTY-SEVEN

The beautiful moment we wanted it to be

I'd suffered from some sciatica and back problems during my pregnancy, so my obstetrician at the Portland Hospital was the one who'd initially suggested a caesarean birth. From my side, I was thrilled with the idea of being able to plan a specific date to give birth, particularly as Lee was still away on tour. Yes, it was a luxury, but it meant there'd be no need for him to have to dash back from somewhere if I suddenly went into labour. Towards the very end of my pregnancy, however, I started to feel more and more uncomfortable. My fingers and toes had swollen up so much that I was in quite a lot of pain, particularly in my hands. On a visit to my obstetrician to discuss all this, he had a suggestion.

'Your baby's cooked,' he said. 'She can safely come out anytime now. Why not bring the date forward?'

We decided that on 1 May I would go into the Portland to have our baby. It was a couple of weeks earlier than my due date, but my doctor assured me that it was perfectly safe. As well as the pain I'd suffered in my hands, I'd also become aware of a few photographers hanging around outside my flat. I knew they just wanted a snap of Lee and me with our new baby, so a few of them had been hovering from time to time, waiting for the moment when I went off to the hospital. The last thing Lee and I wanted was a big fuss around our child's birth. We tried to keep everything as private as we could until we were ready, so I called on my friend Lucy, who I've known since my time with Jay, when she dated Jamiroquai's bass player, Nick. Lucy was now a successful artist manager and quite adept at dealing with privacy issues and the media.

'Come and stay at mine the night before you go to the hospital,' she suggested. 'No one will follow you from my place. I'll make sure of that.'

The night before the planned birth, I crept out of my flat and drove to Lucy's, managing to get away without any fuss. Lucy drove me to the Portland the following day at 6am, and I settled in. I'd suggested that Lee arrive later in the day when the baby was due to be born, rather than hanging around all day. Everything felt calm and planned, which is just the way I wanted it. It's the way I am; I can't help it. I just like to be organised down to the last little thing. I'd even chosen my baby's birthday as 1 May because it was a bank holiday, meaning there'd always be an option for a bank holiday Monday birthday party as she got older. That said, things all moved quicker than expected when a change in my doctor's schedule meant the time for my caesarean was suddenly brought forward by a couple of hours. In the end, Lee ended up rushing across town in a panic anyway. Before I knew it, he was standing in front of me in a set of medical scrubs, which, at the time, looked very odd. It's funny now when I look back at the pictures of that day because Lee went on to play nurse Ben 'Lofty' Chiltern in both *Casualty* and *Holby City*. Now I've seen him dressed in scrubs just like that dozens of times.

Planning down to the last detail meant that I'd even made a playlist of music to play during the birth. I love Burt Bacharach's music, so I'd compiled a selection of my favourites. I thought it would be nice if Betsy had come into the world during 'Magic Moments', but in the end, she arrived to 'Raindrops Keep Fallin' on My Head'. My memories of Betsy's birth are always tied up with the sound of that phrase and that melody going round and round as I watched her come into the world. Lee got to clean her up and cuddle her, and I remember looking down at him, sitting on the floor with Betsy in his arms. It really had turned out to be the beautiful moment we wanted it to be. I was ecstatically happy.

Later, back in my room, the nurses told me I needed proper bed rest post the caesarean and that I wasn't to move around too much. Well, that lasted about five minutes with me. I was in my tracksuit in the bathroom, putting a bit of lip and some mascara on before anyone could stop me. Look, I'm an Essex girl; if I was going to have visitors coming in to get a first glimpse of our new baby, I needed to have at least a modicum of glamour. There was no way I would greet guests sitting there in a hospital gown without a lick of make-up on. Forget that idea!

That evening, before visitors arrived, Lee ordered a pizza, which we had in the room. At the same time, one of the big Saturday-night TV shows flickered on the telly in front of me. I remember looking over at Betsy lying in her little cot next to me, thinking about how amazing and wonderful it all was. Also, how weird it all was. God, I was a mum!

I have to admit, I got told off quite a lot that evening. The nurses kept telling me to sit down and rest, but when our families turned up, I couldn't sit still; I was too excited.

'You don't look like you've just had a baby,' Mum said, looking at my full face of make-up. 'You look like you're going out.'

'You know me, always camera-ready,' I said.

A couple of days later, my doctor told me I could go home when I wanted. This was just as Lee went back to continue with the tour of his play. All of a sudden, I felt strangely nervous. How could I go back to my flat on my own with a new baby? What would I do? How would I look after her? What time would I feed her? What if she wouldn't stop crying? It's a strange thing to think back on and admit to, but at the time I felt like I didn't know what I was doing. While I was safe within the walls of my comfy hospital room, the outside world seemed a scary place. So far there had been people on hand to help me, but the thought of being on my own with Betsy filled me with dread. I felt vulnerable, scared that I might not cope; the fear was genuine at the time. I had never felt such an overwhelming sense of protection towards another living thing. The thought that I might do something wrong or that some harm might come to her took over. Being in a private facility, I was lucky because it gave me a safety net most people wouldn't have had.

In the end, I spoke to one of the nurses about my concerns.

'How long do patients usually stay after a caesarean?' I asked.

'Well, if they recover normally, maybe two or three days,' the nurse said.

I ended up staying for ten days. Ten. Honestly, they told me it was one of the longest post-baby stays they'd ever had. I don't know how it happened. I think it was because Lee was away and I felt secure there, so I just kept thinking, *Shall I just do one more night? Just to be on the safe side.* I know people who have been in and out in the blink of an eye when they've had a baby, but I didn't feel ready or able. As much as I'd been looking forward to becoming a mother, I felt anxious to the point that I didn't want to leave the sanctuary of the hospital, despite the financial implications.

'Don't you think you ought to take Betsy home?' Mum said to me one evening.

'I should, but I just feel so anxious about it,' I said.

I knew Mum was right, but there was another underlying reason why I was in no rush to get home. The tenant who lived above me in Hampstead was having major work done on his flat, so scaffolding had gone up right across the building, and there was a lot of noise. With my flat being on the ground floor and basement, the scaffolding had plunged my flat into virtual darkness. The thought of all that wasn't appealing at all, although I knew I'd eventually have to face it.

My anxiety continued once I was home from my postnatal mini-break. It was quite some time before I felt confident enough to take Betsy out into the world for a walk. I was actually quite surprised to discover what a nervous mum I was. I'd never imagined feeling like that, but here I was. Friends of mine with babies were tearing up and down the high street with them or strolling in the park just as soon as they could get out of the door. Meanwhile, I spent six weeks being paranoid and trying to find my feet with it all. Of course, Lee came back during that time, and things were better then, but as soon as he'd gone back to work, I was thrown back into a bit of a panic.

One sunny morning, I settled Betsy into her new Bugaboo stroller. I decided to head to Hampstead and get myself a coffee. As most new mums will tell you, it took me about an hour to get out of the door that first time going solo, making sure I had everything packed into the changing bag. When I got to the front door, I realised she needed changing already, then she was sick, then I couldn't get her to stop screaming. Suddenly, staying home for all that time seemed to make sense; I only wanted to get out for a bloody coffee. There was a moment before I left the house when I picked up the change bag and then went to grab my handbag. It suddenly dawned on me that I didn't have enough hands for both bags and a pram. It was really at that moment when I realised that my life had forever changed. I was a girl who'd always loved a matching handbag and shoe combo, but that wasn't possible any more. What's more, it didn't seem necessary. It wasn't about me any more; it was all about her. I remember standing at the front door, thinking, *God, I won't need a handbag for ages*.

It's one of the things I always tell my friends that are having babies. 'Trust me, you won't use your handbag for years!'

Once I finally stepped outside on my own with Betsy, I breathed in the fresh air, feeling really proud. As I pushed my pram up the hill, I had a flashback to being a child, pushing a doll's pram and pretending to be a mum. Recalling its innocence, I realised that I was feeling it all over again – that childlike innocence of not really knowing what I was doing but feeling happy and optimistic. I'd always been a person who was so capable and competent, but here I was starting from scratch, learning a new and essential life skill.

After that first trip out, things changed. I loved taking Betsy out; in fact, I wanted to take her everywhere. After what happened with *Over the Rainbow*, I'd told myself that being a mum wasn't going to stop me from carrying on or taking on new things as far as my career went. My plan was to make motherhood a part of it all and have Betsy with me for as much of it as possible. In that first couple of years, she came to photo shoots with me, and I'd have her with me if I was in a TV studio. Of course, she was always well looked after while I was working, but then I'd have her close to me during any downtime. I even took her to V Festival, and she came with me on a trip to LA. We were inseparable, and it was lovely.

Lee was also very hands-on as a dad. He was and still is a brilliant father to Betsy. Even since we've separated, I couldn't have asked for a better outcome to the way we work together as parents. That's been a real blessing.

When Betsy was about five months old, I embarked on another West End show. I told you, I can't sit still for five minutes. Lee was in the West End doing *Wicked* at the time, so I took on the role of the feisty Paulette in the musical version of *Legally Blonde* at the Savoy Theatre. The show starred Sheridan Smith, who I loved working with, and was directed by Jerry Mitchell. It was already a huge success when I joined the cast and a fabulous fun production to be a part of. To be honest, I was loving life at that point. True, I worked in a theatre every night while doing night feeds for my young baby, so there was a certain amount of tiredness and sleepless nights. Still, my part in *Legally Blonde* wasn't so big that I didn't have time to be a mum. Sometimes, Betsy would even come to the matinees with me and snuggle up in my dressing room. I loved having her with me during that time, being a working mum and having the support of my colleagues and the people around me. The production company was happy for me to have Betsy with me, and there was always a crew or cast member happy to sit with her while I did my thing onstage.

It's funny, I remember wondering what she must be thinking sitting there in that strange place, surrounded by all my brightly coloured costumes. Then, when I was in full 'Paulette', with my spiky wig, she must have thought, *Hang on, that's not my mum. The voice is the same but the clothes and hair don't match!*

It felt like a great time to be working in the West End because there seemed to be so many great productions happening, and I felt lucky to be part of such an incredible, successful show. Being able to do all that while having Betsy in my life made it all the more satisfying. I guess I felt like I had it all at that moment in time.

CHAPTER TWENTY-EIGHT

Like an Essex angel

In 2012, when my agent Claire called to tell me that the BBC wanted me to go in for a meeting regarding the tenth series of *Strictly Come Dancing*, I was thrilled on several levels. Firstly, it meant that all that negativity of *Over the Rainbow* had been well and truly forgotten. Secondly, I was such a massive fan of the show and loved the idea that I might get to be part of it.

There's so much secrecy around who's going to be a contestant on the show. After I was offered my contract, I had no idea who the other contestants were, let alone that one of them was to be one of my closest friends. I'd met Kimberley Walsh from Girls Aloud when we'd climbed Mount Kilimanjaro together, and we'd become instant friends. She became someone I could always call if I wanted an honest opinion about something or advice. I like to think I'm the same kind of friend for her. Still, while I was preparing for the show, doing all my dance trials and negotiations, I had no idea that Kimberley was doing the same, despite us talking regularly. As much as we loved a bit of a gossip, we both stuck to the rules of the show. Neither of us let on to the other that we were doing it. The first I knew about Kimberley's involvement was when that year's contestants were revealed to the press. For this, we were all gathered in a TV studio for the big reveal.

Personally, I was dying to know who else was doing the series and who'd I'd be up against. The first person I saw was Nicky Byrne from Westlife. *Thank God*, I thought, *somebody I know*. It's always lovely to have a mate or someone you can chat to when you're on a project over so many weeks. Other contestants were supermodel Jerry Hall, actors Lisa Riley and Colin Salmon and Olympic gymnast Louis Smith, who went on to win the competition. Suddenly, there was Kimberley, and the two of us rushed across the room and hugged.

'Oh my God, this is going to be so fab, doing this together,' I said.

In the past, we'd discussed between us whether competing on *Strictly* might be a good or fun thing to do, but we'd also both been a bit nervous about the idea. This was the biggest TV show in the UK; it was and still is the Saturday-night staple leading up to Christmas. It's also a huge commitment with a lot of training over many weeks – depending on how long you stay. We both knew you had to be fit, focused and dedicated if you were going to cut it with a professional ballroom dancer in front of millions of viewers every Saturday night.

On the day of the contestant reveal, Kimberley was confident we'd be OK.

'Look, we've climbed Mount Kilimanjaro together, so I reckon we can do this.'

She was right – but hang on! That's a story for another chapter.

I absolutely loved my experience on *Strictly*, but it was hard! Of course, I'd trained in dancing when I was little, and I'd danced at Sylvia's, but it certainly wasn't a skill I'd nurtured or kept up. I think people thought I was much more of a dancer than I actually was. There was even some negativity about me doing the show, being a 'trained dancer', having been on the West End stage and Broadway. The truth is, I hadn't trained for years, and never for something like ballroom. Even in *Chicago*, the part of Roxie Hart isn't the big dancing part. Velma Kelly is the character that carries that side of the show. Still, I did have to put up with a fair bit of sniping about me having an unfair advantage. The funny thing is, Kimberley would have done far more choreography and dance training than me. Have you ever seen Girls Aloud in action? They really go for it with the choreography, and Kim was always amazing. She said as much in a TV interview. In my defence, she said that if I was being touted as a trained dancer, then so was she. Her support made our friendship even stronger, but the truth is neither of us was trained in dances like the tango, the jive, the samba, American smooth and the like. They're entirely different disciplines, and we didn't have a clue what we were doing when we started. I mean, who the hell trains in doing the Charleston? I guess it was just the usual thing. There always has to be a controversy, and if there's one going, I always seem to be able to find it. I did my best to ignore it. Still, the perception that I had an unfair advantage led me to conclude that I was never going to win the competition. This notion hit me fairly early on in the proceedings, so I just decided to relax and enjoy it. I loved the performing side of my career, and I saw *Strictly* as a way of keeping a bit of that old magic alive. It was something glamorous; it was training and learning a new skill.

I worked hard with my professional partner, James Jordan, and we got on well. To be honest, I think he was relieved he'd got a partner who could dance, and he certainly seemed to appreciate how hard I was willing to graft. He confided in me one day that he thought I was going to be difficult; he'd had this pre-conceived idea that I was going to be a bit mouthy and hard to handle. What, me? Mouthy? It made me smile when he told me that I'd turned out to be the opposite of all that, but then again, I never gave him reason to be angry or pissed off at me. I wanted to learn, so I tried to take in everything he taught me, and if he was critical of something, I'd go away and try to work on it.

Whenever possible, I tried to organise to train in an adjacent studio to Kimberley and her dance partner, Pasha Kovalev. That way, Kim and I could encourage each other and watch our respective routines. Neither of us felt like we were competing against the others, and our mutual support continued through the series. Kimberley and I ended up as joint runners-up, which I don't think had ever happened before. That was a lovely way for the series to end.

As well as walking away with the runner-up title, I took something else away from my *Strictly* experience, which really wasn't so nice.

Just before the end of the series, I'd had an accident that I didn't think was all that serious at first. Our show dance for the final was 'Flashdance ... What a Feeling'. This routine included a very daring and difficult lift, which James had only done with his professional dancer wife, Ola. The move involved James lifting me up over his head by the hips while I flew above with outstretched arms, like an Essex angel. A big audience-cheering moment, for sure, and one that worked brilliantly on the night. However, during one rehearsal leading up to the performance, James had lost his grip on me, and I'd fallen to the ground, banging my head. The show's camera crew actually captured the moment, and the clip of me hurtling down and my neck going 'click' was shown on the final.

After it happened, I was sent for some physio and told I probably had whiplash. I didn't know it at the time, but I should really have had an MRI. Instead, I had a course of steroid injections to numb the pain to get me through the final show. Typically, I just brushed it off as a minor injury, like the other little ballroom war wounds I'd collected throughout the series. I had no idea that, down the line, I'd live to regret my casual attitude towards what turned out to be a severe injury.

As much as I'd enjoyed my time on *Strictly*, all had not been well in my personal life, and things didn't seem to be getting any better. As fond as Lee and I were of one another, we had been drifting apart for a while; I don't really know how else to put it. There were none of the big dramas of past relationships; it was just a fact neither of us could ignore. We were not on the same path. We didn't want the same things. Betsy was our one genuine connection, but even our mutual love and care for our daughter wasn't going to be enough to sustain a relationship that wasn't working any more.

Doing a show like *Strictly* can take over your life. You don't have time for much else. I was lucky. As well as Lee being a great dad, I also had my best friend Tamara, who helped me out as far as looking after Betsy was concerned. As for my relationship, however, I guess it's when I started to notice how wide the cracks had become. It had been coming for a while, but I think my time doing the show cemented it. I felt pretty low after I'd finished *Strictly* – post-show blues, I suppose it was. For a while, Lee and I tried to make things work, but they really weren't.

I still had the bug to be out there performing, and so agreed to do the *Strictly* tour in 2013. After that, there was no question that things were coming to an end as far as my marriage was concerned. I just didn't feel the same. It was a hard truth to accept. Things like that can make you feel like a failure, and God knows I'd gone through that with some of my relationships in the past. In fact, in some ways, it would have been easier if there had been a big drama, something to really pinpoint what had gone wrong. I didn't have that, though, just my gut feeling that I shouldn't be with Lee any more. Friends suggested I stick it out, like friends do, telling me that we both might feel differently one day soon. That might have been true, but surely we'd just be settling for something that wasn't right. That wouldn't be fair on anyone, even Betsy.

I have to hold my hands up on this. One of the main reasons my marriage to Lee ended was because of my itchy feet. It's not something I like about myself, but it's something I know to be true. As time went on, I just didn't feel the same any more. Despite our similar upbringings, the differences in our personalities and in the things in life we enjoyed doing became more and more apparent. Of course, we tried to make it work for a while for Betsy's sake, but in the end, I had to give in and be honest with myself, as tough as that was.

When I sat down with Lee to tell him how I really felt, he was more upset than I'd imagined he'd be. Despite everything, he still wanted to try, but I couldn't go along with it. I'd watched other friends carry on in relationships where they weren't happy, and it wasn't pretty or, indeed, helpful. On some occasions, they'd soldiered on for the sake of their children, which, of course, I understand, but mostly it was at the expense of their own happiness. In my heart, I knew that if Lee and I separated now, we could stay friends and still be good and loving parents to Betsy. If I'd let things drag on, that may have changed, and then everyone loses.

Once the split was announced, there was a certain amount of speculation as to what had happened. Some areas of the press tried to create a shitstorm that wasn't there, with Lee as the sweet boy who'd played Joseph and me as the hard-nosed career woman who'd left him behind. I even got a tip-off from a friend in the know, who warned me a tabloid had organised an enormous bunch of flowers to be delivered to my front door. The idea was that I'd open the door to take in the bouquet, and a waiting photographer would snap a photo of me accepting the flowers. The story would be that the blooms were from a heartbroken Lee, attempting to win me back. The tip-off turned out to be a good one, but I sat sadly in my bedroom when the flowers arrived and refused to open the front door. Not today, thank you!

I've always wanted Lee to be happy, and he's now in a relationship with a person who I'm sure he would say is much more suited to him, just as Eddie is to me.

Looking back, the two of us meeting, getting married and having Betsy all seemed to happen in the blink of an eye, but we were together for almost six years, all told. That was much longer than my previous relationships. It was also a time of significant changes for me: marriage, motherhood, experiencing a whole new life with my own family. Still, I certainly didn't imagine that I'd be a divorcee before my fortieth birthday. I'd always thought of marriage as a forever thing. No one settles down and marries someone with a view to it ending, do they? Also, my mum and dad have been together for over 50 years, so I guess that was my benchmark. It wasn't to be, though, because of me and my itchy feet.

When I think and write about all this, it makes me think of my relationship with Eddie, which is now seven years strong. The weird thing is, it doesn't seem like seven years, and there's not an itchy foot in sight. The two of us always seem to be very much in sync with each other: our humour, moods, likes and dislikes. Many friends have said that I'm the female version of Eddie, and he's the male version of me, and I think that's probably on the money.

As a father, I can't fault Lee, and what we've managed to do as far as Betsy is concerned is quite remarkable. Despite separating and then divorcing, we've created an environment that is loving and stable for her, and I know Lee is as proud of that as I am. We're still friends, and he'll still come in for a chat when he drops Betsy home, and sit and watch the football with Eddie from time to time. We even did a holiday together with Betsy long after we'd split up. I spent a week in Dubai with Lee and when he flew home, Eddie flew out to join me for the second week. This was much to the amusement and bemusement of the other families around the hotel pool. I explained to some of them how well Lee and I still got on and how we always wanted Betsy to have the best of both of us. We didn't want her to miss out on the moments a child might have if their parents were together. For instance, we'd made a pact that whatever happened, we would all be together on Betsy's first trip to Euro Disney. Despite being separated, we both had to be there on her first meeting with Mickey Mouse – and we were! Betsy got to have that experience with both of us, which is how we felt it should be.

CHAPTER TWENTY-NINE

A hard truth to accept

After a holiday in Ibiza with some friends, I was featured in a newspaper article where I was compared to the model and socialite Tamara Ecclestone and a few other celebrities. The piece was a 'who's been on the most holidays this year' feature. Apparently, I was fourth after Tamara, Rita Ora and Tulisa Contostavlos. The idea of it made me uncomfortable, and there were other stories with a similar slant. The inference seems to be that I'd dumped my husband, left the baby at home and now I was a wild party girl again. In truth, I'd gone on a few mini-breaks with friends I hadn't connected with for ages, while Betsy was with her dad. Yes, I felt like I needed to let loose a bit, but none of it was particularly wild.

Christ, I didn't have the energy to be wild! Still, after pictures of me enjoying myself at the Ocean Beach Bar in Ibiza were splashed across the tabloids, I decided enough was enough. Maybe it was time to lie low for a while. I'd never really done that before: purposefully kept my head down and stayed out of the limelight. It always seemed to find me, even when I didn't want it to. The last thing I wanted was for Lee to be hurt, seeing me living it up all over the place. It wasn't fair. After our break-up, everything had been very amicable, and I didn't want to do anything that might jeopardise our friendship. So, I decided I would keep my head down, enjoy dedicating all my time to Betsy, and stay single.

Of course, I couldn't just do nothing as far as work went; that was impossible for me. I decided that I wanted to try writing because it was something I could do under the radar. Nobody would see the results until I was ready – if I was ready. At first, I didn't know what form this writing would take. All I knew was that it had to be something that I could immerse myself in and something that other women of my generation would enjoy. I wasn't sure I had a book in me at the time, but maybe a play of some kind.

The idea for what would become my one-woman show, *Some Girl I Used to Know*, first came about because I wanted to prove something to myself as much as anyone else. After the critical disaster that was my Edinburgh Fringe show, *Blondes*, I felt like I needed to redeem myself. In my heart, I knew I hadn't put all my energy and effort into that show, so I wanted to do something I could feel proud of. I wanted to show people that I could still carry a theatrical presentation on my own, as I had with *Tell Me on a Sunday*, and that I was good enough to lift up an audience and take them on a journey. Whatever it was, it *had* to be good. No, not just good – great!

It wasn't easy; I had to think long and hard about what this new and fabulous thing could possibly be. In the eighties, I'd loved the play and the movie *Shirley Valentine*, with Pauline Collins. Many women had watched this beautiful story of an unfulfilled housewife who travels to a Greek island to follow her dreams and see something outside the four walls of her kitchen, and they'd connected with it. I wondered what the equivalent of that might be in 2013. I came up with the idea of a successful businesswoman who'd put everything into her career and her marriage but put her own wants and needs on hold. It wasn't necessarily based on me or anyone I knew. Still, I'd gathered so many stories and experiences talking to my friends, I felt like I already knew this person.

I'd recently bumped into a friend of mine, Terry Ronald, at Kimberley Walsh's thirtieth birthday party. He'd worked as the vocal arranger on *Rent* in 2007 but had since started writing and recently published his first novel. As much as I wanted to write myself, I knew I would need some help and guidance, not really having done it before. I called Terry for a chat about my ideas. He loved the idea of helping bring my character to life, and we ended up meeting in a tiny coffee shop in Fulham to hash out some ideas. Over the next few months, we developed the story and layered the ideas. We sat reading bits out to one another over lunches at Soho House, laughing out loud at our own lines and doing funny voices. At the same time, the other guests looked at us as if we were weirdos. We both shared the same mischievous sense of humour, so there were a lot of laughs, but as the idea grew, there was more and more poignancy to the piece. Eventually, I took my idea to Charlie Parsons, who'd started the production company Planet 24 and pioneered *The Big Breakfast*. He was also now involved in producing theatre with his business partner Tristan

Baker. They loved the idea and brought on a director called Michael Howcroft to help us workshop it further.

Charlie and Tris reacting so positively to our little play meant a lot. But, as much as I wanted it to happen, there was always this nagging doubt that it might come to nothing, despite all the hard work. I guess the doubt was in myself, really. I wanted to believe that I could do it, but it was hard to shake off some of the setbacks I'd had in the past few years. I don't think I'd have felt the same if this was a TV presenting gig or something I'd been employed to do, but *Some Girl I Used to Know* was my baby. I was really putting myself out there this time, which made the fact that it was actually happening both exciting and daunting.

I don't think I can overstate how much I put into *Some Girl*. For so long, I'd been looking for that special thing, a vehicle that would allow me to act and sing, which I could have a big part in creating, and here it was. I spent hours committing the many pages of dialogue to memory, walking around saying the lines over and over, choosing a new scene to focus on each day. I swear some of my neighbours thought I was bonkers, wandering around my garden having conversations and rows with myself.

It was a long process. In fact, from its incarnation in a café in Fulham, *Some Girl I Used to Know* took nearly two years of writing and workshopping before we finally previewed it at the Leicester Curve towards the end of 2013.

Finally, my character had come to life. Stephanie Canworth was a successful lingerie designer in an unhappy marriage who's tempted into an affair with her first love. Her story is a monologue covering her school days, first love, holidays in Ibiza and the great loss she suffered but has buried for years. It's a one-women piece, so I literally had to immerse myself and become Stephanie. There was music in the show, produced and arranged by another friend who'd worked with us on *Rent*, Steve Anderson. These were all songs from the eighties and nineties, when the story is set, stripped back to beautiful torch songs. Doing this show was a very different discipline to *Tell Me on a Sunday*, which is a song cycle. On *Some Girl*, I was basically talking for almost two hours, just me, with the songs peppered throughout. It was a lot to learn, and the only way I could do it was by repetition. Luckily, I've always had a good memory when it comes to scripts. Even back in my presenting days, I was known as 'one-take Denise' because I could look over a script once and usually get it down in one go. Betsy is the same, funnily enough. She can read something once and then pretty much recite it back.

As it was all set in a hotel room, I also used the things around me to cue me for certain things in the script. I was very particular about the set and everything being placed in precisely the same place for each performance. I'm sure the stage manager must have thought I was just being mega-fussy. Still, every prop and every movement became a cue for where I was in the show and my next piece of dialogue. I was picking up phones and computers, getting undressed and re-dressed, packing and unpacking a suitcase. Every new task connected to the specific part of the story I had to deliver. If I was picking up a pen, I knew exactly what I was supposed to be saying when I was doing it. It was the only way I knew how to do it. Then, in the moment of emotion, I'd burst into song. The show had everything: laughter, tears, drama and music – all the things I love about theatre.

We opened the finished version of the show at the West Yorkshire Playhouse, as it was called at the time, a lovely theatre and quite prestigious but a much bigger venue than I'd initially wanted to be in – sold out or not! During the technical rehearsals, Michael Howcroft told me I wasn't projecting enough. The truth was, I simply hadn't pictured an intimate show like ours sitting in a 1,100-seat theatre. It certainly took some getting used to.

In early 2014, we toured *Some Girl* around UK theatres before taking it to the West End later that year. It went down a storm. Just as I'd hoped, the show connected with so many women; men too, I've been told. Some people came back to see it over and over, but that was another issue. I would never let anyone I knew tell me when they were coming to watch the show, not even my family. It was such an immersive thing to do that if I knew a friend or family member would be in the audience, I was scared I'd lose my train of thought or slip out of character. I'd be thinking, I wonder if they're enjoying it, while I was supposed to be immersed in the role. And God forbid I saw anyone I knew; that really threw me off. I told all my friends to not mention to me when they were coming, and to sit at the back of the stalls or up in the circle.

'Don't sit in the first few rows, smiling up at me, because I'll cock it up for sure!'

When you're doing something like that, where it's just you onstage, you can't lose your momentum for a second.

When we eventually transferred to the Arts Theatre in London after a successful tour, the 350-seat capacity felt much more comfortable. The show felt like it belonged there.

The part of it I never looked forward to was being reviewed, particularly in London. I've never wanted to perform or create shows for critics. I don't think anyone does. I want to do it for my audiences. Every performance of every show has a unique audience, with wildly differing tastes. After the reaction I'd got with *Blondes*, of course I had my concerns about what people might say, but I tried not to think about it. I knew *Some Girl* was something much better, and I didn't feel like I needed confirmation from some stuffy broadsheet critic. In fact, when the show eventually went into the Arts, I put a ban on journalists coming unless they'd paid for a ticket. I figured they might invest in the story a little more if they'd forked out for a seat.

With *Some Girl*, I finally felt like I'd washed away the disappointment I'd had after *Blondes*. It actually turned out to be one of the biggest achievements of my career, and I'm still very proud of it.

CHAPTER THIRTY

'I can't, I'm playing golf'

I spent a whole year happily single and working on *Some Girl I Used to Know*. I guess it was a way of gathering myself and getting myself ready for whatever came next. Betsy was a wonderful distraction from life in the spotlight. My other distraction was a bit of surprise, but something I've come to love and enjoy ... I took up golf!

Now, if someone had told me when I was 25 that I'd one day fall in love with the idea of hitting a little ball around a green, I'd have laughed in their face, but that's precisely what happened. I was approaching my fortieth birthday when my friend Zoe Hardman, a keen golfer, invited me to spectate a celebrity pro-am tournament, where both professional and amateur golfers compete. She was playing in the tournament along with another friend of mine, Kirsty. The event was at Stoke Park Country Club. While I was there, I got chatting to some of the other participants, many of whom I knew: Anton Du Beke, Brendan Cole, and Brian McFadden, who I'd known for years. I had a lovely day and really got into the atmosphere of the thing. Zoe suggested afterwards that, as I'd enjoyed myself so much, I should get myself a set of clubs, and she would teach me to play.

'It'll give you a nice little hobby and something to do,' she said. 'Keep you busy on the weekends when Betsy's with her dad.'

Zoe was aware of how hard I found those weekends when Betsy wasn't around. It was fine in the week when I had bits and pieces of work to focus on. Still, it was a big adjustment being alone on alternate weekends when I'd got used to having a family around me. As lovely as you'd think it might be, having time to yourself felt weird to me and a bit unsettling. It's not like I was thinking, *Right, Betsy's away, I'm off out on the lash!* Who would I go with anyway? Most of my girlfriends were also 40 or close to it, and many had kids. They weren't always up for boozy nights any more, and neither was I.

Anyway, I did end up getting a set of golf clubs. Before long, the golf course became my sanctuary away from the world whenever I needed it.

First up, I joined the Grove Golf Club in Hertfordshire – no mucking about. True, it was a bit pricier than your regular pitch-and-putt type of place, but I thought, *What the hell?* I wasn't spending money on expensive nights out; I could afford to treat myself, surely. I also took on a coach called Kevin Merry, who I'd heard great things about. The lessons were going to be extra on top of the club membership fees, but it wasn't about just hitting balls and learning to play for me; this was something that was giving me a new focus. Something to occupy my mind, rather than worrying about work and my break-up with Lee. As much as I knew parting ways was for the best, it had been much harder than I'd imagined adjusting to a new normal, and as resilient as I thought I was, I was still hurting. Getting out in the fresh air and learning a new skill was just what I needed.

Kevin was more than happy to take me on, but he got a bit of a shock on our first lesson.

'I'm playing in a pro-am tournament in a few weeks,' I told him. 'I've already signed up.'

'What? Are you serious?'

It was true. I'd got chatting to Brian McFadden at the Stoke Park tournament, and he'd asked me if I played. Feeling like it was something I'd like to get more involved with, I'd fibbed and told him I played a bit but would love to do more. I know, I know! I've got form on bending the truth to suit a situation, albeit in a very harmless way. I'd done it ever since I was a kid auditioning for shows, making myself shorter for a part in *Les Mis*, or telling an auditioning panel that I'd been directed by Roman Polanski when in truth I'd never once set eyes on him. In that respect, I hadn't changed at all. It was typical of me.

When Brian told me he was organising a charity tournament called Golf Rocks, I told him to 'sign me up.' I mean, I had the golf clubs now; how hard could it be? Golf Rocks was in aid of the Bubble Foundation, which raises funds for the treatment of babies and children born with defective immune systems or suffering from leukaemia and severe forms of arthritis. As I've said, I love a challenge, especially when it's attached to a good cause, but I hadn't for a second anticipated how hard it was to learn and play the game. No wonder Kevin looked so alarmed when, on my first lesson, I'd announced that I already had my first tournament booked.

'You do know how hard it is to learn golf, don't you?'

'Oh, it can't be that hard,' I said cheekily.

'Right, come with me,' he said.

I literally missed every ball on that first go, but I enjoyed the process of trying. Kevin was an ex-pro player, and the two of us got on really well, but he knew that the task of getting me ready to play in a golf tournament was monumental in the time we had.

'I've got to do it; it's for charity, and I've committed to it,' I said.

Kevin didn't look as confident as I'd hoped he might. 'Look, I can get you to the stage where you can hit the ball and not make a fool of yourself, but I'm not sure how much more we can do in the time,' he told me.

'That'll do,' I said. 'As long as I can turn up and play and show my support, that's good enough.'

I'd booked ten hours of lessons with him, but the first lesson flew past so quickly that I asked Kevin if we could do another hour straight away. Luckily, he had the time and agreed. As it turned out, I enjoyed the lessons so much I think I ended up using up my ten hours in about three days. By then, I'd really got the bug. After that, ten lessons became twenty, and it got to the point that I was practically living on the golf course – and I was getting pretty good. In the end, my agents were getting a bit pissed off with me because I started turning down work stuff so I could concentrate on my game. I'd get a phone call saying I'd been asked to do a radio show or a slot on a daytime chat show.

'I can't, I'm playing golf,' I'd say.

Eventually, my agent said, 'Denise, you've got to get off the golf course.'

By then, I understood why people got so into the sport, obsessive even. It's great for focus, it keeps you fit, and it's both competitive and relaxing. Being out on the green in the sunshine, smelling the grass and listening to the sound of the swishing clubs and whacking of balls was good for my soul. And yes, golf might not be the cheapest hobby in the world, but it was still a lot cheaper than therapy!

There was also the social aspect. Aside from a new circle of friends, I reconnected with some old ones who also played. Brian McFadden and Ronan Keating were people I'd known from those wild nights out, back in the day. Now here they were, married with kids, swinging a golf club. We laughingly christened it 'clubbing for the middle-aged'. In the old days, we'd have bumped into each other on a dance floor somewhere, holding a beer or a cocktail. This day it was on grass, with a long stick and a little white ball.

I did end up playing at Brian's Golf Rocks tournament. I didn't play particularly well, but that wasn't really the point. It was a light-hearted pro-am match for charity, and everyone enjoyed it.

After that, I played at the Mike Tindall Celebrity Golf Classic, a charity tournament at the Belfry golf resort in Royal Sutton Coldfield, North Warwickshire. I had friends playing there that day, including my good friend Zoe. For some time, Zoe had been trying to set me up with a friend of her boyfriend, Adam, who she thought I might hit it off with. She'd mentioned him on several occasions over the previous months. Still, I really wasn't ready to get out there and date, even on a casual basis. As I travelled around the course with Zoe that day, it suddenly dawned on me that I might finally be ready. I hadn't seen anyone for over a year now – perhaps it was time.

'So, what about this fella you wanted me to meet up with, Zoe,' I said. 'Is he still knocking around?'

Zoe looked surprised. 'I actually don't know, Den. It was ages ago when I first mentioned it to you, so I'm not even sure if he's still single.'

'OK, it's just that I feel like I might be ready to go on a date now,' I said.

'Well, I could certainly find out, then give you the nod if he's still on the market,' she said.

I left it at that, not thinking about it for a while, but after enjoying a day out at the BMW pro-am tournament with my friend Kirsty, I really fancied a night out. Betsy was with her dad, so my diary was all free and clear.

'Do you fancy going out later?' I asked Kirsty. 'I could really do with a night out.'

Kirsty had prior commitments that evening, so my mind went somewhere else.

I wonder if Zoe ever heard back from that fella. Maybe I should give her a call.

It turned out that Zoe had made enquiries but had forgotten to fill me in. This bloke – Eddie – was still single and up for a blind date.

'That's great,' I said. 'Can you find out if he's free tonight?'

'God, you're a bit keen,' Zoe said, laughing. 'Tonight?'

'Yes, I just really fancy a night out, and why not? The only thing is, I won't have time to go home and have a shower, so I'll have to go straight from the tournament, and he'll have to take me as he finds me.'

Zoe agreed to try to arrange a meeting via Adam and asked where we should meet. I was a member of Soho House, which would be relatively chilled and had a no-picture-taking policy for privacy purposes. I decided that Eddie should meet me there. If I'd stopped to think about what I was doing for too long, I probably would have bottled out and cancelled the whole thing. It's not like I was in the habit of going on dates with men I didn't know. All I'd been told was that Eddie was a really lovely bloke who worked in the city – a work colleague of Adam's.

With the date all arranged, I sat in the back of Kirsty's car, putting a bit of make-up on, en route to Greek Street. One look in the mirror told me my hair really needed sorting out. After a day of being windswept on a golf course, I was giving major Bonnie Tyler vibes, circa the 'Total Eclipse of the Heart' era. That would never do.

When Kirsty dropped me off at Soho House, Zoe called to say that she'd passed my number on to Eddie and then gave me his. That way, we could take it from there between the two of us.

'Well, does he know it's me?' I asked. 'Does he know who I am?'

'No,' Zoe said. 'Adam just told him you're a good friend and that you worked in telly. He's got no idea it's you.'

The whole thing felt absolutely bonkers. Me. On a blind date. I was 39 but felt like a 20-year-old all over again.

After a large glass of wine, I sneaked a look at Eddie's WhatsApp picture. It wasn't a clear shot of his face, but him with a teenage girl sitting on his lap on a sunlounger. I thought, *God, I hope that's his daughter!* My WhatsApp photo was of Betsy, so there's no way Eddie would know who I was by looking at that.

Eventually, Eddie messaged me, asking – as he wasn't a member of Soho House – who he should ask for.

'When you get to the desk, just ask for Denise,' I messaged back. 'And by the way, what do you look like?'

The last thing I wanted was to have to wander up to random men in Soho House asking if their name happened to be Eddie. He sent me a picture so I'd know who to look out for. As I stared down at the image, it was clear that the photo on his WhatsApp had been taken a few years before. In fact, my first thought on seeing his current pic was, *God, he looks well old!*

Eddie's side of the story goes something like this. He had no idea who I was and what I looked like. He arrived at Soho House and told the woman at the desk that he was meeting Denise.

'Oh, you mean Denise Van Outen?' the woman said.

'No,' Eddie said, momentarily confused. 'Well, at least I don't think so.'

Eddie tells me that his mind was racing at that point. He knew that Zoe worked in radio and TV and mixed with celebrities. Had she really set him up with Denise Van Outen and not told him? Surely not . . .

'Er . . . the thing is, I don't really know because I'm on a blind date,' Eddie said.

'Oh, right,' the girl said, and there were raised eyebrows between her and her colleague at the front desk. 'Well, this is exciting!'

Meanwhile, someone approached me in the bar and asked if I was expecting someone.

'I am, but I don't really know who,' I said, laughing.

'Well, if he's a man called Eddie, he's here,' the guy told me.

'Right, give me a minute; let me sort my hair out,' I said.

When Eddie finally sat down in front of me, we laughed about the whole thing. On his way upstairs to meet me, he'd messaged Adam to ask if this was all one big joke and he was being set up. He really had no idea who I was until he'd walked into the bar area and seen me.

It's funny, we talked and talked that first evening. It all felt so comfortable, and the conversation just flowed as we downed cocktails together. At one point, Eddie asked me if there was somewhere I'd like to go that I'd never been.

'Well, no one's ever taken me up the Shard,' I said with a grin.

'Well, I'd definitely love to take you up the Shard,' Eddie giggled.

It was clear right then that Eddie and I shared the same risqué sense of humour. Eddie promised faithfully to take me up the Shard the first opportunity he got, and we laughed our way through the rest of the evening. I remember thinking, *This guy gets me, and I think I get him too*. After a year of not seeing anyone and going it alone, it was a nice feeling. We drank and chatted late into the night. In fact, I think we were almost the last to leave. At one point in the evening, after drinking our body weight in cocktails, I'd made the suggestion that we should at least try to eat something. The bill we received as we left Soho House is a testament to that valiant effort. It reads something along the lines of '22 x Margaritas, 1 x Chipolatas'. It was 22 May 2014, and I still have that bill somewhere.

That first night, Eddie stayed at my place in Hampstead. It was so late, and he lived in Essex but had to be in the city the following day. Well, there was no point in him going home at 3am, was there? After that, there was no game playing or trying to be cool. Eddie messaged me and said, 'Let's get another date in the diary', and I was happy to do so. That was the start of my now seven-year-strong relationship with Eddie Boxshall.

• • •

I dated Eddie for quite a while before I introduced Betsy to him. It felt right to take things slow, so that's the way I went with it. One of the best things about my new fella was that he also loved golf. He ended up coming to all my golf tournaments with me, and everyone immediately fell in love with him. In fact, it got to the stage when my golf friends were messaging to ask me if Eddie was coming along to this event or that. They didn't seem all that bothered about whether I was going or not, just Eddie!

I met Eddie's children, Jordan and Leah, at V Festival. Jordan is now 26, and Leah is 22. They're lovely, and if there's anything positive to come out of the recent lockdown situation, it's that I've got to know the two of them even more. With work much quieter for both me and Eddie, we had a lot more free time, and we all got to hang out and cement our new family. In fact, Leah ended up 'locking down' with us here in Essex, where Eddie and I finally bought a house together in 2018. Now we have two beautifully blended families as well as a couple of French bulldogs.

And just in case you're wondering, he's still never taken me up the Shard. Even after all these years!

CHAPTER THIRTY-ONE

The simpler things in life

Now, I'm a girl who has always loved a challenge. In truth, if I set my mind on doing something, it's nigh on impossible for anyone to dissuade me from getting out there and doing it. For instance, not long after Betsy was born, I'd decided it was a good idea to fly to Peru and trek up a mountain. As you do! Well, it was for a good cause.

The idea was to put together a team of amazing women, some of whom had suffered breast cancer, to trek Machu Picchu to raise money and awareness. The trip had actually been arranged before I was pregnant, and although Betsy was only three months old at the time I was due to go, I didn't want to let the team down by bowing out. Charity work is, and always has been, important to me. As well as raising money for good causes, which is the main thing, it's also a great leveller. It gives me balance and makes me realise how lucky I've been to do the things I've done because of my career. You know, private jets with Jon Bon Jovi and Chinese takeaways in Vegas with Elton John – that sort of thing!

* * *

The first really big charity thing I'd done was climbing Mount Kilimanjaro for Comic Relief in 2009. To be honest, it wasn't something I'd ever imagined myself doing, as much as I loved the charity.

This was set to be an epic undertaking. Organised by Take That's Gary Barlow, my climbing mates were Alesha Dixon, Fearne Cotton, Kimberley Walsh, Cheryl, Ben Shephard, Ronan Keating, and Chris Moyles, and we were all expected to train hard before the event.

For that, the credit must go to my dear friend and personal trainer, Nicki Waterman. Nicki is sadly no longer with us, having lost her battle with an aggressive brain tumour in 2016.

Nicki was a great friend and a superb trainer who helped me prepare for what was to be a momentous and gruelling challenge. The central part of my training was, of course, walking, and God, did we walk! I walked further than I ever thought I would during our sessions, with heavy backpacks to emulate the kind of experience I'd be faced with on the mountain, carrying supplies. I also trained with Fearne and Ben, walking for hours around Richmond Park.

An essential part of the prep was learning to cope at a high altitude, which meant training in an altitude chamber. I remember doing this with Chris Moyles, and just how strange it felt. When you're exercising at altitude, your heart rate goes up and the body slows down, so running on a treadmill for a short time felt like a marathon. It was as if there was a weight against me as I ran, and I had to work much harder than I usually would on a regular jog.

As the trek got close, my legs were my mode of transport wherever I went. If I had to get into the West End for work, I'd get my hiking boots and walk from Hampstead rather than getting the tube or a taxi. In fact, when the time came to leave for Tanzania, I felt very prepared for what was to come. Chatting to all my fellow climbers on the journey there, it seemed as though Fearne and I were probably the least nervous and the most excited. Ben Shephard was also extremely gung-ho. My dear friend Kimberley Walsh, on the other hand, was absolutely petrified. Kimberley's Girls Aloud bandmate, Cheryl, was equally nervous. In fact, I spent a fair amount of time geeing them up with words of encouragement and pep talks along the way. Like everyone, the girls were both completely dedicated to the idea of raising money for Comic Relief. Still, as the time came nearer, many of the group were understandably apprehensive about the idea of scaling a massive mountain. I mean, people have died on Kilimanjaro, so this was no small thing.

There was something else in the back of my mind at the time. The doctors had recently told me that to elevate my chances of getting pregnant, I should be as physically fit as possible. So, secretly I had two mountains to climb.

We laughed a lot, especially on the first part of the climb. Alesha Dixon constantly had us in fits. Having joined the group late, she hadn't done as much training as the rest of us. I remember on the first day, she called out to the rest of us, 'Oh, this is just like Hertfordshire!'

She wasn't wrong; it was a bit like strolling in the woods back home at that point. Of course, that all changed as the days went on. Most of us were pretty broken by the end of it.

We all had our moments, and they came at various times. Poor Alesha suffered the most awful stomach cramps at the final stages, going up the mountain on her hands and knees, determined not to give up.

Like many of us, I struggled the higher we got. There was a point one day when my heart was racing so fast I thought it was going to burst out of my chest. I just didn't know how to make it stop. The only thing I could think of was to be still. But even then, my overriding fear was that I would have to give up and be taken back down the mountain, having not completed the journey. I really didn't want that. Luckily, we were all looked after by our wonderful porters. My porter had the nickname Heaven because he said the higher up the mountain he went, the closer to heaven he felt.

Our food was carb-loaded: hearty, healthy porridges, plus loads of pasta and potatoes. Most climbers had brought along loads of healthy snacks: nuts, seeds, protein bars and the like. Not me. I had a backpack full of Percy Pigs and wine gums. I quickly became the 'treat-dealer' asking, 'Does anyone fancy a Percy?' whenever we made a pit stop.

I shared a tent with Fearne, and one of my overriding memories of the trip is her becoming quite seriously ill with altitude sickness.

We'd been briefed by our medics on what to look out for as far as altitude sickness went and told to always keep an eye on our tent-mates for warning signs. On this particular evening, Fearne really didn't look all that well. As we spoke, I could hear that her speech was slurred, and she seemed as though she wasn't entirely with me. At times, she was almost dozing off mid-sentence.

'You're freaking me out a bit, Fearne,' I said. 'Just keep talking to me, can you?'

She told me she was just tired, and it was time for bed anyway. Still, I decided to stay awake and keep an eye on her. I was too scared to sleep and just remember her looking really pale. Mind you, everyone looked pale compared to me; I think I even applied my fake tan halfway up the mountain.

Things got worse, though, and Fearne started vomiting. Obviously this wasn't something and nothing, so I rushed out and called the medic, Raj, who came into the tent to check on her. By then, I was panicking.

'On a scale of one to ten, how bad is she?' I asked him.

'Eight,' he said without pausing.

'Eight?' I yelled, thinking that ten must be death.

'This can happen very quickly,' Raj told me.

He looked after Fearne wonderfully, but poor Raj ended up sleeping wedged between Fearne and me in what must have looked like some bizarre mountainside threesome. Thankfully, Fearne recovered. The two of us still talk and even laugh about it now; the memory of us all crammed together in a two-man tent, with poor Fearne as sick as a dog, three-quarters of the way up Kilimanjaro.

We've stayed really good friends, and she's since told me she can't imagine what might have happened if I hadn't been with her that night. It was certainly something I won't forget in a hurry.

The summit climb was particularly tough, walking for many hours through the night on a tiny track. We were close to the edge of the mountain, without seeing it, and had to walk slowly due to the altitude. With my head torch on, all I could see was the feet of the person in front of me. At daybreak, when we reached the summit, a group photo was, of course, called for, but it was minus 20 in a glacier, and we didn't all arrive at the same time.

It was no surprise that Ben was one of the first to reach the top, and I was hot on the heels of Fearne. I remember Kimberley and Cheryl completing the last bit together, clinging to one another with tears in their eyes.

'Come on, girls,' I called out to them. 'You're made of tougher stuff than this!'

Ultimately, we just wanted to hold up our banner and get down; it was much too cold to hang around. Looking back, I wish I'd stayed up there for longer. It was such an incredible, life-changing moment, something I never imagined I could have done. Still, apart from the fact it was bloody freezing, I, like everyone else, was exhausted.

What I hadn't expected, however, was how hard it was going to be coming down. I was using a different part of my legs, so my shins were killing me all the way back. We'd done it, though. What an achievement.

All in all, Kilimanjaro was an amazing experience, not least because we raised £3.5 million for Comic Relief, and the fact that I made some lifelong friends in Kimberley and Fearne. Still, I think I can safely say that 70 per cent of the team would say they wouldn't do it again. Not me though; I got the bug!

My experience up a mountain gave me the urge to do more things, to be more adventurous. Since then, these far-flung adventures for causes have been real bright spots in my life, and I look forward to them. Like many people, it's one of the things that I've found really frustrating during the pandemic, not being able to get away to experience other parts of the world. I've missed those trips.

• • •

After that first journey, I started to organise trips myself through a company called Charity Challenge. I've since trekked the Great Wall of China, and Machu Picchu, walked and cycled across the Himalayas and also Rajasthan. It's a beautiful and incredible way to see the world and something I'm so grateful for.

Of course, the training for one of these treks is a commitment in itself. For the Rajasthan trip, we were going to be peddling over challenging terrain in the sweltering sun, so plenty of hard bike training was in order. That trip was christened the 'Essex to India' cycle. I took along Lydia Bright from *The Only Way Is Essex* and another friend, Kirsty Williams. I didn't really know Lydia, despite having done the voice-over for *TOWIE* for some time. We met at an event where I told her about my plans to cycle across India.

'God, I'd love to do something like that,' she said.

'Well, why don't you? Why don't you do it with me?'

The goal was to raise money for Great Ormond Street Hospital to help provide equipment and fund research into new and better treatments for sick children. We started training for the trip in January 2012 with hybrid road and mixed terrain bikes and top-of-the-range indoor exercise bikes. I never imagined I would, but after a few training sessions I got pretty hooked on cycling. Still, that's me, I suppose. If I'm going to do something, I throw myself into it completely.

During our mammoth ride, we cycled for 300 miles through unbearable heat. Most days, we were on the road for 6–8 hours, but we'd be winding our way through villages along the way.

Jaipur, the capital of Rajasthan, is popularly known as the Pink City, and is the most colourful city in India; a pulsating, crazy mix of Indian culture, both traditional and modern. To me, everything about it felt magical. I loved seeing the hustle and bustle of it all: young guys getting their hair cut in the middle of the street; vibrant wedding parties trailing alongside us; cows crossing the street as we cycled past. There was a visual feast waiting around every corner.

It wasn't just the heat that made things challenging, but the unfinished roads. We had to swap between two bikes: a mountain bike for rough terrain and road bikes for the smoother roads. I always wore two pairs of cycling shorts with gel inserts, so I'd usually end up walking around looking like I'd had bum implants. I imagine I looked a bit like an Essex Kim Kardashian from behind.

I laughed a lot on that trip and really bonded with Lydia, making a friend for life. We ate fantastic food, stayed in a maharaja's palace, and giggled our way across India in the sweltering heat. Best of all, we'd always finish our day with a well-deserved Bombay Sapphire gin and tonic.

On any of the adventures I've been on, I've never really felt like I wanted to give up. Still, if there was one moment that I ever came close to it, it was on the cycle ride across the Himalayas. This was the one I did to raise money for brain tumour research in memory of Nicki Waterman in 2017.

•   •   •

Ever since the injury I'd suffered on *Strictly*, banging my head and jolting my neck in rehearsal for the final, I'd suffered fairly regular spells of shoulder and neck pain. Sometimes the pain was quite bad, but at other times it was relatively manageable. Still, it was now three years on from the original injury, so I should have known something had gone seriously awry.

Rather than addressing it, I just adapted to it. I suppose I even got used to it. When it was bad, I'd try not to sleep on my left side or move in a certain way. I worked around the pain, and avoided any kind of exercise or activity that might cause it to flare up. It was stupid, really, but on some days, I felt fine, so I just kept going. I told myself it would get better soon enough and that I didn't need to see anyone about it.

As time went on, the pain got worse, and when one day I found myself struggling to turn my head to the left, I thought I might be in trouble. By then, I was on strong painkillers to mask the pain, but even just sitting down and watching TV was uncomfortable. I always seemed so busy, though, and although I told myself that I would get it sorted, there never seemed to be enough hours in the day. Looking back, I suppose I'd been burying my head in the sand for ages, but then hindsight is a wonderful thing, isn't it?

Breaking point came when I found myself struggling to pick up my own child. Then on my way to the car one day, I tripped up a small step outside my house and froze in the most excruciating pain, unable to move, speak or do anything. Finally, I had to admit that something was seriously wrong.

After a scan at the hospital, I finally found myself in front of a doctor, a surgeon called Adrian Casey. God, I remember at one point lying in a foetal position on the floor of his office, in absolute agony, terrified of what might be happening to me. I was in a real state.

Mr Casey took no time in telling me that he needed to operate as soon as possible.

'I can't believe you've been walking around like this, Denise. You are one very lucky lady!'

As Mr Casey spoke, I could hardly believe what I was hearing. He told me that I'd slipped two discs in my spinal column and that I was only a millimetre away from total paralysis from the neck down. A slight jolt or slip at that point would have almost certainly meant permanent injury. The way he described it was that my scan showed that my spine had been squashed in the same way a marshmallow would be if you stepped on it. That was pretty sobering, I can tell you.

The resulting operation was quite major spinal surgery: anterior cervical discectomy and fusion including bone grafting, the aim of which was to remove the herniated discs in the neck. They had to go in through the front of my neck and remove my voice box to get to the damaged discs, which also meant substantial scarring on my neck. Before the operation, I'd been warned there was a possibility of some damage to my voice, and that I could even lose my upper range.

Mercifully, the operation fixed the problem, but I went through plenty of painful moments and 18 months of quite intense physiotherapy, plus vocal exercises to get my voice back into shape and help prevent any lasting impairment. That said, I still have some nerve damage on my left side, which looks like it may be permanent. In fact, someone could put a cigarette out on my left arm and I probably wouldn't be able to feel it.

Like the lunatic I am, I did a charity walk across London for a breast cancer charity in memory of my nan just a week or so after the operation. Of course, I asked Mr Casey if he thought it would be OK first.

'I'd say it wasn't the best idea, but seeing the way you are, I'm pretty sure it would be falling on deaf ears with you,' he said. 'Just make sure you walk very slowly and that nobody knocks you or bangs into you along the way.'

In the end, my friends and cousins who did the walk with me created a protective ring around me just to make sure I didn't end up back on the operating table. I proudly completed the walk and got my gold medal, all with a chorus of 'you're absolutely mental' ringing in my ears.

Once that was done, I did take time to rest up and do what the doctor told me. I had to. I don't know what I would have done without Betsy's child carer, Laura, during that period of rest.

She was so hands-on with Betsy, doing almost everything while practically nursing me through it. An absolute angel.

As I was starting to get back on my feet, I got the chance to see just how lucky I'd been, close-up. Leafing through a local newspaper, I came across an article written by a young woman talking about her best friend who really needed help. She'd suffered almost exactly the same injury I had after slipping down the stairs while chasing her two-year-old toddler. Things had become very tough for her as she was now incapacitated.

I contacted the writer of the article through Twitter, asking how her friend was. Unfortunately, her friend's spinal injury had gone that tiny but irrevocable bit deeper, and she'd been left paralysed for life, aged 27. Now, the woman who'd written the piece was trying to raise money to convert her friend's home to meet the needs of her and her family. I ended up setting up a Depop page under an assumed name and selling off loads of my clothes to help raise funds for the things she needed. It really moved me hearing what this poor young woman had gone through, and meeting her truly brought it home to me how fortunate I'd been.

● ● ●

Having had such a serious operation meant that, leading up to the cycle trip across the Himalayas for Nicki, I hadn't been able to train at the level that I usually would, and it seemed I'd underestimated how long my recovery would take. The region is very hilly and mountainous, and there were times I really struggled with the climbs. On several occasions, I ended up getting off the bike and pushing it up steep slopes, gritting my teeth and sweating buckets. It wasn't just me; my cycling partners – which included Kate Thornton, Michelle Heaton from Liberty X, and Lydia's sister, Georgia Bright – also found it gruelling. Nicki's daughter Alex also took part in the challenge.

It wasn't just the physical side of things that almost beat me either. I'd determinedly organised this challenge for the dear friend I'd lost, which meant that there was a lot of emotion at play. I desperately didn't want to let Nicki down or fail the challenge I'd set myself in her memory. Looking back, I think I was still very much grieving for her, so the combination of mental and physical anguish was sometimes almost too much to bear.

There were times when I'd stop and get off the bike, lift my head to the heavens and talk to Nicki as if she were there with me. 'I'm sorry I'm finding this so hard, Nicki. I'm doing my best. I really am.'

On my other treks and bike rides, I'd felt like I was one of the stronger ones, always helping and encouraging those who needed it. But this time, I found it tough, and it was me who needed help. It wasn't something I was used to.

We were all overjoyed when we crossed the finish line after 187 miles. I'd fallen off the bike and twisted my knee, Kate got heat stroke and Georgia had several panic attacks along the way, but we'd done it! All in all, we raised £43,000 for the Brain Tumour Charity, all in honour of Nicki.

• • •

I grew to love India on those trips: the people, the colours, the smells and the sights. It's a place that's so magical and spiritual. Machu Picchu is another place that fills you with awe. Looking out across a fifteenth-century Inca city high in the mountains of Peru is breathtaking beyond comprehension. Of course, I'd seen pictures of it, but nothing prepared me for actually experiencing it first-hand. How did they build it? It's incredible.

Writing about all this has made me realise how much things have changed since Covid hit. Taking trips across beautiful, faraway places feels another world away amid a global pandemic. I've found myself wondering if I'll ever be able to do those things again.

What really surprised me during those adventures is how much happiness there is in simplicity. How a person can be happy with the most basic essentials and little to none of life's luxuries. And when I say luxuries, I mean everyday things we simply take for granted. I have always come back from those trips changed somehow, perhaps a bit more thoughtful about what really matters.

Look, I'm not going to pretend I don't end up slipping back into my old ways. Like many of us, I don't think twice about popping out and spending too much on overpriced cups of coffee most of the time. I'm certainly not averse to occasionally treating myself to a handbag I don't need.

That said, those changes and the things I've experienced do stay with me. They've helped me see the beauty in the simpler things in life. I've seen families living high in the mountains, with nothing but the basic necessities – but they were smiling, and they were living fulfilled, happy lives. That's why I'm still keen to do more and to see more. I'd never want to lose the joy of those experiences, especially if you can help others while doing it. I know how lucky and privileged I am, and if I can share some of that and pass it on then why not?

CHAPTER THIRTY-TWO

More than just a touch of impostor syndrome

I've had a bit of a TV bonanza over the past few years, landing on a few iconic shows I never imagined I would. It started in 2015 when I joined the cast of *EastEnders*. I think it's safe to say that if there was any gig that had been on my bucket list of shows to do, this would have been it. I'd loved *EastEnders* right back from when I was a kid. The glory days of Den and Ange and Pauline and Arthur; it was very popular in the Outen house back in the eighties. I'd always thought that it would be a nice role to have when I was a bit older, behind the bar at the Queen Vic, just like the brilliant Barbara Windsor as formidable landlady, Peggy Mitchell.

A close friend of mine, Chris Parker, had been in the show from 2002–05, playing Spencer Moon. Chris is now a media lawyer living in LA. Knowing him as I do, I felt like I'd gotten a little insight into how it all worked at *EastEnders* over the years. Still, I don't think anyone can ever really be prepared for just how full-on it can be, working on a show which airs four nights a week.

There had been whispers about me doing a cameo role on the show for years, going right back to the nineties. Still, for one reason or another, it never panned out. Now, I'd been given a chance to play the character of businesswomen Karin Smart. She arrives on Albert Square searching for Phil Mitchell and ends up in bed with Max Branning. It was only a four-episode stint over the space of a month, but certainly enough time for a classic 'Enders dodgy deal and a bit of seduction. It was a fun part, but I suppose typical of the sort I'd get cast in. As in, five minutes after I'm on-screen, the clothes are off! I certainly got to display something, but I'm not sure it was my acting skills.

I had been looking forward to doing the show, but it wasn't what I'd expected. I'd been used to working on shows with a happy, buzzy atmosphere, and during my time on *EastEnders*, that wasn't really the case. I hadn't been aware of anything before I started, but there seemed to be some underlying tension once I was on set. Not towards me, thankfully. Apart from one cast member, who wasn't particularly welcoming, I didn't have too much of a problem. It was just that the mood was a bit sombre for my liking. From what some of the cast members told me, it had been that way for a while between a few of the actors.

There seemed to be a certain amount of discontent too. I remember one of the female cast members warning me, 'You're going to fucking hate this.' I'll admit, it did put me on the back foot a little bit; I felt pretty uneasy sometimes. I'd breeze on to the set all bubbly and ready to go, only to meet with people who looked like they didn't want to be there. Of course, this wasn't everyone by any means, but I think the unhappy actors seemed to be dictating the mood and the atmosphere for the rest. From what I've gathered, it was just bad timing and a bit of a rough patch. Still, it definitely wasn't my favourite work experience. It put me off the idea of wanting to work on a soap or a long-running drama altogether. I didn't really make any new friends; I just did my stint, and then I was gone.

I've always had a bit of a laugh at the jobs I worked on and usually made friends and stayed in touch with one or two people. Making a film or a TV show can be quite an intensive process. Consequently, relationships can be formed relatively quickly. I've always been one for making friends on jobs; in fact, I think I've sometimes been a bit too keen. I recall telling Tamara once how I struggled to keep up with all my friends during a busy period and how guilty I felt when I failed to get back to someone speedily.

'Den, every time you go on a job you leave with new friends, sometimes more than one. You need to stop making friends,' she said. 'Just keep a handful of friends rather than befriending everyone you meet.'

I do find that difficult, at least most of the time.

Despite my reluctance at the idea of working on another soap, I caved when it came to the chance of a part in *Neighbours* in 2019. The producers at Fremantle, who make the show, asked me to record an audition tape when they were looking to cast a new British character on the show. My role was Prue Wallace, the hippy-dippy mother of Harlow Robinson, the on-screen granddaughter of the legendary *Neighbours* character Paul Robinson, and the real-life daughter of another *Neighbours* legend, Jason Donovan. My brief was to be like Joanna Lumley in *Absolutely Fabulous*, so it felt like something I'd enjoy. I was also going to get to work in Australia, on actual Ramsay Street!

I'd known Jason since I was about 17 when he was starring in *Joseph and the Amazing Technicolour Dreamcoat* in the West End. My mum was working as a chaperone for the children in the show. Of course, I messaged him with the news about working with his daughter, Jemma, on *Neighbours*. She was only 19 at the time and had recently left her family and relocated to Melbourne to take on the role of Harlow on a three-year contract. Jason was thrilled that I was going out to work with her and could bring a bit of home along with me. Jemma hadn't been away from home before, and knowing she'd be homesick, Jason was comforted to know that he'd have a friend out there looking out for her.

I filmed my first scenes in London with Stefan Dennis and Rebekah Elmaloglou in a London park. Stefan remembered me from his time as a guest on *The Big Breakfast* in the nineties.

'You're the bed girl!' he'd said on meeting me, recalling the numerous celebrity interviews I'd conducted from the show's infamous bed.

I'd smiled. 'That's me!'

Three weeks later, I flew to Melbourne to start filming at Global Television Studios, Nunawading, and at Pin Oak Court, the very famous, real-life cul-de-sac that doubles as Ramsay Street.

TV presenter Richard Arnold, who also had a cameo role on the show, had recommended a lovely little apartment complex in South Yarra for the duration of my stay, and pretty soon I was all settled in, ready for a month of filming. What I didn't know at the time was that *Neighbours* is known for being the fastest-moving soap in the world, shooting the greatest number of episodes in a given time frame. The schedules are crazy but brilliantly organised. There are two units on the go the whole time, one location and one interior. These units might be filming different episodes simultaneously, so you might well find yourself filming two separate episodes on two different locations on one day. As I was only there for a limited time and had quite a lot to get through, I worked very long hours. Plus, it was August at the time, so mid-winter in Australia. Some of my friends had suggested I'd be basking on the beach the whole time I was there, or learning to surf, but it was bloody freezing. Every morning, I'd be up at the crack, picked up at six o'clock and in the make-up chair by seven. Most mornings, I'd be into shooting scenes by 7.30, and I'd often be going right through till eight, sometimes nine o'clock at night. After that, I'd head back to my apartment with a pile of scripts to learn for upcoming episodes and the following day's shoots.

Despite all that, *Neighbours* was a wonderful experience. I couldn't have been made to feel more welcome by the cast. They were all so lovely. The first time I'd stood on the set of Albert Square for *EastEnders* had been iconic, and being in the Waterhole and on *Neighbour*'s famous cul-de-sac felt equally so. These locations have been on the telly-box in my lounge for so many years, and now here I was, right inside it all.

One of the funniest things was how, every Friday, the *Neighbours* tour bus would go past, full of fans who'd paid for a tour of the show's locations. Inevitably, many of the people on the bus were British fans who all looked a bit confused when they spotted me on the set. At that point, my appearing in the show hadn't really been made public, so you can imagine the confusion of some of the Brits on the bus.

'It's Denise Van Outen! What's she doing here? This is *Neighbours*!'

When I did have some downtime of an evening, some of the cast took me out for dinner or drinks. I became very close with Colette Mann, who'd played bartender Sheila Canning in the show for nearly ten years. Colette is great fun; a proper old-school Aussie actress who's appeared in so many famous Australian TV shows across her long career, including *The Flying Doctors* and the late-night classic *Prisoner: Cell Block H*. While I was there, I gave Colette *Some Girl I Used to Know* to read. She adored it and told me she'd like to direct it if I ever thought about taking the show to Melbourne. That's something I'd love to explore, as the Aussies do enjoy a bit of British theatre.

I ended up staying longer than planned to be part of a late-night version of the show – *Neighbours: End Game* – in celebration of the soap's thirty-fifth anniversary. This racier package with more adult content ran concurrently with the teatime show over a week in March 2020.

As well as a bedroom scene that would never have happened in the regular version, I also got blown up in a car bomb during one of the episodes. Still, despite my supposed fiery end, there was talk that I might end up coming back for another stint on Ramsay Street. As the show's producer Nat Lynch told me, in the land of soap, if you don't actually see a body, there's no reason to think a character has truly been finished off. Who's to say I was actually still in the car when the bomb went off? Unfortunately, a global pandemic and Australia's strict lockdown have put paid to Prue's return anytime soon, which is very sad. In fact, I ended up watching all my *Neighbours* scenes on TV right at the start of the UK lockdown. It brought back lovely memories; I had a brilliant time on the show, and I would love to return one day.

• • •

I have to say, one of the best things to come out of my recent TV work was getting the unexpected opportunity to sing onstage again. Mind you, I'd never have imagined I'd have to dress up as an animal in the process!

I'd watched the Australian version of *The Masked Singer* while I was filming *Neighbours*, so when I was asked to take part in the UK version, I jumped at it. The utter ridiculousness of a show where famous people from across all fields of sport and entertainment adorned outrageous costumes and sang in disguise, while a panel of judges tried to guess who on earth they were, was right up my street.

While some of the other celebrity contestants had no idea what they were signing up for, I knew exactly what to expect, having been a fan of the Aussie version. My character was Fox. I loved dressing up in my slinky costume, plus doing all the vocal training that would enable me to project my singing voice in the outlandish costume while not giving away my identity. Happily, there had been no lasting damage or change to my voice after the spinal surgery I'd had a few years before, despite my voice box having been taken out and put back again. The nicest thing about the show for me was that it laid to rest some of the old demons I had about singing and about my voice. I'd always been reasonably confident when singing as a character, from Éponine in *Les Mis* and Maureen in *Rent* to Roxie Hart in *Chicago*. In those shows, I could immerse myself in the part and hide behind a character while performing. It was as if it wasn't me singing, and therefore I couldn't be judged. It was why one-woman entities like *Tell Me on a Sunday* and *Some Girl I Used to Know* were so perfect and enjoyable for me; I could sing my heart out as somebody else without feeling exposed. My problem always came when I was singing as Denise Van Outen. Just me. It was this weird fear I'd had for years about believing in myself as a singer, a doubt in my ability. Maybe it was a knock-on effect from my past, being cast as 'the pretty one' in Those 2 Girls, back in the day, rather than the serious singer. Maybe it was the memory of Jay standing in his kitchen telling me that I'd make a fool of myself. I'd somehow convinced myself that I was a TV presenter that did a bit of singing but didn't deserve to be taken seriously because I wasn't a good enough singer. Whatever the case, I definitely had more than just a touch of impostor syndrome.

You might think that being dressed up as a giant sexy bejewelled fox would be the most perfect cover of all. However, it was still me underneath, and when it came down to it, it was my voice that was being judged by a panel. The fact that I did so well on the show and got so far really did the trick. Every new song I did gave me more confidence, especially with the great feedback

I was getting. When presenter Davina McCall said my rendition of 'On My Own' gave her goosebumps, I felt like a kid at Christmas; I was buzzing.

My experience on *The Masked Singer* has led me to conclude that I would like to finally record an album of my own, as Denise Van Outen. To this end, I've been recording songs with my dear friend – and Kylie Minogue's musical director – Steve Anderson. I've been surprised at how much I'm enjoying the results. Listening back to the songs, which range from pop to theatrical, there are none of the usual internal monologues about not being good enough to just be me. Who'd have thought that I'd finally find confidence in myself by donning an animal head and singing on Saturday-night telly?

CHAPTER THIRTY-THREE

I've always found it's better to be honest

In 2017–18, I enjoyed being a regular on the panel of *Loose Women* and, of course, made more new friends there. I got closer to Andrea McLean, who I've always really liked, and Nadia Sawalha was a massive help to me with all the issues surrounding Betsy's learning difficulties, which had come to light in the early years of her life. Nadia was also great when it came to helping us choose a new school for Betsy, and, as she homeschooled her children, she offered the most brilliantly helpful tips and strategies for homeschooling Betsy during lockdown. I'll always be grateful to her for that.

As well as having ADHD and finding it hard to focus, Betsy has mild forms of several conditions: dyslexia, dyscalculia (difficulty with numbers) and dyspraxia, which affects motor skills and coordination. These all came to light gradually, often through my wonderful child carer, Laura, who helped me so much in those first years when I was a working single mum. Laura was very astute when it came to that sort of thing; she also ran a nursery and had vast experience in childcare. I remember her talking to me about Betsy and maths.

'She just doesn't get it. She can't seem to make sense of anything to do with numbers.'

'Isn't that just because she's young?' I said.

'No, I think there's a real issue here,' Laura said. 'Even the simplest thing is like gobbledegook to her when it comes to counting.'

At nursery school, it wasn't long before the teacher started pointing out specific issues to me; little things they thought I needed to look out for, particularly regarding Betsy's lack of focus.

All this led to a fair few appointments at the Portland, who did all sorts of tests and assessments. I consider myself extremely fortunate to be in a position that I could make this happen. I've seen first-hand how frustrating it can be when children with conditions like Betsy's, or even more pronounced conditions, are swept aside and left to fend for themselves. I was pretty vocal about what we were going through on social media. Hearing other parents' stories is always so helpful. I was surprised by how many people there were, asking how I'd gone about getting a proper diagnosis because they'd been struggling with getting support as a result.

I knew only too well how it felt to be lacking support. At Betsy's first school, I was unhappy with some of the ways they dealt with her. For instance, she was taken out of the music class for intervention and extra help with her work. I assumed this was fine, but when I was invited to attend a school concert, I realised that the school really hadn't thought it through. I sat in the audience watching my child sitting on her own at the side of the stage while all the other kids in her class performed in the concert. I tried to put myself in her place and think about how she must be feeling. It was as if she'd been singled out, like there was something wrong with her. I accepted that, yes, this was a music concert, and her sense of timing might not be as good as the other kids'. She also struggled to learn and retain things as quickly as some of her classmates. However, couldn't they at least have given her another job to do? Give her a triangle if she can't play the recorder, but don't just sit her at the side of the stage on her own and tell her she can't join in.

I took Betsy out of the school and found a specialist school in Finchley, but even that didn't feel like the right fit for her needs. Her time there was short-lived anyway, as the school couldn't get the funding needed to stay afloat. By then, she was getting a bit older, and despite everything she was dealing with, there were so many positives. Eddie has encouraged me to be a bit more relaxed about it.

'She's got learning issues, but it's not that bad,' he said. 'She's such a great, funny little character.'

I smiled in agreement. 'She's definitely got strengths in other areas, that's for sure.'

'Exactly,' Eddie said. 'You've just got to find her somewhere that will play to those strengths, and that might not need to be a specialist school.'

Betsy now goes to a wonderful little school in Essex. It's an independent school that has support within, while not specialising in those kinds of conditions. Here, she's come on in leaps and bounds. She knows the areas where she struggles, and she even jokes about them with me.

'Mum, I know I'm rubbish at maths, but I don't want to be a mathematician, so I'm not bothered,' she says.

I've always found it's better to be honest, and talk to her about it, rather than pretend it's not there. I want her to know what she's dealing with but not be ashamed or embarrassed about it. I tell her that if anyone is mean to her about her conditions, she should stand up for herself and say, 'I just learn things in a different way to you. It doesn't mean that I'm any smarter or any less smart. I've just got a different way of learning.'

I'd always suffered terrible problems with anything mathematical and with problem-solving. Even now, Eddie will say to me, 'How can you not work that out?' when it comes to a problem, mathematical or otherwise, that he finds very simple.

'Ah, but look at all the things I *can* do!' is my stock answer.

To be honest, I think if I hadn't had such a strong focus on the performing arts when I was a child, things might have turned out very differently. Luckily, the realisation that I was a creative and not an academic came early to me, so I didn't beat myself up too much about the things I couldn't do well. This has helped both Lee and I positively handle Betsy's conditions. We always had to play to her strengths rather than focus on the things she struggled with.

Betsy has sensory toys and fidget-clickers to help with the fact that she always needs to be moving – they help with focus. I sometimes think I need to get Eddie one too. He's a fidgety sod; there's always one part of him moving. If he's sitting at the table, I can usually feel his leg jiggling up and down. We're a family of fidgets.

CHAPTER THIRTY-FOUR

'It's all right, this telly lark, isn't it?'

I imagined I'd do *Celebrity Gogglebox* with one of my famous friends; someone I had a bit of banter with, a pairing that the viewers might get a kick out of. I was quite surprised when Channel 4 told me they wanted Eddie to be my TV couch potato partner. They'd seen us do an interview together and thought he was hilarious and that we'd be a great team on the show. Eddie was quite apprehensive at first, not having done any TV work, but I told him he'd be fine if he was just himself in front of the camera. That was what people wanted to see. It's funny; it took Eddie quite a while for the penny to drop at just how famous he'd become after the show went out. After the first series aired, we made the second one during the first lockdown, so we never got out much to gauge the viewing public's reaction to us. I suppose I knew what to expect, but Eddie didn't have a clue what being famous meant.

His first real taste of it was when he went to get fish and chips. He arrived back with a big grin on his face. "'Ere, look! They gave me extra chips 'cause the woman recognised me from *Gogglebox*. It's all right, this telly lark, isn't it?'

• • •

Like everyone, I've found various aspects of the pandemic and subsequent lockdowns tough. For someone like me who finds it hard to sit still and always has to be doing something, the first few weeks were bloody torturous. I could see it coming, as we all could. In the weeks leading up to the first lockdown, I performed in my cabaret show at Proud Cabaret on Embankment. Proud is a venue that showcases singers, circus performers, burlesque artists, drag queens and all sorts of other fabulous performers. It's set in a glamorous, dimly lit underground club that's straight out of the forties. You can go there to have dinner or sip cocktails while witnessing a unique, colourful show that's usually sexy and outrageous without being sleazy. It's a great venue, and I'd come on board for a series of shows as the host and headline act. I loved performing and engaging with the audience at Proud; I'd so missed that side of my career. Of course, it was heartbreaking for all the performers when we had to shut up shop due to the pandemic; we were all devastated.

Watching the news every day, at first it seemed like it was all happening to other people, but then we lost people we knew. A close friend's father died, and then the lovely lady who worked in our local shop passed away. Most devastating of all was that Mum lost her best friend Janet, who'd been a dear friend to our family for many years. Losing people we knew, or people we might see every other day, really brought it home. This thing was everywhere. It didn't matter who or where you were; it touched us all in so many ways.

On the other hand, I will always try to find positives in any given situation. For me, homeschooling Betsy wasn't the easiest thing in the world, but I enjoyed getting to see her learn and complete her work. We drop our kids off at school every day and rarely get to see how they function in a class environment, but now I was getting a glimpse into that side of her. I should imagine many parents experienced something similar. For me, the most surprising thing was how alike I discovered we were; I learned almost as much about myself as I did about her. As I said, I've never been diagnosed with ADHD. Still, the more aware of it I've become, through Betsy and through other children I've encountered with the condition, the more traits I recognise in myself. Obsessing over certain things and hyper-fixating are both characteristics associated with the condition. That was something I could really identify with. I thought about my recent golf obsession, which had started off as a hobby but then quickly became everything. I'd immersed myself in it totally, to the point where I just wanted to be on a golf course all the time, even at the expense of work and other commitments.

I was two weekends, four shows, into my run at Proud Cabaret as lockdown approached. There'd been no official announcement yet, but I knew it was coming. After that second weekend, instead of leaving all my stuff in my dressing room as I usually would have, I packed everything up and took it with me. One of the doormen laughed at me.

'Where are you going with all that? Are you not coming back?'

'We'll be in lockdown this time next week,' I said.

'No, we won't,' he said.

'I'm telling you, it's going to happen.'

Before it all went down, my last job was playing the voice of opinionated inventor/scientist Professor Polonium in the Fireman Sam movie, *Norman Price and the Mystery in the Sky*. I thoroughly enjoyed doing the voice-over sessions for the film, but something didn't feel quite right as time went on. For a start, I had a really runny nose. This was followed by bouts of exhaustion and feeling really shivery. As I arrived at the recording studio one morning, I felt like I used to after I'd been to an all-night rave, except I'd had a whole night's sleep. Even with everything that was going on, I didn't put two and two together or suspect that I might have Covid. As far as I knew, I hadn't been around anyone who'd had it, and the list of potential symptoms and ways of catching it was still a bit sketchy. Everyone was talking about breathing difficulties and a cough, neither of which I was suffering from. While I was in the booth recording that morning, I asked if the heating could be turned up.

'Are you joking?' the studio assistant said. 'It's like Jamaica in there; the heating's full-on.'

'But I'm freezing,' I moaned.

I think that's when I really knew things weren't right, cough or no cough. By then, I was achy, and my nose was streaming. This was on the Tuesday before the government announced that the country was going into complete lockdown, right before Mother's Day, 2020.

Back at home, my sense of smell wasn't what it should have been. I have this one strong perfume that I have to be sparing with. It's lovely but quite potent, and if I pile it on, Eddie always says it gives him a headache and makes him feel sick. It's actually my favourite perfume, so that's nice!

On the first morning of the lockdown, I remember thinking that I needed to 'keep myself nice' despite being shut in the house, so I put a lick of make-up on and spritzed myself with my favourite fragrance.

'Oh my God, you stink!' Eddie said as I came out of the bedroom and descended the stairs to the kitchen. 'You've well overdone it with that gear; you're making me feel sick.'

'Really? I can't smell it at all,' I said, slightly miffed.

I went back upstairs and tried spraying it on my wrist, inhaling deeply. Nothing. Before long, I had my head jammed in the fridge, trying to smell all the food. Nothing. What was worse was I couldn't taste anything either. I could tell if something was hot or cold, but nothing had any flavour. It was bizarre.

It was then that I phoned the NHS helpline, who told me that a loss of smell and taste wasn't a known symptom of Covid.

They told me to keep an eye on things but didn't think I needed to go for a test at that point. It was only a few months later that I turned out to be antibody-positive when I was tested before a job. I'd had Covid without knowing it, but, of course, by the time I had the tests, the loss of taste and smell were known symptoms.

During the summer, when things opened up, I managed to finish my run at Proud. In fact, my show at Proud Cabaret was the first in London to open after the lockdown. The venue spent money going to great pains to make sure everything was as safe as it could be, with limited capacity and mandatory mask-wearing when you weren't sitting at your table. It was pretty momentous being the first performance venue to open up again. I do remember stepping out onstage for the first time in months, feeling very emotional. The audience were so enthusiastic, so hungry for what they'd been missing: live entertainment and the buzz of a show. A night out at last. Given how much the arts and theatre had suffered, it felt quite special to be working with a team of people again. However, it was sadly relatively short-lived because of the second lockdown.

CHAPTER THIRTY-FIVE

Was I not enough? A new and unexpected chapter

My book was originally due at the end of 2021, but then my seemingly perfect life took a sharp turn, and a new and unexpected chapter opened up before my eyes. It isn't a happy one, and, in writing, I'm mindful that there are families and children to consider, including my own. So, I'll be as honest as I can be.

In the seven-plus years I was with Eddie, I never secretly checked his phone or emails. I know it's a thing in some relationships, but it's something I've never done with anyone. I assume honesty in a relationship, as I did with him. In early November 2021, something happened to change that.

It was a Friday afternoon, and I was rushing around after the school run, getting ready to head to London for my show at Proud Cabaret. The previous week, I'd filmed a little skit with my fellow performers there. It had since been edited, so I'd invited them all to my dressing room at five o'clock to premiere the finished video. Now, I'm not tech-savvy – I do everything on my phone – and for this, I needed a bigger screen. I'd asked Eddie if I could use his iPad, and he'd agreed, but when I was due to leave, he didn't seem ready to hand it over.

'I'm charging it,' he said.

'I'll charge it when I get there,' I said. 'I'll be late if I don't leave now.'

Eddie took ages upstairs with the iPad; it struck me that he was stalling for some reason. I laughed to myself, thinking he might be getting rid of something he didn't want me to see – some dodgy memes or banter with his mates. When I arrived at my London flat and met my friend Alfie, I joked that we should take a peek at what Eddie had seen fit to delete.

I guess I wasn't expecting to see much, perhaps just something that made me giggle. That wasn't the case. In among photos that had been deleted from the photo library, but not from the 'recently deleted' folder, there was a screenshot ... of a woman's breasts – and they definitely weren't mine! As well as the screenshot, there was a flirty text exchange between Eddie and this woman, which, of course, set off alarm bells.

'Best get ready for bed', the message – sent at midnight – accompanying the picture said.

There was also a name and phone number, clearly visible.

I noticed that the exchange had happened the same week I'd booked a mini-break for Eddie and me, at the apartment I'd bought us in Spain. I'd been working hard all year; being the main breadwinner meant saying yes to most jobs just so I could pay to get the house finished. Eddie and I planned on getting married in 2022, and I loved the idea of a simple registry office ceremony followed by a big party at the house for friends and family. I even made light of my determination in a newspaper interview, saying that I wanted to get my patio sorted before thinking about a wedding!

As it turned out, Eddie decided not to come to Spain because he didn't feel well. While sympathetic, I was slightly confused about why he couldn't chill with me beside the pool but could still manage to go to the pub.

There was more. After I got back from Spain, Eddie told me there had been a 'bit of trouble' with a woman he'd met in a pub. I didn't know it then, but the trouble in question apparently involved a confrontation between Eddie and the woman's boyfriend.

At the time, I just rolled my eyes and thought little of it. But now, looking at his iPad, I asked myself, was this the reason he didn't go to Spain? Was this the reason he was always going out doused in aftershave?

There were other pictures in the deleted files folder. Selfies of Eddie with a different woman in a bar – I could tell she was different by the boobs! These were taken on a day when Eddie said he was in London for a business meeting. That might have been true, but he certainly hadn't mentioned meeting a woman for a drink afterwards. My head was reeling by now, but the detective in me went into overdrive. The selfies were taken at 4pm, and I remembered I'd booked that night off from Proud so we could spend the evening together. That night, Eddie hadn't come in until 1am, and he'd slept in the spare room so as not to disturb me.

The weirdest thing about these selfies was that he'd set one of them as a screensaver at midnight that night. It had been saved to his photos and later binned.

Unfortunately, that wasn't the end of it. There were also Instagram messages alluding to phone sex with a third woman. I quickly found the woman's profile by her screen name, only to discover I'd previously blocked her on my Instagram account – which struck me as odd. This was a woman I didn't know, who'd clearly had an online connection with my boyfriend. Why would I have blocked her from my Instagram account?

Straight away, I unblocked her and sent a message asking how she knew Eddie.

'Oh, you've unblocked me then,' came the fast reply.

'I don't even know you. Why would I block you?'

She suggested that Eddie had probably gone into my phone and blocked her so she couldn't message me. Her name was Tracy, and she'd apparently spoken to Eddie over FaceTime and text for a long period – often from our home and sometimes from my flat in Hampstead, which she seemed to think was his. They'd never met in person, but she said the conversations had become sexual in nature reasonably quickly – some of the stuff I found on the phone seemed to support that. However, she was upset with Eddie by then because he'd apparently ghosted her.

'I hope you're not angry with me,' she wrote. 'I'm not a homewrecker.'

I didn't want to rant at her, but I couldn't believe she felt this was acceptable. She was a similar age to me, with a child of her own, and in my book, sexual chats on FaceTime and text and continued communication over a long period amount to cheating. Especially when it's done from the home that I'd strived to build for us as a family. A home that Eddie found and I bought for us. A home we'd only just moved into when it all started. It was disrespectful and devastatingly hurtful.

That night, I had to put on my showbiz head and do my show, but my mind was all over the place. The day after, when I confronted Eddie with what I'd found, I came up against a wall. As far as the woman showing her boobs went, Eddie denied anything had happened, saying that he didn't know why she'd sent the picture. Apparently, she'd done the same sort of thing with other men. I wasn't convinced. If that was the case, why no sign of a response from Eddie, asking her why she'd sent the picture or reminding her he was in a relationship?

Down the line, when the story eventually came out, I received messages from people who knew her, confirming they'd seen them together.

As for the second woman, I asked again and again who she was, but he wouldn't answer. 'A friend' was the best he could do. It transpired she was an ex-girlfriend from back in 2013 who he said he hadn't seen for almost 10 years. He swore it was innocent and that he'd met up with her because she'd just been to her father's funeral. I later discovered her father had died a year and a half earlier.

If there was nothing in it, why all the secrecy? Why delete all the photos if she was just a mate? And having one of the shots as his screensaver was the biggest red flag of all!

Eddie denied even knowing Tracy, but by then, I just couldn't trust what he said. So, I asked him to leave for a couple of weeks while I tried to make sense of it all.

I was confused and hurt; the life I'd shared with Eddie felt like a lie. Then came the second-guessing, the self-doubt. Was some of this my fault? Had I been working too much for too long? Is that why he so often went off to the pub when I got home from a day's work? Was I not enough?

A week or so later, my agent got a call from the *Sun* newspaper saying that a 'persistent woman called Tracy' had offered them the story about her 'relationship' with Eddie. For the sake of making Betsy's Christmas a happy one, I fobbed them off by telling them she was just some random woman messaging Eddie. But in my heart, I knew it was all true. I kept going over it in my head, the idea of this woman watching me as a *Loose Women* panellist and saying to her friends, 'Guess what! I was chatting to her fella last night!' I felt humiliated.

Eventually, I asked Eddie to come over because I wanted to give him the chance to tell his side of the story. I wanted him to be honest and to help me understand what was going on with him. All of it. He sat down with me, but all I heard were denials and deflections. He knew nothing of this Tracy, who'd been messaging him over three years, or the woman showing her boobs, or the ex-girlfriend. None of it was true, he said. It got to the point where I felt like it must be me and I was losing my mind.

That day, I'd given him the chance to open up and be honest, but he didn't take it. The thing I battled with most was that it wasn't just one person, one mistake or one drunken night. This was something that had gone on for more than three years. I felt betrayed. In the end, I told Eddie he had to leave the house.

Later, I spoke to my mum, crying my heart out. I was in pain and shock, but I didn't want anyone else to know what had happened until I'd had time to accept it for myself. I'd thought we had the perfect life. I'd thought this was it, my family.

When he finally admitted to knowing Tracy, he said he'd never meant it to happen, that he was in a dark place. If that were true, then I wish he'd spoken to me, his partner, rather than turning to another woman. I've always been honest with him about my problems, so his words just felt like a sorry excuse. It was incredibly painful.

After that, I ploughed into my work, but there were moments when I stood onstage at Proud ready to burst into tears. I'd sit in my dressing room after no sleep, trying to work out a way forward. The fact that I was keeping this big secret from almost everyone was also taking its toll. Christmas cards to Eddie and me and messages wishing us both a happy New Year stung like paper cuts.

I wasn't ready to tell everyone. Not until I knew how I might move forward as far as Eddie was concerned. After all, I'd had friends who'd made it through situations where a partner had been deceitful. But could we? Those same friends had told me they'd never fully trusted their partners again. It made me ask myself, *Am I the sort of person who can brush it under the carpet to make my relationship work?* The answer is no, I'm not! I've got too much self-respect and I just can't live like that. I'd created a home that was a place not just for the three of us but for his children, and his family, and our dogs. We'd had summer barbecues and parties where the house was buzzing with life and laughter. Now I felt like, in a few selfish moments, he'd ruined it. I couldn't imagine it ever feeling the same.

I spent Christmas Day alone, with Betsy going to Lee's. It was a world away from the Christmas I'd planned, but somewhat of a milestone. I realised that if I could get through the day alone – dressed in a Christmas pudding onesie – I could get through anything. And that, in the end, I was going to be OK.

The worst part of it all was telling Betsy. It tore me apart watching her cry while I tried to make her understand. Breaking up with a partner can be like a death in many ways. You're grieving for the person you loved and grieving for the family you once had. I know she feels that as much as I do.

I knew I couldn't go into 2022 with this hanging over my head. I felt like I was lying to my friends by staying silent. So, in the end, I decided to announce my split with Eddie on my Instagram page. I was done.

After that came more rumours about Eddie and the woman I'd seen on his iPad, and more people telling me what they knew.

It's funny; there are so many good things that come with a career like mine. So many perks and opportunities. The downside is that when things go wrong in a relationship, I have to see it splashed all over the newspapers. I'm sure it's equally horrible for Eddie's family and his children.

My mum keeps saying what a terrible shame it is, and she's right. How people saw Eddie and me on *Gogglebox* is how we were. We had a laugh, we had banter and we were a family. But any kind of relationship has to be built on trust, and once that's gone, there's no way forward. The truth is, if I hadn't looked in that folder of deleted pictures, I'd be planning a wedding right now. Instead, I've simply got to move on.

CHAPTER THIRTY-SIX

I'm Essex and I'm proud

Now, I don't want to get too spiritual with my final chapter, but I feel as though I need to get down some things I've learned in life, now I'm cantering towards 50.

If there is one thing I'd like to pass on, it's to never deny or ignore your life's passions. Most of us know the kinds of things we love and enjoy from a young age. To me, those things are a calling ... signposts that we should follow. While writing this book, I realised that things might have turned out very differently if I hadn't accepted the signs and taken my chances when they arose, like being scouted to audition for *Annie* as a kid or breaking my shoe on the top deck of a bus and landing my first presenting job. Even crazy stuff, like finding the shiny quarter in the doorway of my flat, which I took as a sign I should go to America, and saying yes to climbing a mountain. These were the opportunities I ran towards and reached out for, and I'm so glad I wasn't afraid to do that. Taking those risks and chances are the things that will ultimately shape a person. And it's never too late to create your own destiny.

On the flip side, gut and instinct are the things I've now learned to trust implicitly, but that took a while! Of all the relationships I've had in my life, the ones that ended up going sour were the ones I'd pursued despite all the evident signs that they weren't right.

We're all guilty of it, I suppose, even at the start of a relationship. We might go on a first date and then not get a phone call or a reply to a text the day after. Still, when we like someone, we sometimes make excuses for them. 'He or she was probably busy; I'm sure it'll be fine the next time.' No. If someone likes you, they'll let you know.

I've been in a few relationships where I did not trust my gut or listen to the signs. I knew things weren't right but clung on in the hope that they would be. It's very easy to blame other people for our heartache, but we're only adding to it if we don't face up to hard truths and trust our instincts.

Over the years, I've had fantastic times and met some fabulous people, but I've also had my fingers burned with friendships. Sometimes, a friend can break your heart, which can be just as painful as a lost love. Friendship is essential for all of us, but I'm learning that it has to be a two-way street as time goes on. I like to think I'm someone who'll go the extra mile for a friend. I'll always jump in the car and travel to see someone who needs support, and I'm always on the end of a phone when a friend needs an ear to bend. That said, I had a bit of a 'friend clear-out' a few years back. I sat in my house in Kent and made a list of people who had bothered to visit me while I was living in the countryside. It dawned on me that there were a few so-called friendships where I always made the effort and did all the legwork. I'm sure many people reading this will recognise the same thing. After that, my friendship group got much smaller, and I'm sure there are a few people out there wondering why I stopped calling them. It wasn't easy. I felt guilty about losing people I'd once created memories with. Still, it was something I had to do because these relationships were one-sided. So, yes, I think our friendship circles do get smaller as we get older, and I think that's fine; we're just being more selective.

• • •

I still love my work, and I don't seem to be slowing down as I get older. It's almost 30 years since I got my first TV role on *Kappatoo*, and I guess my face has been popping up on the nation's TV screens fairly regularly ever since. I've run the gamut, and that variety is what keeps me fired up. I suppose the thing that's stood me in good stead is having several different tools in my toolbox to work with and the fact that I've tried to keep them all sharpened. Whether performing or singing live, acting, recording or presenting, I still thrive on all of them.

I suppose you could say being busy is in my bones and therefore my nature. Ever since that first day when I walked into Sylvia Young's – maybe even before that – I knew what I wanted to do, and I've tried to keep doing it.

One of the most wonderful things to come out of my career is the platform it's given me to give back and raise money and awareness for important things. My mum messaged me a while back to tell me that my teenage nephew has been working with disabled children and found it fun and really rewarding. How lovely to hear that about a teenager! It was especially nice to learn from Mum that he'd been inspired by some of the things I've done in the past.

I couldn't do all the mad, crazy show business stuff I do without balancing it out, using the platform I'm so blessed to have to help out where and when the need arises. In fact, my most significant achievements are some of the things I've done to help raise funds for various charities, and they've usually been the most fun too. Those experiences I've had and the people I've met are the things that have enriched my life more than any glitzy night out or high-profile job. So do it, I say! You don't have to climb a mountain or even leave the country. There are plenty of challenges and people in need of support on all of our doorsteps. Try it! Step out of your comfort zone and take that leap of faith. You won't regret it.

• • •

I'm in a very fortunate position that, even while living as a single mum for five years, I could carry on working and still be there for Betsy throughout. She's 11 now, and where there used to be tears whenever I had to go off to work somewhere for a few days, Betsy's now at a stage where she's very relaxed about me being away for work.

'Yeah, that's fine, Mum; I'll go and stay with Dad.'

It's funny . . . in the past, I'd always go away feeling wracked with guilt and not enjoying the jobs I was on, but now, seeing how resourceful and at ease my daughter has become is a lovely feeling. I've always tried to be relaxed, open and honest with Betsy, and hopefully that has paid off.

I was always a very confident child, so, as a mum, I want to instil as much of that in her as I can. I learned from my own mum that it's vital to focus on what a child is good at and encourage them. Everyone has their own individual strengths in certain areas. So I try to look at whatever she excels in or loves doing and support her in that, rather than something else that might not be as important to her as it is to her dad or me. For example, Betsy struggles with maths but is the most expressive and brilliant reader. So, as much as I know she has to keep her maths up, my focus is on cheering her on in the areas where she flourishes. If there's a school production, I'll always encourage her to audition because I know she'll be brilliant.

• • •

It also feels good to have gotten to a stage where I don't worry too much about what people think of me or what the public perception might be. True, I've had my share of drama, and there was a time when some of the things that happened in my private life almost overshadowed my work. Back in the nineties, everyone seemed to have an opinion about who I was and what I represented without seeing the bigger picture. Those are the areas of the entertainment industry that I really don't miss. I believe it was Bette Davis who famously said, 'What other people think of me is none of my business.' I think that's a pretty good way to think, whether you're a Hollywood A-lister or a rock star or whether you work in a bank or drive a bus. As a public figure, you could spend an eternity looking online at comments people make about you, but none of it really means anything. With social media being as pervasive as it is, we're all under such scrutiny all the time. All you can really do is be kind, be yourself and do what you do as best you can. Well, that's my plan for the future anyway.

● ● ●

Right now, I feel as though I've come full circle. When I left Essex as a teenager, I felt like I needed to be free and forge my own path. Not because I didn't love home; I guess I just had this drive to be independent and put my own stamp on life. Living back in the old 'hood' has proved to me the old adage that home really is where the heart is. Whether it's saying hello to people in our local shops or popping to our local pub, there's a warmth and humour in Essex people that I love and appreciate. As so many of them are originally from the East End of London, there's no doubt a heavy dollop of that old cockney charm in there somewhere as well. It feels like humour that's unique to here. They work hard too, Essex people. We're a county of grafters!

I also love the fact that I'm so close to my family. In the past, I spent a lot of time away from them, missing out on important family moments, like weddings, christenings, milestone birthdays – all because of my career. Now, I prioritise those things because they're the things that make memories. And the fact that Betsy gets to spend quality time with her extended family and new friends is brilliant.

In truth, it was Eddie who found the house and persuaded me to come home. And despite everything that's happened, I'll still cherish the best memories of our time together: the laughter, the bond he had with Betsy – and I hope he finds his own happiness.

I intend to approach the future with a positive attitude and an open heart, and maybe one day I'll find my happy ever after. In the meantime, I'm focusing on building a wonderful life and home for Betsy and me. I've been happy here and I don't think that's going to change anytime soon.

After all, I'm Essex and I'm proud. It's a bit of me!

ACKNOWLEDGEMENTS

There are a few people I'd like to thank who have supported me and enriched my life, personally and professionally. People I love and value, and who have become lifelong friends. Sylvia Young, for guidance and invaluable advice which has stood me in such good stead throughout my career. Lord Waheed Alli, who gave me my big break on *The Big Breakfast*, continues to support me, and never forgets my birthday wherever he is in the world!

My family: Mum and Dad, you have always supported me. Your encouragement to reach for my dreams and be myself gave me such confidence. Everything I do in my career is for and because of your love, kindness and support. Lee, for being a good friend and a wonderful dad to Betsy, and for helping me surround our daughter with love. Laura and Tamara, dear friends who cared for and nurtured Betsy while I was a single mum, working away from home. Likewise, Julia, who is an absolute marvel as far as childcare help goes and not bad with the dogs either! My management team, Rebecca, Grant and Abbie, for looking after me, and for everything we've achieved together and will continue to achieve. Thanks for putting up with my random late-night voice note ideas! Lorna Russell and all the team at Ebury Spotlight for letting me tell my story. Simon Jones, who looks after my press relations and has always kept me out of trouble – he's certainly had his work cut out for him at times! Simon Albert at Charity Challenge, who has helped orchestrate all of my trips and treks with his incredible team, keeping me safe and giving me some of the most enriching experiences of my life, in aid of some wonderful, deserving causes. Cockney Vik and Anna Kedgley, who I've known since *Big Breakfast* days, for always being at the end of a phone when I need them. We are the three amigos!

Steve Anderson, who always encouraged me to pursue music and singing, even when I'd lost my confidence. Terry Ronald, my writing partner in crime, who 'gets me' and is the only person I trusted to write a one-woman play with me – mainly because he's as naughty as I am!

Dear friends who've helped me get through a tough time: James aka Alfie. I've chewed your ear off on some dark nights and you've been so wonderful – keeping me positive. Zoe, thank you for all the house stuff and for getting me back on track. Tamara for coming over at the drop of a hat when I was sad and lonely. And to Michelle Visage. Your powerful voice note from LA was the light-bulb moment I needed to help me realise I needed to move forward and just look out for Betsy and myself.

My greatest, most fulfilling achievement and biggest role in life is being a mum to my beautiful daughter, Betsy, who, as she gets older, is also becoming my best mate! Betsy, I love you more than anything else in the world. There are many others I could thank too – you know who you are! I feel blessed and lucky to be surrounded by wonderful people.